162

Messages Given during

The Resumption of Watchman Nee's Ministry

Volume 1

Watchman Nee & Witness Lee

Living Stream Ministry
Anaheim, California

© 1991 Witness Lee

First Edition, 4,000 copies. November 1991.

ISBN 0-87083-627-7

Published by
Living Stream Ministry
1853 W. Ball Road, Anaheim, CA 92804 U.S.A.
P. O. Box 2121, Anaheim, CA 92814 U.S.A.

Printed in the United States of America

CONTENTS

Title	Page
Volume One	
The Reason for This Book	9
Foreword	11

**Section One—Talks in Foochow
(September 1947)**

1 The Mercy of God
   W. N., Sept. 5 — 13

2 On Not Being Caused to Stumble
   W. N., Sept. 7 — 17

**Section Two—Messages in Hong Kong
(December 1947 and January 1948)**

3 God's Vessel
   Special Conference (1)—W. L., Dec. 26 — 21

4 Allowing God to Live Himself Out of Us
   Special Conference (2)—W. L., Dec. 27 — 27

5 The Indwelling of Christ
   Special Conference (3)—W. L., Dec. 29 — 33

6 The Grace of God
   Special Conference (4)—W. L., Dec. 30 — 39

7 God's Satisfaction and Man's Satisfaction
   Gospel Message—W. L., Dec. 28 — 45

8 Spiritual Reality and Obeying the Leading
of the Holy Spirit
   Fellowship Meeting (1)—W. L., Dec. 26 — 49

9 How to Abide in Christ
   Fellowship Meeting (2)—W. L., Dec. 27 — 53

10 The Proper Person
   Special Fellowship Meeting—W. L., Dec. 28 — 59

11	Obeying the Inner Feeling Fellowship Meeting (3)—W. L., Dec. 29	65
12	A Fellowship—W. L., Dec. 30	71
13	A Testimony—W. L., Jan. 2	73

**Section Three—Messages in Swatow
(January 1948)**

14	God Gaining Man Conference (1)—W. L., Jan. 7	75
15	Image and the Tree of Life Conference (2)—W. L., Jan. 8	79
16	Two Trees, Two Principles, and Two Results Talks (1)—W. L., Jan. 9	85
17	The Four Laws Conference (3)—W. L., Jan. 9	89
18	The Work of the Holy Spirit and Man-made Works Talks (2)—W. L., Jan. 10	97
19	Three Kinds of Lives and Three Kinds of Livings Conference (4)—W. L., Jan. 10	101
20	God Working Himself into Man The Lord's Day Morning Message (1)— W. L., Jan. 11	107
21	The Center of God's Truth Talks (3)—W. L., Jan. 11-12	113
22	The Way God Works Himself into Man Conference (5)—W. L., Jan. 12	117
23	The Testimony of the Church Talks (4)—W. L., Jan. 13	123
24	God's Central Work Conference (6)—W. L., Jan. 13	125
25	How to Follow the Inner Leading Conference (7)—W. L., Jan. 14	133
26	God's Ultimate Goal and His Present Need Talks (5)—W. L., Jan. 15	141

27	Concerning the Way of Life Open Talks—W. L., Jan. 15	149
28	Gospel, Revival, and Life Talks (6)—W. L., Jan. 16	153
29	Confession and Fellowship Talks (7)—W. L., Jan. 17	161
30	God's Speaking and Man's Satisfaction and Rest The Lord's Day Morning Message (2)— W. L., Jan. 18	165
31	The Service in the Body and Listening to Others Talks (8)—W. L., Jan. 19	173
32	Serving by the Whole Body Conference (8)—W. L., Jan. 19	183
33	The Way to Perfect a Person Talks (9)—W. L., Jan. 20	189
34	Migration Talks (10)—W. L., Jan. 21	197
35	Living by the Lord Talks (11)—W. L., Jan. 22	205
36	How to Build Up the Services Talks (12)—W. L., Jan. 23	213
37	On Being a Practical Christian Talks (13)—W. L., Jan. 24	215

Section Four—Messages in Shanghai
(April and May 1948)

38	The Service of the Priesthood Church Conference (1)—W. L., Apr. 9	225
39	The Way of Our Service Today and Its Crucial Points Co-workers' Meeting (1)—W. N., Apr. 9	229
40	The Recovery of the Body and the Authority of the Ministry Co-workers' Meeting (2)—W. N., Apr. 10	235

41	The Way of the Church Co-workers' Meeting (3)—W. N., Apr. 11	249
42	The Requirements of the Kingdom The Lord's Day Morning Message (1)— W. L., Apr. 11	265
43	God's Work of Recovery Co-workers' Meeting (4)—W. N., Apr. 12	273
44	God's Work of Recovery (Continued) Co-workers' Meeting (5)—W. N., Apr. 12	293
45	Testimonies of Co-workers and Comments Co-workers' Meeting (6)—W. N., Apr. 13	313

Volume Two

46	The Whole Body Serving and the Recovery of Authority Co-workers' Meeting (7)—W. N., Apr. 14	317
47	The Leading of the Body and the Whole Body Serving Co-workers' Meeting (8)—W. N., Apr. 15	329
48	A Brief Report on the Work in Foochow Miscellaneous Notes (8)—K. S. Chan, Apr. 16	345
49	The Treasure in the Earthen Vessel and the Principle of Jerusalem Co-workers' Meeting (9)—W. N., Apr. 17	347
50	The Absoluteness of the Truth and the Relationship between the Body and Its Members Co-workers' Meeting (10)—W. N., Apr. 17	361
51	The Consecration of Our Bodies Church Conference (2)—W. L., Apr. 16	371
52	The Church as God's Dwelling for His Corporate Expression The Lord's Day Morning Message (2)— K. S. Chan & W. L., Apr. 18	377
53	The Body in 1 Corinthians 12 and the Way of the Work Co-workers' Meeting (11)—W. N., Apr. 18	385

54	Money and Occupation Co-workers' Meeting (12)— W. N. & W. L., Apr. 19	395
55	The Desolation of the Church and the Advance of the Church Church Conference (3)—W. N., Apr. 19	413
56	Dealing with Mammon and Serving God Co-workers' Meeting (13)—W. N., Apr. 20	423
57	Fellowship and Exhortations (1) Co-workers' Meeting (14)—W. N., Apr. 21	435
58	Fellowship and Exhortations (2) Co-workers' Meeting (15)—W. L., Apr. 21	441
59	Fellowship And Exhortations (3) Co-workers' Meeting (16)—W. L., Apr. 22	447
60	Handing Oneself Over for the Service in the Body Co-workers' Meeting (17)—W. L., Apr. 23	453
61	The Service of the Whole Body Co-workers' Meeting (18)—W. N., Apr. 24	461
62	Being Crucified with Christ and Bearing the Cross The Lord's Day Morning Message (3)— K. S. Chan & W. L., Apr. 25	471
63	Things That a Co-worker Should Pay Attention To Co-workers' Meeting (19)—W. N., Apr. 25	477
64	The Whole Body Serving Co-workers' Meeting (20)—W. N., Apr. 26	487
65	Deliverance from Mammon and Ministry and Authority Co-workers' Meeting (21)—W. N., Apr. 27	499
66	The Exercise of Authority in the Body and the Body Consciousness Co-workers' Meeting (22)—W. N., Apr. 28	507
67	Voluntary Poverty and Submission to Authority Co-workers' Meeting (23)—W. N., Apr. 28	517

8   THE RESUMPTION OF WATCHMAN NEE'S MINISTRY

68	Brother Nee's Word of Farewell to Brother K. H. Weigh Co-workers' Meeting (24)—W. N., Apr. 29	525
69	Brokenness and Ministry Co-workers' Meeting (25)—W. N., Apr. 30	527
70	Report on the Work (1) Co-workers' Meeting (26)—W. N., May 1	537
71	Zaccheus' Salvation The Lord's Day Morning Gospel Message (4)— W. L., May 2	549
72	Report on the Work (2) Co-workers Meeting (27)— W. N. & W. L., May 2	555
73	Prayer for the Gospel Church Prayer Meeting (1)— W. N. & W. L., May 4	567
74	A Talk with Those Who Are Engaged in Business Church Conference (4)—W. N., May 6	569
75	Concerning Contending or Yielding Church Prayer Meeting (2)—W. L., May 7	579
76	Testimonies by the Saints and Words of Exhortation Church Meeting—W. N., May 8	581
77	A Transparent Person (1) The Lord's Day Morning Message (5)— W. L., May 9	583
78	The Relationship between the Church and the Work, the Meaning and Authority of the Church and Identification with the Church Co-workers' Meeting (28)—W. N., May 15	591
79	A Transparent Person (2) The Lord's Day Morning Message (6)— W. L., May 16	601

THE REASON FOR THIS BOOK

By the mercy of God, in 1947 the church in Shanghai in China experienced a great revival. When the news spread to other places, the churches in the provinces of Fukien and Kwangtung, together with the church in Hong Kong, invited me to visit them. At the same time, co-workers from northern and southern China, together with co-workers from the West, decided to come together in Shanghai the following year for a co-workers' conference and to share the Lord's grace one with another. Consequently, toward the end of 1947 Sister Pearl Wang, Rachel Lee, and I first went to Hong Kong. Afterwards we went to Canton, Swatow, and Amoy. Finally, in March the following year we went to Foochow. In all these places we held special revival conferences. After the meetings in Foochow, the two sisters and I went according to our previously-arranged schedule to have some private fellowship with Brother Nee at his home concerning the future of the Lord's recovery. When the news went out, about thirty to forty co-workers around the Foochow area unanimously requested that they be admitted to the fellowship also. Upon Brother Nee's approval, they all attended those meetings. During these meetings, it was brought out one day the need of "handing over" oneself. All agreed enthusiastically to do this. Subsequently, this move brought in the recovery of Brother Nee's ministry. First, Brother Nee took care of the need of the meeting in Foochow. After that, he went with me in April of that year to Shanghai to conduct a nation-wide co-workers' conference. Throughout this period, Brother Weigh Kwang-hsi and his wife were in most of the meetings. The content of this book is their brief records of these meetings in various places.

Of all these meetings throughout this period of the recovery of Brother Nee's ministry, I was present in all except the first two meetings, and I was even helping to conduct the meetings. I sat face to face with our brother and heard these messages with my own ears. The light that was released was like the shining of the midday sun. Forty-three years have since elapsed. There is indeed the need at present to let its light shine forth once again as the rising sun. Fortunately, under the Lord's sovereignty, we have with us the remaining manuscripts of the brief records by Brother Weigh and his wife. When I read them again, every message was filled with the dawning light. What impressed me the most and rendered me the greatest help are eight things: (1) the knowledge and realization of the Body of Christ, (2) the knowledge and denial of the self, (3) the knowledge of and submission to the authority in the Body of Christ, (4) the knowledge and acceptance by the co-workers of the "line of Jerusalem," (5) the service and coordination of the whole Body of Christ, (6) the need and practice of handing over oneself with all one has, (7) the leading and coordination among the co-workers, and (8) the importance of the Holy Spirit in the service in the Body of Christ. May the Lord grant us the mercy, the grace, and the blessing, that all the above points would be abundantly realized in our work and service of the Lord's recovery.

Witness Lee
Anaheim, California
July 19, 1991

FOREWORD

This book is a translation from Chinese of a collection of messages taken from brief meeting notes of Brother Weigh Kwang-hsi and his first wife, Lin I-tien. Except for some slight adjustments in sentence structure, the majority of the material is presented as found in the manuscripts. The main speakers of these messages are Brother Watchman Nee and Brother Witness Lee.

The first section comprises notes of private fellowship between Brother Nee and Brother Weigh in Foochow during September of 1947. The notes are comparatively scanty in content.

The second section, except for the last chapter, is a record of Brother Witness Lee's first visit to Hong Kong in December, 1947, and the help he rendered to the church there. It includes four conference meetings, four fellowship meetings, one gospel meeting, and one account of private fellowship. The main burdens of these meetings are the believers' living by the life of God and the proper way to serve in the church. The last chapter is Brother Lee's testimony given in Canton.

The third section is a record of Brother Lee's words given to the church in Swatow in January, 1948. It includes eight conference messages, two Lord's Day morning messages, one open talk, and thirteen private talks with a small number of individuals. The main burden lies in God's way of life and the way to help the whole church to rise up to serve.

The fourth section comprises fellowship and messages of a nation-wide co-workers' conference in Shanghai during April and May of 1948. The first chapter begins on April 9, and the final chapter ends on May 16. In total there are thirty-eight days of meetings and fellowship, covering forty-two chapters. During this period, most of Brother Nee's talks were given in the co-workers' meetings rather than in the church meetings. Only a few times did he speak to the whole church in the church conference meetings. This fellowship is weighty, full of light, sober, and direct. The main burdens are the way of recovery that the church takes on earth today, the recovery of the Body life, the coordination of the co-workers, ministry and authority, the relationship between the local churches and the work, release from the bondage of money, the way to preach the gospel, and the way to arrive at the universal priestly service. The materials covered are precious and invaluable. Due to the size of this work, we have divided the series into two volumes, with chapters one to forty-five as the first volume, and chapters forty-six to seventy-nine as the second volume. May God bless His church through these messages.

Andrew Yu
October, 1991

CHAPTER ONE

THE MERCY OF GOD

Date: September 5, 1947
Place: Foochow, Fukien
Speaker: Watchman Nee

EVERYTHING DEPENDING ON THE MERCY OF GOD

When we read Romans 9, we have to pay attention both to its principle and to its application as well. This chapter reveals the principle that everything depends on God's mercy. The apostle applied this principle to the Israelites. He showed us that everything that happened to the Israelites was of God's mercy. Today, not only do we need to pay attention to the application, but we need to pay attention also to the principle behind the application.

Here it says that "it is not of him who wills, nor of him who runs, but of God who shows mercy" (Rom. 9:16). Zeal and pursuit are of no use. Neither will the absence of zeal and pursuit be of any use. To wait too long, not to wait long enough, to be too quick, or to be too slow—none of these is of any use. To be in one place or another, to hear much or to hear little—none of these is of any use either. Everything depends on the mercy of God. Only the Holy Spirit is able to lead men to a proper standing. There must be at least one time that a person sees God's mercy. Concerning this matter, your eyes must be opened at least once. Of course, it is good if your eyes can be opened more than once. But there must at least be one time when you see that everything depends on God's mercy. Whether you see this matter all at once, or you realize it through a process, the minute you touch this matter, you touch a fact—not a feeling, but a fact. This fact is that everything depends on God's mercy.

God's mercy is a fact. A fact is not dependent on feeling. Take the matter of regeneration as an example. We often tell sinners that they must have a one-time definite experience of repentance and believing in the Lord. To the believers, we say that they must have a one-time definite consecration of themselves to the Lord. In principle, it is the same with regard to man's understanding of God's mercy. There must be at least one time when a person definitely touches God's mercy.

THE NEED TO DEAL WITH
THE MIND, THE EMOTION, AND THE WILL—
BEING TEMPERED UNDER
THE DISCIPLINE OF THE SPIRIT

Three kinds of people need God's dealings: those who are strong in their will, those who are strong in their emotion, and those who are strong in their mind. Many people are controlled by these three kinds of conditions. These three things must experience God's breaking. God deals with man's strong points more than He deals with his weak points. Many times, man's strong points hinder him from spiritual progress, more so than his weak points. Unless a man is dealt with in these three areas, he cannot know God's mercy.

After a man has been dealt with by God, he will be tempered in his spiritual life. In many things, it is inappropriate either to be too much or to be too little. Some people wait for too long, while others do not wait long enough. All these require tempering. Some people are not strong enough in their inner man; their outer man is too strong. This is like a man's head taking up one-fourth of his body or one-sixteenth of his body; neither is proportionate. The right proportion should be one-seventh of the body. Some people are too strong in their mind. Others are too strong in their emotion or their will. Their inner man is not strong enough. These conditions require tempering.

Once I took a leader of the China Inland Mission to hear Brother T. Austin-Sparks. After the message, others would usually ask about the message just given. But on my way home with this brother, I did not ask him anything. In the end, he opened his mouth. He felt that Mr. Sparks was too strong in his will. I told him that my will was also quite strong. This leader, Mr. Baker, asked, "How then are you able to get along with him?" No doubt those who are outwardly strong in their will do not easily get along with others. But this brother did not realize that we are one because of our inner man; it is not because of our outer will. Today, in order for our inner man to match our outer man, our inner man must grow. When the inner man grows, it can control the outer man. Some people are too strong in their minds. Their minds need to come under the control of the inner man. I have read the New Testament a few hundred times. Although I cannot say that I have read it more times than everyone else, I can at least say that I have read it more than many people. I could find over one hundred passages that contradict each other. However, I have not done this because my mind has been under the control of the Holy Spirit.

If we want our spiritual life to be well-tempered, we need to attune our condition to a proper balance. We must neither be too much nor be too short. This can be compared to shooting a pinball machine; there are pins to the left and to the right, and the balls must be directed at the optimum angle before they can score. There are many pitfalls in our spiritual journey; our mind, emotion, and will can all become our hindrances. If we are too much or too short, we fall into danger.

Everything depends on God's mercy. Before I was saved, I planned to go to America. Had I left two months earlier, I would not have met Sister Dora Yu, and I might never have been saved. Even if I were given the chance later, I might not have believed. It was God's mercy that I met Miss Dora Yu at that time. It was neither too early nor too late.

Only God can do things in just the right amount. We are prone to speak either too much or not enough. No one can preach a message that will meet everyone's need. Even the apostle Paul and the apostle Peter faced the same problem. When words come out of a person's mouth, it is difficult for the words to come out just right. This is why it is easy for people to misunderstand words.

Only God can bring man to a state of true humiliation.

Sometimes a little cross and a little dealing make a person proud instead of humble. Only severe crosses and severe dealings will make a person humble.

Some people are too spiritual; they think that the Lord dwells only in our spirit. But Ephesians 3 says that by faith Christ dwells in our hearts. He dwells not only in our spirit, but in our hearts also. This is something that a person can feel. John 15 says that Christ abides in the believers, but it does not say that Christ abides in our hearts. Only Ephesians 3 mentions Christ dwelling in our hearts. Some people are too spiritual. They think that the heart does not mean much. However, many of the Psalms mention the heart. In order to be tempered in spiritual matters, we need to pay attention not only to the spirit, but to our hearts as well.

THE WAY OF THE CHURCH—LOOKING TO GOD'S MERCY

The way of the church during the past two thousand years is a way of looking to the mercy of God. Only God's mercy can temper us. I have often told the young people that they may have to wait for five years before they will realize that everything is of God's mercy. On the average, a person has one hundred forty thousand hairs. The Bible says that God has numbered every one of our hairs. He knows us more than we know ourselves. When God wants to save us, we are saved. If God does not show mercy on us, no one can be saved. Once D. L. Moody was preaching the gospel, and a lady was about to be saved. Just then an umbrella fell; it caused a distraction, and in the end the lady was not saved. Whether or not a man can be saved is not the responsibility of the preacher. The responsibility of the preacher is simply to present the way to others. Only God's mercy can put a person on the way. It is God's work that puts a person on the way. It is also God Himself who takes men on, on the way.

CHAPTER TWO

ON NOT BEING CAUSED TO STUMBLE

Date: The Lord's Day morning, September 7, 1947
Place: Foochow, Fukien
Speaker: Watchman Nee

Hymns, #144, stanza one, says:

> Lord of glory, we adore Thee!
> Christ of God, ascended high!
> Heart and soul we bow before Thee,
> Glorious now beyond the sky:
> Thee we worship, Thee we praise—
> Excellent in all Thy ways.

Here the hymn says "Christ of God." We are familiar with the term "Son of God," but we seldom say "the Christ of God." The Christ of God means the One anointed by God and sent by Him to accomplish His work. In the original language, the word for Christ is *Christos,* and the word for Christians is *Christianos,* which indicates that Christians are those who belong to Christ.

Hymns, #38, stanza one, says:

> Of all the gifts Thy love bestows,
> Thou Giver of all good!
> E'en heav'n itself no richer knows
> Than Jesus and His blood.

Here the hymn tells us the vastness of God's riches. We have to wait until that day before we can fully prove the value of God's love. Some people think that it is good enough for God to give us heaven. However, heaven is not the best thing that a person can have. If a man is satisfied with heaven only, he is limiting God's love. He is in reality limiting God's love to heaven. Some people say that they will be satisfied with just a small corner in heaven. Such people are limiting God's love to a small corner. However, our God is not stingy. His grace is abundant, both in the past and at the present, and in the future as well. God sends the rain and the wind in free and full measure. God does not mind giving us a little more than we need. If God were to exercise restriction, it would be a terrible thing for us. Miss M. E. Barber once wrote a hymn that says:

> There is always something over,
>   When we taste our gracious Lord;
> Every cup He fills o'erfloweth,
>   Rich supply He doth afford.
> Nothing narrow, nothing stinted,
>   Ever issued from His store;
> To His own He gives full measure,
>   Running over, evermore,
> To His own He gives full measure,
>   Running over, evermore.

(*Hymns*, #595, stanza one)

The water that Christ gives is living water. What man has is only well water. Well water can never be compared to living water. John 4 says that "the well is deep" and that there is "no bucket" (v. 11). Under such circumstances, man continues to be thirsty.

Scripture Reading: Matthew 11:1-19

NOT BEING CAUSED TO STUMBLE BY THE LORD

The passage we just read records how men were caused to stumble by the Lord. Here John the Baptist must have been extremely puzzled by Christ. Why would Christ not do something spectacular, such as healing the blind and the lame? Before this time, John the Baptist gave a strong testimony for Jesus, declaring that Christ is the Lamb of God and that He came to take away the sin of the world (John 1:29). A second time he declared, "Behold, the Lamb of God!" (John 1:36). When Christ was baptized, John saw the Holy Spirit descending upon Him (John 1:32). However, here John was caused to stumble by the work of Christ. Formerly he told others that he was not worthy to untie the thong of Christ's sandal (John 1:27). Now he was sending men to

Christ and was pressing Him to answer honestly if He was the Christ. At the same time, it would have been possible for Christ to be caused to stumble by John the Baptist as well. John was supposed to be Elijah. He was supposed to be very successful. Why is it that he ended up in prison now, and why is it that he failed today? However, the Lord was not caused to stumble by John.

Today, many people are caused to stumble by the Lord. They are caused to stumble by the way Christ lived. John's food was locusts and wild honey; his clothing was of camel's hair (Matt. 3:4). You cannot find such clothing even in a fur store. Yet when Christ came, He ate and He drank. He was absolutely the opposite of John the Baptist. For this reason, men were caused to stumble by Him. It is easy for a person to have a preconceived idea of what a spiritual man should be, and if anyone does not fit such a pattern, this person would be caused to stumble.

NOT BEING CAUSED TO STUMBLE
BY ANYTHING OR ANYONE

Around 1921, there were about fifty students in Trinity College in Foochow. They all became Christians through my preaching. At that time, I was trying to use Miss Barber's baptistry to baptize them. Miss Barber asked who the baptizer would be. I told her that the Bible indicates that whoever preaches to another is qualified to baptize that one. Miss Barber said that it was better to let Leland Wang baptize these ones because he was older than I was. Later I tried to recommend Brother Dan-wu Wu, for he was twelve years older than I was, and he was of course older than Leland Wang. However, Miss Barber insisted that Leland should be the baptizer. When I brought up the matter of age, Miss Barber remained unchanged about her choice. I then said, "Since you had already made up your mind in the first place to have Leland do the baptizing, why did you bring up the matter of age?" In spite of this, I was not caused to stumble.

Once Miss Barber wrote me a letter and told me definitely not to come to one of her meetings. Nevertheless, when the time of the meeting came, I went, by forcing my way through the door, so to speak. When Miss Barber saw me, she said, "It is so good that you have come. I have many things to talk over with you. I need your help." In this instance, I was not caused to stumble by Miss Barber either.

THE WAY TO AVOID BEING CAUSED TO STUMBLE—
LAYING ASIDE THE OUTWARD APPEARANCES
AND REALIZING THE SPIRITUAL REALITY

We have to realize the spiritual reality behind everything that God has arranged. We should not consider merely the superficial outward appearances. There may be a thousand things along the way that could cause you to stumble, but what you have to do is to lay aside all these things and look straight ahead at the spiritual reality, rather than to be affected by the apparent errors.

In 1926 at White Teeth Lake, one day I saw an article by Mr. Jeffrey in the magazine *Witness and Testimony*. After Miss Barber saw that same article, she told me that Mr. Jeffrey would soon be separated from us. I did not quite agree with her, and I said to her, "You just like to make big assertions and outlandish remarks. This is your temperament." However, after one or two months, Mr. Jeffrey did indeed separate himself from us. Later, when I was in India, I met him and asked why he left. I told him what Miss Barber had told me. After he heard those words, he resolved to take care of the problem on that very day. Immediately, he bought a ticket and sailed home to England to apologize to Mr. Sparks, because at the time he left the latter, he had spoken something against him. Today, men are easily caused to stumble by small things. We need the grace of the Lord that we will not be caused to stumble by anything or anyone.

CHAPTER THREE

GOD'S VESSEL

SPECIAL CONFERENCE (1)

Date: Evening, December 26, 1947
Place: Hong Kong
Speaker: Witness Lee

Scripture Reading: Phil. 2:12-13; 3:8-10 (note the words "obeyed" and "operates" in 2:12-13)

MAN'S SPECIFIC USE—TO BE FILLED WITH GOD

Man is a specific creature. He is created for a specific use. A light bulb can only shine when it is placed in the proper place. If it is not placed in the proper place, it will not shine; if the bulb could speak, it would tell you that it was senseless that it should be there. In the same way, unless a man exists for a specific purpose, that man is empty. Man's specific use is to be filled with God, in the same way that the light bulb is used to shine forth light. In this universe, man should be filled with God and should shine for God. Some people are filled with money, education, family, and position. But after they are filled with these things, they are still empty. Lands and houses are but turmoils and headaches. Man does not live for these things. The specific purpose of man's living is God. Whether a person is young or old, rich or poor, male or female, as soon as a person touches God, he is satisfied.

GOD'S PURPOSE IN MAN—
FOR MAN TO CONTAIN HIM AND TO EXPRESS HIM

Within every one of us, we need God. Without God, we feel empty, unsatisfied, and sad. God needs us also. He needs us more than we need Him. God not only created man; He also sought man out. After Adam fell, God asked him, "Where are you?" When the Lord came, He came to seek and to save the lost sinners. In the story of the prodigal son, we see God's need for man. The father needed the son. Parents need their children more than the children need their parents. Why did God create man, love him, and save him? Some say that God is love, and that He has prepared many places in heaven. They say that if we do not go to heaven, heaven will be empty: "All things are ready; come to the feast"—this is the calling of God's love. But what is the purpose of God's loving us and saving us? God's purpose is to receive glory through man. His purpose is to express His life through us. When a light bulb is connected to the electric current, it shines forth light. This is the meaning of glory. When God enters you and is expressed through you, it is glory. God desires that we be filled with Him within. Every saved believer has God within him. We need to see this before the Lord, and we need to present ourselves to God in this way to be His vessel.

CONSECRATION NOT FOR GOD'S WORK, BUT TO BE GOD'S VESSEL

Many times we want to do this and that kind of work for God. I have been to a number of places in northern and central China, and I have seen some very zealous workers for the Lord. Although they are very zealous, few among them know that they are God's vessels. To them, there is not much difference between being God's vessel and working for God. But I have to say that there is a big difference between being zealous for God and being God's vessel. To those among you who have consecrated yourselves to the Lord, I would like to ask a question: "Why did you consecrate yourselves to the Lord?" God wants us to be His vessels so that He can put Himself inside of us.

GOD'S WAY—
CALLING MAN TO BE HIS VESSELS

It is natural for us to work much for God and to save souls. There are over one million people in Hong Kong. If there are ten or twenty brothers and sisters here who are filled with God within, in two to three years, you will definitely see many people saved. But more than that, those who will be saved will be very different from those who are saved today. As long as God fills Hong Kong, blessings will be here. I arrived here on Tuesday (December 23). By now I have been here three to four days already. I have met many brothers and sisters who are very zealous. I would like to ask if among these many brothers and sisters there are some who are God's vessels. Here is an elderly sister. She has been meeting with us from the very beginning. Let me ask, "What are you doing here? Are you here merely to meet, to listen to messages, and to pray?" If that is what you are doing here, God cannot have a way here; He will not be able to spread out from here. This is why in the past there have been so many revival meetings, spiritual conferences, and other meetings, and yet after these meetings are over, no one has changed. In the nineteenth century, there were many conventions, sermons, conferences, and revivals. But these things are not God's way today. Only when some answer God's call will God have a way today. There are those who are zealous for God. There are also those who work for God. But how many are there who will truly answer God's call?

THE WAY TO BE GOD'S VESSEL

A. Removing Hindrances and Emptying Out Oneself

God desires to gain man so that He can put Himself into man. God desires to have such a vessel that can contain Him and express Him here and now. This may sound very simple, but actually it is not simple. To pour water into a glass is simple because the glass has no will, emotion, or inclination of its own. If you want to pour water into it, it will not object. If you do not want to pour water into it, it will not complain. However, if you want to pour water into me, it will not be a simple matter. This is because I am a living creature; I have a will, an emotion, preferences, inclinations, choices, a mind, and imaginations, not to mention the many sinful and evil things that are within me. Even for us who are serving God, there are so many things. In the case of the unbelievers on the street, it is difficult to have God put within them. In the case of us who are serving God, it is likewise difficult to have God put within us. Therefore we must empty ourselves, obey God, and consecrate ourselves to Him.

B. Fellowshipping with God and Walking according to the Spirit

The meaning of consecrating ourselves to God is not to work for God, but to become God's vessel, and to allow God to fill us up. From morning to evening, are you led by the Holy Spirit in everything you do? Many times, we have good prayers in the morning. But soon after that, we find ourselves doing more than a few things contrary to the leading of the Holy Spirit. If you measure these things according to the letter of the Bible, these things may not constitute very serious mistakes, but your conscience will condemn you. A voice within will tell you that you have not turned to God enough, that you have not been godly enough, and that you have not obeyed Him enough. If you want to love the Lord, there is no need for you to beg, to fast, or to pray for three days. The simple thing to do is to receive the Lord into you. We are not Christians in an outward way. We are Christians in an inward way. We are not Christians according to the biblical teachings and doctrines. We are Christians according to our inner feeling. If we are such Christians, we will surely touch God all the time. If you fellowship with God, you will become God's vessel. All the time, God will fill you up and will shine His light through you. No doctrine can be our way. The most important thing for us to do is to be a vessel of God. All that God wants is to gain some people who will live before Him. Zeal, love, and emotional sentiments are useless. Only one thing is useful: to take care of the feeling within moment by moment.

C. Not a Result of Teaching, but a Result of Living

For example, Brother Hwang may hit Brother Hsu on the face one day. Perhaps Brother Hsu does not strike back. If you ask him why, he may tell you that the Bible teaches him not to do that. If he says this, he is not a first-class Christian.

We should be Christians not by teaching, but by living. Confucius taught people to honor their parents and to love others, but that kind of honoring and love comes out of teaching. Today, we do not eat because others teach us to eat, but because we have a taste for eating. For you to eat rice today is not a decree of the government, but a choice based on your taste. If you ask me why I am speaking on this subject tonight, I will tell you that it is not the Bible that tells me to speak this way, but the inner feeling that tells me to speak this way. The more I speak this matter, the more I feel happy. In the New Testament, there are many passages with the little word "in" in them. Many outsiders do not understand what this word means. I only wish I could go to the streets and shout to people, "I have God *in* me! Do not touch me, for I have God *in* me!"

Man is God's vessel. God's work today is to put Himself into man. This is God's purpose.

CHAPTER FOUR

ALLOWING GOD TO LIVE HIMSELF OUT OF US

SPECIAL CONFERENCE (2)

Date: Evening, December 27, 1947
Place: Hong Kong
Speaker: Witness Lee
Scripture Reading: Phil. 2:12-13; 3:8-10

GOD'S PURPOSE IN MAN—WORKING HIMSELF INTO MAN

If we read through the Old and the New Testament, we will see that God has one specific purpose in man. Whether in creating man or in redeeming man, God desires to achieve this purpose. This purpose can be considered the center of the universe. If a man does not meet this purpose while he lives on earth, he will feel empty. Even a Christian who does not see this purpose will feel that his life is meaningless. God has shown us in many ways through His word what this purpose is. God's purpose is to work Himself into man. At the end of Revelation we are told that in the new heaven and new earth, when God's work is completed, He will have worked Himself completely into man. By that time, God will be fully in man, and man will be fully in God. God and man will become one. We may think that we were destined for perdition and hell. After we are saved, we may think that now, as a saved person, we are satisfied as long as we can go to heaven. However, this is not the highest purpose of God, His ultimate purpose. God's highest purpose, His ultimate purpose, is to work Himself into man.

SALVATION BEING GOD ADDED INTO MAN

God created man according to His image (Gen. 1:26). What is the meaning of an image? When you see a picture, you recognize the person represented by the picture. There are many great men in this world; it is difficult for us to meet them face to face. However, we can recognize them from their pictures. Man is God's picture. At the time of creation, man had only God's image; he did not have God's life. At that time, man bore only God's outward appearance. After he is saved, he possesses God's life as well (2 Pet. 1:3). Salvation means that God comes into us. By this, we become a man with God, having received nothing other than God and nothing less than God Himself. Salvation is not a matter of turning an evil man into a good man, or turning a filthy man into a clean man. No matter how much man cleanses himself, he is still only a man. The meaning of salvation is God added into man. Man's number is seven, and seven is three plus four. Four is the number of the creatures, and three is the number of God. Three plus four means God added into man.

In 1932, I was meeting in the denominations. There were many people in my denomination, and not a few were saved. One older gentleman was a professional man in the law. Although he was old, he was very healthy. I noticed him in the services, but I had never had a chance to talk to him. One day I met him on the street, and I asked him, "Have you believed in the Lord?" He told me happily that he had. I asked, "Are you saved?" He said that he was. I then asked, "How do you know that you are saved?" He said, "I know I am saved because God and I have become one." This word was marvelous. Even if you were to give the whole world to me, I would still be one individual person, an empty person. But one day I was saved, and God entered into me. From that time on, the two became one. This is like an electric light. Before the switch is turned on, the light does not shine. But once the switch is turned on and the electricity comes, the light comes on. When we are saved, God is added into us. The two have become one. This is not something for the future, but something that is for the present. What does this mean? It means that God is added into man. In the future, who will the perishing ones be? The perishing ones will be those who are empty, those who do not have God inside them. Who are the saved ones? They are the filled-up ones, those who have God inside them. On the day of salvation, God entered into us. Many times, I considered myself an evil person. Sometimes I have even hit myself. But then I would remember that the God within me is marvelous.

THE PROPER LIVING
OF THE BELIEVERS AFTER SALVATION—
ALLOWING GOD TO LIVE HIMSELF OUT

After a person is saved, all his spiritual experiences consist of allowing God to gain the proper ground within him. They consist of allowing God to live Himself out of him. Let me illustrate this in another way. Suppose there is an empty glass here. This depicts the condition of man before he is saved; he is empty within. After he is saved, he is filled within, in the same way that the glass would be filled with water. Do not say that salvation is to bring us into heaven. Salvation is to put God into us. The Lord washes us with His own blood for the purpose of putting Himself into us.

Some of us had bad tempers before we were saved. Now that we are saved, we have a "housekeeper" within us. You will discover that there are now two persons within you, one on the outside, and the other in the inside. This can be compared to putting on our clothes; we are the clothes, and God puts Himself inside of us. When I sit down, my clothes sit down with me. When I come here, my clothes come with me. When I go home, my clothes go home with me. Sometimes, we may be afraid outwardly but not inwardly; we may be confused outwardly, but we are clear inwardly. We may feel pressed outwardly, but we are at ease inwardly. This is because God is living within us. For God to live out of us is true spirituality; this is growth, and this is the true spiritual reality.

THE WAY TO ALLOW GOD
TO LIVE HIMSELF OUT OF US

A. Taking Care of the Inner Feeling

Brothers and sisters, I look to the Lord to gain a group of people in Hong Kong who will answer God's calling to allow Him to live Himself out of them. How can God gain ground in us? How can we live out God? When God operates in us, He gives us feelings. You need to take care of these feelings. You have to take care of every feeling from God. Brothers and sisters, if you neglect these feelings, you will not grow even if you read your Bible all year round. This is because God does not have any ground within you; He cannot live out from you. God desires to mingle His nature, desires, thoughts, inclinations, and will into man. However, Satan tries to usurp man with his own devices also. Some people are fully occupied in their mind, desires, and emotions with fashions, position, fame, parents, children, or marriage. This is the reason the Lord calls us to deny our children, wife, parents, houses, and lands (Matt. 19:29). You have been attending revival meetings and spiritual conferences for many years. But you are still the same you; you have not changed. No wonder you do not grow. The reason you do not grow is that you have ignored the inner feelings. You have only added to yourselves some outward practices, doctrines, and knowledge. I do not believe that the teaching tonight will help you. Brothers and sisters, if God grants mercy to you, and He touches you or visits you, you will begin to take care of every inner feeling.

B. Giving Oneself to God

How many people here tonight would like to take care of their inner feelings? You need to go to God in a specific way, to set aside a time. It may be midnight tonight, but do not wait until tomorrow. Give yourself to God. I do not say consecrate yourself. I say give yourself to God. Say to God, "Lord, from now on, I would take care of every feeling from You. Mingle Your inclinations, emotions, desires, and thoughts into me." If you would give yourself to God in this way, and if tomorrow morning while you are putting on your clothes, the Lord says to you, "Don't put on this piece of clothing," what will you do? This is an important matter. We all look very zealous; we are busy running to and fro. But when God puts a demand on us, many times we will not obey it. If you are such a Christian, how can you grow? Not only are you deceiving God; you are deceiving even yourself.

C. Having an Ambition to Obey God Absolutely

Many Christians walk according to their own tastes. This is like those who have a sweet tooth devouring sweet things when they see them and rejecting spicy things that are served to them. A person can be fussy with food, but he cannot be a Christian in this way. A person can be a "pew-Christian," a "Sunday-going Christian," but such a one will never afford God the way to go on. You may say that you are willing and that you hope the Lord will help your weakness. God will surely not listen to such a prayer because by praying in this way you have opened a back door already; you have made provision for yourself to disobey already. You should have the ambition to say, "Lord! I do not need Your help. As long as You give me a feeling, I will obey."

The gospel has been preached in Hong Kong for over a hundred years. Here are over a million people. But too few people are saved. Even among us tonight, we have only one to two hundred people. What is the reason for this slow increase? It is a small thing for you to answer my question today, but how would you answer the Lord that day at the judgment seat? There is no need to wait for that day; even today, it is hard for us to give an answer to ourselves. There is no need for those who do not obey their inner feelings to vindicate themselves; there is no need for them to tell God that they are serving Him. There are many who have proclaimed themselves to be believers, and it is not necessary for you to tell others that you are zealous. However, if you truly give yourselves to the Lord, you will see many people saved through you. If you want to love the Lord, love Him in an absolute way. If you want to love the world, love it all the way. A man can only be one person at a time; he cannot be two persons at the same time. He cannot love the Lord and love the world at the same time. Some people are eight different persons all at one time; their hearts are in eight different places. One place may be their children. Another place may be their money. It is better for these people to put their hearts in one place and to love God with a single heart.

D. Being Simple, Not Analyzing, and Walking Step by Step according to the Feelings of the Spirit

In order to be a Christian, a person must be simple. As soon as a feeling comes, we should obey. As soon as another feeling comes, we should obey again. This is the Christian way. You do not need to worry if this or that is wrong. Even if you are wrong, you need not be afraid. As long as you feel peaceful in your heart, you can go on. As long as you remain simple, and as long as you are for God and are pure toward Him, you do not need to analyze too much. You have to realize that sometimes God gives us uneasy feelings within; He also makes us uncomfortable. Whenever you feel uncomfortable about something, do not do it. If you practice this, after a while, your emotions, desires, and thoughts will become one with God, and spontaneously God will fill you up.

E. Studying the Bible to Allow God's Word to Check the Feeling in Your Spirit

At the same time, you must study the Bible thoroughly. This allows the Holy Spirit to have a chance to enlighten you. The Bible confirms our feelings and tells us whether they are right or wrong. To be a Christian, a person must not only walk according to the teachings of the Bible, but walk according to the inner feeling. A weighty and proper Christian is one who reads the Bible, on the one hand, and walks according to the inner feelings, on the other hand. If you do not walk according to your feelings, you are merely a dead Christian. We must all learn to take care of this crucial matter: to go along with the inner feeling.

CHAPTER FIVE

THE INDWELLING OF CHRIST

SPECIAL CONFERENCE (3)

Date: December 29, 1947
Place: Hong Kong
Speaker: Witness Lee

Scripture Reading: Matt. 28:20; John 15:5; Eph. 3:17; Phil. 2:12-13; Rom. 8:26-27

WHERE IS THE LORD JESUS TODAY?

Where is the Lord Jesus today? This is a very interesting question. Some say that the Lord Jesus is at the right hand of the Father in heaven. Others say that He is in our hearts. Let us consider what the Bible says.

There are four Gospels in the New Testament. Where was the Lord Jesus in the book of Matthew? Where was He in the book of John? In Matthew 26, He was betrayed. In chapter twenty-seven, He was crucified, and in chapter twenty-eight, He resurrected. I remember that when I was in Nanking a brother answered me promptly that in Matthew, the Lord Jesus is in ascension, whereas in John, the Lord Jesus is in the Father.

A. Being with Us

The end of Matthew tells us that the Lord Jesus is "with you all the days until the consummation of the age" (Matt. 28:20). In the book of Matthew, we see two names, Jesus and Emmanuel. Emmanuel means God with man. No doubt God is God, yet He is now with man. It is true that He incarnated, grew up, worked, was betrayed, was crucified, and has resurrected. But today He is still with man. Today the Lord is here with us. He is with us by being within us. Suppose we have two hundred fifty people here today. Our physical eyes do not see the Lord. Today the Lord is not in our midst; He is not the two-hundred-fifty-first person. He is with us by being in us. He is not mingled among us, but He is within us. Outwardly speaking, men see us. But inwardly speaking, there is the Lord. In every age, wherever the Lord's disciples are, the Lord is there. Wherever there are believers, the Lord is there.

B. Being in Us

Where has the Lord gone in the Gospel of John? He has come into us. John does not have chapter twenty-two. In chapter twenty, He was resurrected. Originally, He was God, coming in the flesh and living among men. Now through the Holy Spirit, He enters into man. Today, we do not merely have Jesus among us, but we have Jesus within us. Outwardly we are a man, but inwardly we have God. God was once in Jesus the Nazarene. Today He is in us. The Scriptures reveal to us that God in Christ has come into man. Oh, what a glorious fact! As a little man, I have God living within me. Today I have become a great man. Do you know who I am? I am "great." I am greater than the king of England. This is so much higher than the forgiveness of sins! I wish I could shout. Do you know who I am? The Jesus who is the King is now living in me. The One who is the eternal life has come to live in me. On the one hand, He is in me as life. On the other hand, He is ruling as the King. When I am sad, He comforts me. When I am confused, He enlightens me. When I am in darkness, He shines on me. When I rebel, He disciplines me. Today He is within me.

OUR RELATIONSHIP WITH THE INDWELLING CHRIST

Whether or not you are a proper Christian, and whether or not you carry some spiritual weight with you depends on the way you take care of the Lord. If you take care of Him properly, you will be a proper Christian. If you do not take care of Him properly, you will not be a proper Christian. To be a Christian is fully a matter of your relationship with the Christ who is within you. It is not a matter of how much work you do or how much love you have. It is a matter of having the proper relationship with the Lord.

FELLOWSHIPPING WITH THE LORD, ALLOWING HIS ELEMENTS TO OCCUPY AND REPLACE US

Suppose you treat a person well and render him much help. Can you say that this is spiritual? Outwardly speaking, this is very spiritual. Actually, it may not necessarily be spiritual. How then can something be considered spiritual? While you are fellowshipping with the Lord, He may tell you to help a certain person. If you obey His word to help this one, this is spiritual. Furthermore, while you are helping such a one, you do so by trusting in the strength of the Lord all the time and acting according to the inner feeling. You are not only performing what is after His heart; you are also acting according to His feelings and His thoughts, and you are taking Him as your content and as everything to you. Day by day, you will have more of the Lord, and gradually your thoughts and your natural disposition will decrease. Up to a certain point, your own elements will disappear, and the Lord will occupy your whole being. Finally, you will be able to say that it is no longer you, but Christ the Lord.

THE PURPOSE AND PRINCIPLE OF GOD'S WORK— WORKING HIMSELF INTO MAN

When you have God's life, nature, thoughts, and love within you, and when you are filled with Him, God's desire will be accomplished. God desires to mingle Himself with man. God has taken on man's form. Now He wants man to take on His form. He has put on humanity, and He has ascended to heaven with His humanity. He is the God-man, and He is the Man-God. He desires to see that man has God, in the same way that He as God desires to put on man. God can now say, "O man! I now have the human nature." Man can also say, "O God, our great God! I now have Your nature." This is God's eternal purpose. It is for this purpose alone that God created man, redeemed him, forgives his sins, regenerates him, and lives in him. God desires to work

Himself into man. What is God's work? God's work is to work Himself into you. This is God's principle, and it is God's law.

THE GOVERNING PRINCIPLE OF A CHRISTIAN'S LIFE AND WORK

All our living and works have to be measured by this rule. Only then will they be up to standard. For example, here may be a brother who is very capable in leading the hymns. If he has never allowed God to pass through him, and if God has never worked on him before, his leading of the hymns will not carry much weight. But if God is added to him, his hymn-leading will carry much more weight. A person can save a large number of souls without allowing God to pass through him and without much mingling with God at all. A person can do many good works, help others, and visit many people. But the question is whether or not he has allowed God to pass through him. The same is true even with the reading of the Bible and praying. Many readings of the Bible end up being without God. If you study the Bible much, yet you do not fellowship with God in your studying, your Bible study cannot be considered spiritual; it can only be considered mental. It is useless to study diligently the letter of the Bible without having any fellowship with God. A proper Bible reading is one in which a person fellowships with the Lord through his reading. This kind of reading becomes a kind of "gold plating," in which God is "plated" onto you. This will not be mere knowledge, but will become life.

Sometimes even our prayers can take God away from us. At the beginning of the prayer, we may still be fellowshipping with the Lord. But after a while, the presence of the Lord is gone. Prayers that are merely in the mind or in the flesh, that have no spirit in them, are useless. No wonder so many prayers are not answered. If a person is not proper, even his prayers will not be answered. The real problem is with the person himself. In reading the Bible, in praying, and in working for the Lord, the most important thing is that the person has to be right. A person cannot pray according to the mind. Whatever he feels within, he should pray according to that feeling. If he has only a few words, or if he feels to pray for a certain particular person, he should go ahead and pray accordingly. This is prayer in the spirit. The important thing is not that your prayer be beautiful, but that while you pray, God has one more chance to pass through you. In the end, not only will you have your prayers answered, but by praying you will become like God. Your view will be like God's view. Through prayer, you will allow God to work Himself into you.

**ALLOWING THE LORD
TO BE THE HEAD OVER ALL THINGS**

All those who have a heart for the Lord and who will answer His call will realize in eternity that what we are talking about during these meetings is something very precious. Do not be concerned whether a thing is good, bad, right, or wrong. Instead pay attention to what lies behind the thing itself, to whether or not in doing such a thing, you are allowing the Lord to be the Head.

CHAPTER SIX

THE GRACE OF GOD

SPECIAL CONFERENCE (4)

Date: Evening, December 30, 1947
Place: Hong Kong
Speaker: Witness Lee
Scripture Reading: John 1:16-17; Rom. 5:21; 6:14; 1 Cor. 15:10; 2 Cor. 12:9; Phil. 4:23

GOD'S GRACE NOT BEING OUTWARD THINGS

In this message we want to consider what God's grace is. Many times we hear people say, "Thank God for His grace, that I have not had any accident." These people think that God's grace is to keep them from having an accident. Others think that to make a few thousand dollars is grace. Still others think that for a person's whole family to be free from illness and calamities is grace. Some people ask God for a lovely little baby, or a good husband, a good wife, or good children. They think that these are grace. They think that God's grace being sufficient means that they will lack no food or clothing. Still others say that joy, peace, and power are God's grace. All these concepts are not necessarily correct.

GOD'S GRACE BEING HIMSELF RECEIVED BY US

God's grace is God putting Himself into us. To receive grace is to receive something that we do not deserve to have. It is to receive something without a price, something free from God (Rom. 4:4-5). Receiving God is better than receiving everything else. Nothing else is worth much, for all things are vanity of vanities. A bad husband is surely vanity, but a good husband is also vanity. Good children and many riches are all vanities. We must never think that grace is success and accomplishment in our work. If God were to give us things of vanity as grace, He would be deceiving us indeed. When God gives us grace, He is actually giving us Himself. Paul forsook everything for the sake of gaining the priceless treasure (Phil. 3:8). When a person has God, he has the best treasure. This is why the Bible tells us that grace is not some thing. Rather, it is God Himself.

Grace Enabling Paul to Labor More Exceedingly

Do not consider grace as a thing or a matter. Paul became the leading apostle, and he became a diligent and laboring person. He became such a one through grace. It was through such a living person that he was able to do what others could not do and suffer what others could not suffer.

Grace Being God as Life and Power in Us

Those who do not have God within surely do not have grace. When they encounter difficulties, they shed tears easily, and it is easy for them to be sorrowful and in distress. Those who have God within them may appear sorrowful outwardly, but they can rejoice inwardly because of God. All the money in the world could not buy the strength they have. Good children are not grace. Could you still say "hallelujah!" if your child were to die one day? Neither is it grace to have a fortune. If your business were to close down one day, what would you say? Others may hang themselves, or kill themselves by drowning in the sea. What about you? Could you still praise the Lord? To have peace is not necessarily to have grace. If you were to have a car accident one day, could you still thank the Lord? True grace is the inward power to overcome what others cannot overcome.

Do you have this grace? I can tell you that I have it. Everyone who does not live by this grace is living in vanity. If you have God within you, if you live by God, and if God becomes your life and your strength, and He comforts you, supports you, and is with you all the time, you are experiencing God's grace. Never pay too much attention to the things and the works. Even if the whole world were given to you, it would all become vanity after a few decades. All those who know God, the One by whom we live, are persons who know grace and are blessed persons.

ALL SPIRITUAL EXPERIENCES AND VIRTUES BEING A MATTER OF GOD WORKING IN MAN

God's grace is God given to us. The principle of the Christian life and of spiritual experiences is a matter of living by God. Never think that solving the problems of others is a spiritual experience. Spiritual experience is to live by God and to fellowship with God. Through these experiences, you derive strength from God to help others. In this way, God will come in and come out of us. When God is in us, and when He comes out through us, this is spiritual experience.

What is prayer? Prayer is to allow God to come into us and to allow Him to come out of us. We should not pray according to the mind, the memory, or our experiences. Instead we should allow the Spirit of God to operate, and we should pray according to His operation. What is faith? Faith is God coming into us and coming out of us. What is humility? What is love? Humility and love are also God coming into us and coming out of us. Both humility and love are God's nature. When God is added into us, we will match God's nature, and we will have humility and love.

LIVING ACCORDING TO THE GRACE OF GOD

What will you mothers do if your sons stir up your temper? What will you do if your husbands come home tonight with a big temper? Are you going to bear it by the grace of the Lord?

IN THE LORD

Many times, we say that Christians should live "by" the Lord. Actually, the Bible says that we should do things "in" the Lord. We do not rejoice "by" the Lord but "in" the Lord. Consider the example of riding on a bus. Do you come here riding "by" the bus or riding "in" the bus? If you come riding "by" the bus, you would be outside the bus trying your best to hold onto it, and if you were not careful, you would fall down. But if you come riding "in" the bus, then whether or not you hold onto it, and whether or not your hands let go, or you sit down or stand up, the bus will carry you here.

NO NEED FOR RESOLUTIONS AND STRUGGLING, BUT MERELY FULFILLING THE CONDITION FOR GRACE TO OPERATE

At one time, I was just the same as you are. When the children misbehaved, I wanted to lose my temper. I would pray, beseech the Lord, and trust in Him. However, in the end, I lost my temper just the same. It is natural for me to breathe. I breathe without being conscious of breathing. In the same way, as long as you are in the Lord, your victory will come in a spontaneous way. Suppose you are going to eat, and you pray, "Lord, help me to digest the food; I trust in you for my digestion." I am afraid the more you pray, the more you will not be able to digest your food; you have spent too much energy in this matter. Digestion is something spontaneous. When some sisters lose their temper with their husbands, the husbands may say "Praise the Lord" with clenched jaws. If the wives rebuke them some more, they may try to say "Praise the Lord" again. But sooner or later, they will not be able to hold back and will lose their temper with their wives also. Life is spontaneous; you cannot imitate life. Here is an orange tree. If you pray for it, it will bear oranges. If you do not pray for it, it will still bear oranges. This is because the life it has enables it to bear fruit. The tree does not bear fruit through resolutions and prayers. To be a Christian is a simple thing. When you were born, you measured a little over a foot. But now you are over five feet tall. When did you grow to this height? You do not know, for you do not bear the responsibility for your own growth. All you have to do is to fulfill the conditions for growth. Crucifixion is something that others execute upon you; you cannot crucify yourself. A man can commit suicide, but he cannot crucify himself. You can nail your right hand with your left hand, or you can nail your left hand with your right hand. But in the end you still cannot nail both hands by yourself. This is the reason that after twenty years you still have not been able to crucify yourself.

Hence, you do not have to worry about how much you have grown. All you have to take care of is hygiene, normal restrictions, exercise, and proper food. Spontaneously, you will grow. If you love God and fellowship with Him, this is all that is needed. Everything else is taken care of by God. You do not have to reckon, to beg, to crucify yourself, or even to trust. All you have to do is to praise. Is this not very simple?

GOD'S GRACE BEING RESPONSIBLE FOR EVERYTHING

I know what I am speaking, and I know that this is the right way. If you ask me, "Brother Lee, what do you do when your children stir up your temper?" My answer is, "Don't do anything." This does not mean that I do not know what to do. Nor does it mean that I just let the things go, ignoring them and overlooking them. Rather, it means that I have the grace within, and I let grace take over the responsibility. The life within will spontaneously react to the situation. God's grace is my strength. I am afraid that after listening to my messages in these days, some brothers and sisters would think, "Brother Lee is telling us not to lose our temper. Lord! from today on, cause me not to lose my temper. Please help me." If you are such a Christian, you are indeed under a curse. You will not experience any blessing. All those who make resolutions by themselves have fallen from grace (Gal. 5:4). You are saved now, and God is within you. You can experience His blessing without struggling, striving, or making resolutions. In the end, you will be able to say, "By the grace of God I am what I am" (1 Cor. 15:10). Paul was able to overcome all trials gracefully and calmly because he was not the one who was responsible for the overcoming, but God was responsible for it.

To live in grace is like breathing. When a person does this, whatever temptation comes upon him will be calmly dealt with. In the end, such a one will live in God's grace and will be full of God's taste. When others touch such a one, they will touch God, for such a person is full of God.

KNOWING THE ALL-SUFFICIENT GRACE OF GOD

When you encounter difficulties, you have to know God's grace. You do not have to pray, because the Lord's Word says, "My grace is sufficient for you" (2 Cor. 12:9). No wonder the prayer or blessing that comes at the end of each Epistle mentions God's grace and His life. We must realize that God's power and His grace are simply God Himself.

KNOWING, EXPERIENCING, AND ENJOYING GOD AS OUR GRACE

You have to learn to realize how powerful is the God within you. A Christian should be one who lives under such a condition. Ultimately, God will be mingled with you, and all the life, power, light, and every spiritual virtue will be here. May God open our eyes to see that God Himself is our grace, and may we enjoy everything in this grace.

CHAPTER SEVEN

GOD'S SATISFACTION AND MAN'S SATISFACTION

GOSPEL MESSAGE

Date: 10:30 a.m., The Lord's Day, December 28, 1947
Place: Hong Kong
Speaker: Witness Lee
Scripture Reading: John 4:3-35

A THIRSTY UNIVERSE

This passage of the Scriptures tells us of a conversation between our Lord, while He was on earth, and a Samaritan woman. Here the question of water was brought up. Water is something to satisfy man's thirst. A person can live without food for a day. But if he does not have water for a day, he will become very desperate. Without water, man will be unsatisfied. Here was a woman who was thirsty and unsatisfied within. The Lord came and asked her for water to drink. This shows that the Lord was also thirsty and unsatisfied. If He had not been thirsty, He would not have asked for a drink. Both the woman and the Savior were thirsty.

Friends, do you realize that the world today is a thirsty place? Who among us can say that he lacks nothing? You may have much education and money, but you still feel that you lack something. Although you may not know what it is that you lack, you somehow feel that there is something missing in your life. The reason man seeks for entertainment and amusement is that he is bored and depressed, and he has no interest or taste for anything.

GOD BEING MAN'S SATISFACTION

When a man is thirsty, you will not solve his problem by giving him gold. Husbands, wives, children, parents, money—

none of these things can satisfy man's thirst. Only God can solve this problem of man. A wife cannot satisfy a person's heart. Money cannot satisfy a person's heart. But when you come to the Lord with an empty heart, you will be filled. God is man's real need and real joy. A person can have fine clothing, good food, nice houses, an enormous amount of savings in the bank, high position, or great knowledge, but he will still not be happy within. What he needs within is simply a glass of water. This water is God. Without God, man is not satisfied. God is man's satisfaction. Whenever man has God, he is happy, and he is satisfied.

BOTH GOD AND MAN SATISFIED BY EACH OTHER

Not only are the sinners thirsty; even God is thirsty. Man thirsts because he does not have God, and God thirsts because He does not have man. God is man's satisfaction, and man is God's satisfaction.

The Lord Jesus is a sinless Man. Yet He is also thirsty. Today what He wants is you. He is asking water from you. Whenever the Savior meets a sinner, that sinner will thirst no more. Whenever the Savior gains a sinner, the Savior will also be satisfied. You are drawing water, and the Lord is asking you for water. Man is thirsting on earth, and God is thirsting in heaven.

Satan is working on earth today to frustrate man from having God. What we are doing on earth today is to have man gain God and to have God gain man, so that both God and man can be satisfied. This is why both heaven and earth rejoice when a sinner is saved (Luke 15:8-10, 23-24). Both heaven and earth rejoice because both God and man are satisfied.

GOD AND MAN RESTING IN ONE ANOTHER

Not only was the Samaritan woman thirsty; she was also restless. In the same way, not only was the Lord thirsty; He was also restless. He came to earth to seek the sinners. The Lord is not at rest yet because He has not yet gained you. He said that He did not have a place to lay His head (Matt. 8:20). He wants to come into your heart. At the same time, you also do not have rest. You are laden with heavy burdens.

There is the burden of your family; there is also the burden of your job. You may have the best bed there is, but within you, you cannot rest in peace. You are tired. You do not have rest. This is because you do not have the Lord. The Savior is not at rest, and you are not at rest.

GOD AND MAN BEING FOOD TO EACH OTHER

Here is not only a question of thirst and restlessness, but also a question of hunger. What is hunger? Hunger means that a person needs food within him. The Lord's food is the sinner, who is you. Our food is the Lord. The Lord is not only the water of life, but the bread of life (John 6:35). Only He can satisfy our thirst and fill our hunger. Only He can remove our restlessness.

THE CONDITION FOR RECEIVING GOD—CONFESSION

By that time, the Samaritan woman realized her need. She began to ask the Lord for the living water. The minute she began asking, something happened. She asked for the living water, but the Lord asked her for her husband. Why did the Lord ask her for her husband? The matter of her husband speaks of the life she lived in private. She told the Lord that she did not have a husband. This was only a half-truth. She was lying by telling the truth. The husband here also signifies sin. Her husband signifies her sins. The Lord wanted her husband. This means that the Lord wanted her to confess her sins. Do you want the living water? The first thing you have to do is to confess your sins. Although a man may not know what kind of sins he has, the Lord nevertheless knows. Cheating, evil thoughts, craftiness in the heart, and lying are all sins. If you do not take your sins to the Lord, you will not have the living water. Have you told lies? If there is one thing you have done that you have never told anyone about, including your parents, your husband, or your wife, you have at least one thing that is not upright. This is sin. The Lord wants to have an exchange with you. He wants you to give Him the husband, while He gives you the living water. You hand over to Him your sins, and the Lord gives to you His salvation. You do not have to tell me or anyone else what your sins are. The Lord is not trying to give you a hard time. But you have to tell Him everything. Concerning this matter, you must have a proper confession before the Lord.

WORSHIP BEING IN SPIRIT AND IN REALITY

When the Samaritan woman saw that the Lord had exposed everything about her private life, she changed the subject of the conversation. She began to talk about the worship of God. The Lord answered her that one must worship with the spirit and in reality. There is no need to worry about the place. The important thing is for one to worship in spirit.

A TESTIMONY OF GOD BECOMING MAN'S SATISFACTION

In 1940, while I was preaching the gospel in Chefoo, a certain person came every day to listen to my preaching. One day he asked to have a time with me. At that time, this person was working in the Customs Department. I told him that it is a very simple thing to be saved. All that a person has to do is to receive Him as the Lord from the heart and to confess his sins to Him. If he does that, he will be saved. This one asked me to pray with him. After I prayed for him, he prayed, "Lord Jesus, save me. I am a sinner." I told him that when he went home, he should stop whatever he was doing to pray and confess to the Lord alone in his own room. After he did this, he slept peacefully. He was indeed saved. After he was saved, immediately he bore a strong testimony. Formerly, he smoked every day. But after he was saved, he was completely freed from cigarettes. He had two colleagues at work. When these two persons offered him cigarettes, he refused them. His colleagues said, "We have tried to quit smoking but could not cut down to less than twenty cigarettes a day. How can you stand not having even one cigarette?" Nevertheless, from that day on, he stopped smoking. Besides this, he also stopped many other evil habits. Many of his colleagues were touched by his testimony.

Friends, God is waiting for you today. He is waiting for you to accept Him. When you accept Him, you will experience a change in your whole being. Please do not refuse today, and accept Him now.

CHAPTER EIGHT

SPIRITUAL REALITY AND OBEYING THE LEADING OF THE HOLY SPIRIT

FELLOWSHIP MEETING (1)

Date: 10:00 a.m., December 26, 1947
Place: Hong Kong
Speaker: Witness Lee

SPIRITUAL REALITY— THE LIFE WITHIN BECOMING THE LIVING WITHOUT

Brother Weigh asked: What is the relationship between spiritual knowledge and our practical living?

God's Unique Goal Being to Work Himself into Man

Brother Lee answered: Every saved person should be very clear that he has God's life within him. Spiritual reality is nothing other than the inward life becoming the outward living. We must have the basic understanding that God has only one goal, which is to work Himself into man. The significance of salvation is that God has entered into man. This is not merely the forgiveness of sins or deliverance from hell, but the entrance of God into man. When we say that we have received life into us, it means that God has entered into us. If we are clear concerning this point, the rest will be simple. God has put Himself into you in the same way that electricity has been transmitted into the light bulb and has become the shining of the bulb.

Obeying the Operation of God Within

God is living and omnipotent. He is living now. You may not be very impressed by this word, because, although He may be living, to you He may be sleeping. In the Bible, there is a difference between "living" and "being." To "live" is active; the Lord is not merely "being" in you, but He is "living" in you. He is moving and working, and He is very purposeful. Since the day you were saved, God has been living within you (John 15:4). What you have to do now is to go along with this moving within. Suppose a person easily loses his temper with his wife. At the time he is saved, he may not know that God is in Him. Right after he is saved, when he comes home from the meeting, his wife may provoke him again. At that instant, he would surely have a certain feeling. If he goes along with that feeling, he will be all right. However, if he does not go along with that feeling and instead loses his temper, he will feel depressed. The next time, when a similar incident occurs, he will not dare to go against that feeling again. The matter of going along with one's inner feeling may be a small thing, but it is difficult to find one person in a thousand who knows to obey it.

There were two people who were always at odds with each other. Both of them were Christians. One day, both came to me and asked for advice. I turned the question back to them and asked them if they knew what the problem was. They said that they seemed to know, yet they were not clear. In the past, when I encountered such problems, I would try my best to answer them and to list the answers one by one. I would even open up the Bible and explain to others with it. Actually, the ones that asked the questions knew the answers already. In recent years, I do not do this kind of thing any longer. When others ask me a number of questions, I would only answer, "What is your feeling within?"

Paying the Price to Obey

The Lord says in the Bible, "Or do you not know...?" (1 Cor. 6:9, 16). This means that we ought to know such things already, because a living God is living within us. You have to learn to follow closely the inner leading. If God tells you to give up certain things and to forsake them, you should say, "Lord, for the sake of loving You, I would forsake them." Christians today like to listen to teachings. Very few of them listen to the voice within them. I would like to ask the brothers and sisters who are sitting here if there is anyone who has been obeying God from morning until evening today in every matter. If you have a genuine desire to take care of God's word, He will only have to speak once. If you do not have this desire, even if He were to speak many times, it would still be useless to you. If there is a group of people here who are willing to give themselves completely to God, in a year's time this place will have a complete turnaround. But if there is not such a group of people, then even if someone were to preach to the people the whole year round, it would still not be of much use. Every time we want to obey the inner feeling, we have to pay a price, because to do such a thing would cause pain to our self and would inflict loss on us. This will show how much you really love God. If you are not willing to obey, even if you listen to a hundred more messages, it will still not do you any good.

Obeying in a Simple Way

If there is a small number of brothers and sisters who will obey God, His blessing will be brought in through them. Only when we learn to live in the reality of the spiritual things can we have real spiritual progress. This is the only thing that will cause us to live before God and in His light. Our inner feeling and guidance is our spiritual restriction. When we go along with this feeling, we go along with the spiritual restriction. God's way is always simple. If it is complicated, it is because we have made it so.

OBEYING THE LEADING OF THE HOLY SPIRIT

Question: We may know the leading and the restriction of the Holy Spirit. But why is it that we are not able to obey this leading and restriction?

Not a Question of Being Able, but a Question of Being Willing

Brother Lee answered: Actually, the issue is not one of being able or not able, but of being willing or not willing to obey. It is not a question of ability, but a question of willingness. When you are willing, God will manifest His strength upon you. We were all paralyzed and were unable to walk. But when we obey, strength will come upon us. When the Lord called the paralyzed person to stand up and walk, he was able to stand up and walk (Mark 2:10-12). If God says yes, you have to say yes. When God says to put your feet down, you have to put your feet down. The water of the Jordan will spontaneously be divided (Josh. 3:8, 13-16). Your eyes should never be fixed on the water. If you look at the water, you will say, "The Lord must divide the water first before I can put my feet down." If you do that, the water will never be divided.

The Secret of "Willingness"— Being Drawn by the Love of God

How can you become willing? The secret of willingness is to be drawn by the love of God. It is a matter of how much you love the Lord. If you do not love enough, you will feel that you cannot do anything. If you love enough, you will be able to obey what others cannot obey, and you will be able to do what others cannot do. Only those who love the Lord with a single heart can go on in this way. Hence, it is not a question of whether or not you are able, but a question of whether or not you are willing. In order to be willing, you have to love the Lord, and you have to be constrained by the Lord's love.

CHAPTER NINE

HOW TO ABIDE IN CHRIST

FELLOWSHIP MEETING (2)

Date: Morning, December 27, 1947
Place: Hong Kong
Speaker: Witness Lee

HOW TO ABIDE IN CHRIST

Brother Shen asked: How can we abide in the Lord?

A. Knowing the Teaching of the Anointing

Brother Lee answered: First John 2:27 mentions the anointing: "The anointing which you have received from Him...." In Greek, the word *anointing* is a gerund; it is not a simple noun. The anointing as a gerund denotes a moving and an application of an ointment. Within us we have the teaching of the anointing, and we do not need any teaching from man. This anointing is true and is not a lie, and even as it has taught us, we should abide in Him. God abides in us, and we abide in Him. Although these appear to be two different things, yet in fact they are not two things, but one thing.

B. The Lord's Abiding in Us Being Based on Our Abiding in Him

In the New Testament, there is a difference between the two phrases "in the Lord" and "abiding in the Lord." To be in the Lord refers to being saved, whereas to abide in the Lord refers to living an overcoming life, one that is in fellowship with the Lord. To abide in the Lord is to have fellowship with Him. The Lord's abiding in us is based upon our abiding in Him, while our abiding in Him is based upon our being in Him. When electricity is installed to a lamp, it can be considered as being "in" the lamp. But when the switch is turned on and electricity is applied, then the electricity is "abiding" in the lamp. Some people abide in sin, the flesh, and the world. Although such a one may be a person in Christ, he does not abide in Him at all. You may be a person who belongs to Christ, yet you never abide in Him. Some have asked if a person who is abiding in Christ can move out again. Actually, in our experience, we can move in and out more than a dozen times within a day. The fact of our being in Christ is once for all and can never change. But our abiding in the Lord and the Lord's abiding in us is something relative. In the entire New Testament, you cannot find one incident where it says that He will abide in us without us abiding in Him first; these two things are linked together. Romans 8 mentions the Holy Spirit abiding in us. Every saved person has the Holy Spirit in him, but this does not mean that every one has the Holy Spirit abiding in him. The Holy Spirit does not have the complete authority over every one yet. God's abiding in us is based on our abiding in Him.

C. Abiding in the Lord according to the Teaching of the Anointing

How do we abide in God? We abide in Him according to the teaching of the anointing. The Holy Spirit operates in us. This operation is the application of the ointment. Suppose you want to joke with Brother Shen, but there is an inner restriction that tells you not to do it. If you disobey it and keep on joking, you will lose the peace. You will be cut off from the Lord and will not be able to continue in the fellowship. This disruption in fellowship can last for a whole day. Only after you confess your sin will this fellowship with God be resumed. Consider again the example of the sisters scolding their children or their servants. A sister does not need someone outside of her to tell her that this is wrong. Instead, the operation inside of her will restrict her. The greatest punishment to a Christian is not outward sufferings, but being cut off from his fellowship with the Lord.

1. The Anointing Bringing with It a Feeling

A few times I found myself arguing with rickshaw drivers. When I argued, the Lord was gone. There is a difference between what we know and what we feel. You may know that a certain medicine is bitter, but it is only after you put the medicine into your mouth that you feel its bitterness. When God anoints us, this anointing comes with a feeling. If I touch Brother Weigh's forehead, surely he will feel something. Whenever we ignore our feeling, we are cut off from the fellowship. This is very real, and it is very simple. It all depends on whether or not you are willing and whether or not you want to have this experience.

All other kinds of teachings are dispensable, but this matter is indispensable. There is no teaching that can cause something to happen: No matter how proper, neat, clean, and blameless you are as a person, as long as you are living outside of the Lord, you are not worth anything in God's eyes.

2. Walking according to the Sense of Peace

It is true that every genuine Christian has the anointing in him. The Lord is not stingy, but neither is He sloppy. He means business with us. Some sisters may want to buy some bargain fabrics. There is nothing wrong with this, yet the Lord may not want them to do it. For the price to be cheap is one thing. For someone to buy the items is another thing. In the end, when the sisters go ahead and make the purchase, they lose their peace and are unable to pray for a few days. Only when others buy those fabrics from them are they able to gain back their peace.

3. The Depth of Our Experience Depending on the Degree of Our Obeying the Inner Feelings

I have been a Christian for twenty-two and a half years. During the first ten or more years, I did not know anything about this way. During the last few years, the Lord has granted me mercy to discover this way. The more you go along with your inner feelings, the more your spirit will be enlightened, and the more demands you will experience.

These demands will become more and more severe, and you will be more and more restricted by the Lord. Up to a certain point, you will lose the freedom to speak, act, laugh, or cry. You will be restricted in everything. The more we reason, the more the Lord is gone. Only by accepting all adverse conditions willingly and giving up all reasonings will the Lord have a way. The anointing teaches us in everything. This anointing is true and is not a lie. The question is whether or not we are willing to obey.

THE DIFFERENCE BETWEEN THE FEELING OF THE SPIRIT AND THE FEELING OF THE CONSCIENCE

Brother Ho asked: How can we tell the difference between the feeling of the spirit and the feeling of the conscience? Can our conscience be wrong sometimes, since Satan disguises himself as an angel of light at times? (2 Cor. 11:14).

A. Taking Care of the Inner Feeling in Everything

Brother Lee answered: The initial work of the Holy Spirit is to recover the function of the conscience and to point out man's mistakes. After the function of the conscience is recovered, the Holy Spirit can go on to recover man's spirit. Once man's spirit is recovered, surely it will have feelings. A person has to take care of the inner feelings. If he does not have peace about something, he should stop doing it. Only when he is at peace should he proceed with anything.

B. No Need for Too Much Analyzing— Rather, Exercising Much and Walking in Peace in a Faithful Way

In the Gospels, after a person is saved, many times the Lord says, "Go in peace" (Mark 5:34; Luke 7:50). Romans 8:6 says that "the mind set on the spirit is life and peace." After the Ethiopian eunuch was baptized, he went on his way rejoicing (Acts 8:32-39). In taking this way, there is no need to analyze too much. In the course of our experience, spontaneously we will be able to differentiate between the conscience, the spirit, and the flesh. We will develop a feeling for all these things. Sometimes we may make mistakes, but we should not be discouraged. If we are wrong, we can exercise more until we become right. This is like practicing riding a bicycle or practicing penmanship. This way is surely the right way, and as long as our hearts are clean, as long as we are faithful, and as long as we have a heart for God, our feelings will become more and more sensitive.

CHAPTER TEN

THE PROPER PERSON

SPECIAL FELLOWSHIP MEETING

Date: 1:30 p.m., December 28, 1947
Place: Hong Kong
Speaker: Witness Lee
Remark: A meeting for those who are burdened for the affairs of God's house, concerning matters related to God's house. Attendance, about forty or more.

Brother Hsu asked: How should elders serve in the house of God?

THE PERSON BEING GOD'S METHOD AND WAY

Brother Lee answered: The service of the elders has to do with the person of the elder. It does not depend on the method, but on the person. In the New Testament it is very difficult to find out what is the method or way to serve. Some places seem to speak about the method or the way, but actually the emphasis is still the person himself. The person is the way, and the person is the Lord's work. If God does not gain a person, He will have no work, and He will have no way. A way is a course that a person takes. If God does not gain man, He will have no course to take. Man thinks that the most important thing to do is to find a good way. However, God's work does not involve giving us the ways, but is a matter of gaining the persons. If God can gain two or three brothers here, He will have a way. Even if I present to you the best way to be an elder, it will be useless if the person is wrong. We, the person, should be gained by God. We have to learn to be the proper person more than to learn to do the proper things. It is meaningless for things to be done properly without the person being a proper one. What you are is what you do. You cannot serve God beyond what you are as a person. Hudson Taylor said in his book *Union and Communion* that what we are is more important than what we do. This word left a deep impression on me. We should know how to help the brothers and sisters properly.

BEING DEALT WITH BY GOD TO SERVE HIM

What God cares for is whether or not you have been touched by Him. The measure we yield ourselves to the Lord determines the measure we are able to serve Him. If you have been dealt with in your temper, you can help others with their temper. If you have been dealt with in the way you dress, you will be able to help others in the way they dress. The church is not a worldly society. The church is a body (Eph. 1:23). A body is a matter of life. If we can only do the proper things in the church and nothing else, we are failures. It is true that we need to learn the proper lessons with regard to many things, including money and the way we deal with our family. However, in the church, business affairs do not take priority. Rather, life takes priority. Life can meet man's present need. This should cause every servant of God to come before God again. Otherwise, the more right things we do, the more man-made works there are, and the more the church will become a human society or community; it will become something merely human, with nothing other than a common belief and a common philosophy!

BEING DEALT WITH IN LIFE
TO BRING IN THE AUTHORITY

In order to have such a proper life, we need to be restricted in everything and to apply ourselves in a practical way to learn the lessons. The main thing we have to learn is the matter of authority. A person who has authority has life; he is like the budding rod of Aaron (Num. 17:1-10). If you submit to him, you will have life. If you do not submit to him, you will touch death. However, such a person does not put on an air. When the apostle spoke about the elders, he spoke very little about what they do. Mainly he spoke about the kind of persons they should be (1 Tim. 3:1-5). In a degraded church, people pay much attention to the office of the elders and the deacons. A person can be very clever and capable, but he may not be dealt with in the matter of life. Whenever someone brings his knowledge and diplomacy into the church, it is like putting a hole into a ship. Soon the whole ship will be filled with sea water; the world will invade and take over the church. Just because a person has the knowledge does not mean that he can therefore interpret the Bible. When a person engages in visitation work or other affairs, what is needed is not merely to have things done properly, nor to gain others' admiration, but to be a proper person. A proper person has the authority with him. Even if he is not a responsible one, the authority is still with him. Wherever there is life, there is authority. Life is authority. If God can gain one brother here in an absolute way, the saints in this place will be able to advance in great strides.

DOCTRINES BEING USELESS

Doctrines are useless. If doctrines are to give us a way at all, then there is only one way that is useful, which is the way to God. The only way that is useful is the way that brings us to God. The Christians here are spoiled by revival meetings already. This can be compared to putting rice in a cooker and cooking it for a while. Before the rice is cooked, the fire is turned off, and the rice is left half-cooked; nothing more can be done to the rice. If a man has not been dealt with in a practical way in his daily life, what good will doctrines do for him? I wish that there would be no more revival meetings in this place. Every child of God who loves Him faithfully must be broken by Him. How many are captured by God in this way here? We have to realize that the person is God's way.

GOD'S WAY BEING TO TOUCH THE PERSON

During the five or six years between 1938 and 1944, I spent all my time in Chefoo. In 1937 I travelled to other places often. The Pentecostals always tell people that they need the power. I told the brothers and sisters once, "Let them seek for the power. See where they will be after a few years." In Chefoo there were twelve or thirteen denominational churches. At least three or four of them could seat over a thousand people, but their combined attendance did not match our attendance. We did not have pastors, preachers, or seminary students. Although I cannot say that every one among us was touched by the Lord in an absolute way, I can surely testify that some were indeed touched by the Lord. The Communists opposed us very much. But during the New Year, we still preached the gospel in a daring way. One time we baptized one hundred two persons at the same time. The next time after that, we baptized a few dozen. For a city with only a few hundred thousand people, this was quite an outstanding achievement. One village chief warned a Communist cadet not to touch us, because he said that the Communists would not be able to deal with us.

If your heart is attracted by the Lord's love, you will be willing to give yourselves to the Lord. This is a very simple and direct word. The degree you can render others help is determined by the degree you have advanced yourself; it is also determined by the amount of learning you have picked up. If only one-fourth of those among us are used by God in this way, in a few years, the church will increase from one or two hundred people to one or two thousand, and the quality of the people gained will surpass the one or two hundred people that we have today. It is not our ground or our doctrines that will bring in God's blessing. The basic question is the person himself.

A GOOD TREE PRODUCING GOOD FRUIT, A CORRUPT TREE PRODUCING EVIL FRUIT

I do not believe that there is anything that is more real than the things in the spiritual realm. A person cannot cheat God. He cannot cheat himself, and he cannot cheat the saints. In two years' time, you will see the effect of my words today. The kind of person you are determines the kind of children you produce. Those who love the world will produce Christians who love the world. Those brothers and sisters who seek after modern fashions, if they can bring others to salvation at all, will bring in ones who are flippant and shallow. Those who have a hot temper will surely bring in

Christians with a bad temper. A good tree produces good fruit, and a corrupt tree produces evil fruit (Matt. 7:17-18). The kind of person we are determines the kind of fruit we produce.

GOD'S LIFE COMING INTO MAN THROUGH THE PROCESS OF BREAKING

In order for God's life to enter into man at all, there must first be the breaking. This is like giving people an injection: the skin must first be punctured before the needle can go in.

PAYING THE PRICE TO GIVE GOD THE WAY

What this place needs is not doctrine, or zeal, or the so-called power of the Holy Spirit. What this place needs is neither excitement nor stirring up. What this place needs is people who are willing to pay the price. If there are some who would do this, God will have a way here. Brothers and sisters, we must be willing to suffer loss, so that God could have a way.

THE CONSECRATION OF OUR WILL

With regard to the work of the Holy Spirit, the main thing on our part is not whether or not we are able, but whether or not we are willing. Are you willing to allow God to do great things in you? This requires the consecration of the will. Sometimes we have to say to God with tears, "Lord, I am willing." When we do this, though our heart may at times be in pain, our spirit can rise up to praise Him.

CHAPTER ELEVEN

OBEYING THE INNER FEELING

FELLOWSHIP MEETING (3)

Date: 10:00 a.m., December 29, 1947
Place: Hong Kong
Speaker: Witness Lee

OBEYING THE INNER FEELING

Brother Shen asked: As far as the inner feeling is concerned, I realize that we should do something only when we have the peace, and we should stop when we lose the peace. Suppose we are engaged in a business. At the beginning, we did not have the peace. Consequently, we did not proceed with it. But after two weeks, we felt peaceful again. What then should we do?

Walking Only according to the Inner Sense of Peace

Brother Lee answered: First John 3:19-21 tells us that a Christian should not find his heart blaming him. In your business engagement, you were held back at the beginning because you did not have the peace. Two weeks later you had the peace again. Your question is whether or not you should proceed. The answer lies in whether or not your heart blames you. If by going to hell you can have the peace, it is all right for you to go there. Romans 3:17 says, "And the way of peace they have not known." Isaiah 57:21 says that there is no peace to the wicked. The Lord says that peace He leaves with us (John 14:27). The Lord charged his disciples to bless others with peace (Luke 10:5). After He healed someone, He charged that one to go in peace (Mark 5:34). For Christians, peace is something within. If you are seeking for outward peace, you will never be able to be a proper Christian. It is also a very dangerous thing to do. As Christians, we have to be those who have peace within us. If the Spirit of God is not at ease within us, we will not have peace. Others' criticisms, attacks, praises, or debasements can all be ignored. What we need to pay attention to is our inner feeling. The apostle Paul said, "Because of this I also exercise myself to always have a conscience without offense toward God and men" (Acts 24:16). This is a person who fears God and who lives in His presence.

Not in the Letter, but in the Spirit

The only place to be a Christian is in your spirit and your conscience. There is no other place and no other way to be a Christian. Only by being in spirit and in the conscience can a person be a genuine Christian. To practice being a Christian according to the conscience is like shooting in archery; the first time a person may miss. The second time, the third time, and even the tenth time he may miss also. But eventually, he will hit the mark. If you have a lawyer sit down and write out all the laws, you may find yourself blameless according to the laws. But this does not mean that you are a proper Christian. It is possible that you have done the right things, but that you as a person are wrong. If you compare yourself with the Bible, you may find yourself one hundred percent right according to it, yet in fact you as a person may still be off. Do not misunderstand me. I am not saying that I do not agree with the Bible. The Bible says that we have to love others as we love ourselves. If you merely act according to the letter of this word, even if you were to achieve it, you would still be off. If you touch God this morning, you will feel that you have to care for others. You will not only give your coat to others; you will be willing to give even your skin to others. Outwardly speaking, this kind of caring for others appears to be the same as the kind of love mentioned earlier. But in reality, there is a great difference between being a Christian according to the letter and one according to the spirit. Similarly, the humility spoken of in the Bible is not one which bows ninety degrees to others. This will only make your body pliable; what you need is a pliable inner sense. Your inner being needs to be soft. If it is slightly hardened, you will feel uneasy. Those Christians who behave in an outward way feel uneasy only when they lose their face. To be sorry because of an outward mistake is worthless. This is like a thief feeling sorry because he is caught, rather than because he has committed the crime of stealing. If a person feels sorry only because he is caught by others, this kind of sorrow is worthless.

Paying the Price to Forsake Everything

Many preachers tell others that if a person believes in the Lord he will be blessed. They tell others that the Lord is the blessing, and that with Him there is the blessing. Actually, to be a Christian costs one's life. A Christian is one who is blind, who gives up money and position, and who would rather have his own feeling hurt than offend the Lord's feeling. He is one who is willing to give up everything to gain the Lord. All those who are not willing to go on in this way are merely "pew-Christians." All "pew-Christians" are Christians who will not go on in the Lord's way.

OUR HUMAN LIVING BEING A MATTER OF GOD WORKING IN MAN

Mrs. Chow asked: Should we obey our parents if they charge us to do something contrary to the Lord? If we disobey them, are we dishonoring them?

Allowing God to Touch Us in Our Human Relationships

Brother Lee answered: Do not be an analyzing Christian or a rehearsing Christian. You do not need to analyze or rehearse. Whatever your inner feeling, you should simply act accordingly. If the feeling inside tells you that you cannot obey your parents, you should not obey them. In the Old Testament, God ordered Abraham to kill his son, and the Levites to kill their brothers. They would not have committed a sin if they killed those God ordered them to kill.

If you go along with God's feeling, you are pleasing God. However, it is not God's intention for you merely to please Him, but it is His intention to mingle His life with yours.

God's emphasis is not that we work for God. Whether or not we do the right thing is immaterial. What God is after is that in our obeying of Him, He gains the ground in us. He wants to transmit the "electricity" to you. His intention is to put some "gold" on you. God has no intention for us to be rebellious children or submissive children. He has no intention for us to be evil persons or good persons. What God wants is that we allow Him to touch us in our human relationships, in the relationship between parents and children, and between husbands and wives. He wants to put Himself into us in the same way that gold is coated onto an object through a plating process.

Mrs. Chow asked: If my mother-in-law asks me to buy a joss stick for her, should I do it?

Brother Lee answered: If you do not feel peaceful within, you should not buy it. There is always a price to pay. If you do not pay this price, you will feel sorry for a week.

Allowing God's Element to Increase in Our Daily Living

If you take every opportunity to learn the lesson, in the end you will become a person who is saturated with God. You will become a person who lives out God. God has put you in various positions, within your family and in your job. He does so in order that you would allow Him to touch you. God does not care for the success of your career. What He cares for is that through everything He would gain the proper ground. If you have been a good wife for five years, yet God has never increased in you, but has instead decreased in you, you are worth nothing in His eyes. During the five years that you have been a wife, daily you should have allowed God time and time again to anoint you with His desire, His heart, and even Himself, so that you would have His element within, and that this element would increase all the time. This is what God is after.

Everything Being Arranged for the Purpose of God Mingling Himself into Us

The mind of today's Christian is too far away from God's

heart. We should not obey the inner feeling merely for the sake of being a proper man or to please God, but we should do it to allow God to mingle Himself with us. God is exercising His multifarious wisdom to work Himself into us. God loves us. This is why He arranges everything, and He uses our husbands, wives, and children as the means to mingle Himself into us.

Real Grace Being to Possess God

One sister said that God loved her so much that He gave her a lovely little baby. After fifteen years, the lovely baby became a sore mischief. God's greatest love in the universe is His giving Himself to us. Children are not the real grace. Money is not the real grace. The Bible says that everything is vanity, and it is dung. If God gives us these vain things as grace, is He not deceiving us? Some have said that God has blessed them and has given them so much money at the end of the year: what immense grace God has bestowed upon them. How can anyone say that it is grace when his hands are filled with so much dung? The real grace is God. Jesus is the real grace. True grace is when a person gains more of God through his relationship with his wife and when he gains more knowledge about God through his job.

Not a Question of Good and Evil,
but a Question of God Working Himself into Man

Luke 14:26 says, "If anyone...does not hate his own father and mother and wife and children and brothers and sisters...." This shows us that God wants us to hate. He has a heart to hate. How many people have you ever hated? Have you ever hated your daughter-in-law? Have you ever hated your sons? God cannot come into you because you have loved your sons too much. If you would hate a little, God would come in. Your hatred will allow God to gain something in you. In order for God to come into man, it is right sometimes even to hate.

God created everything. He spoke, and things came into being. How beautiful are the flowers in the field. Man does not need to add anything to them. Man can only produce artificial flowers. I am not speaking heresy here. Nor am I joking here. I know what I am saying. The New Jerusalem in eternity does not come out all of a sudden. It is the cumulative masterpiece of God throughout the ages. By nature we are clay. But after God has passed through us, we become gold, pearl, and precious stones. God's presence is within us. His element is in our minds and our emotions. Today, our Savior in heaven still bears His humanity. When the Word became flesh, He brought in a mingling of God with man. Now as the flesh becoming the Word again, He mingled man with God. The result of this is gold and precious stones. If I merely teach others to be good wives and good husbands, my work is surely wood, grass, and stubble. Gold signifies God's nature. Precious stones signify God's glorious image. God is doing only one thing today: to cause the man of clay to become gold and precious stones. God does not try to teach man to be good, in the same way that He does not try to teach man to be evil. All these things belong to the tree of good and evil; they do not belong to the tree of life. To honor one's parents is the good of the tree of the knowledge of good and evil, and to dishonor one's parents is the evil of the tree of the knowledge of good and evil. To love is the good of that tree, and to hate is the evil of that tree. The fruit of the date tree is good, but the branches have offensive thorns. The dates can be compared to the good, and the thorns can be compared to the evil; they all come from the same tree. God is not pleased with either good or evil. From the day that we are saved, God begins to work in us. He continues to work in us all the way until we are glorified and raptured. By that time we will not see our good, in the same way that we will not see our evil. By that time we will see only the gold and the precious stones, which are simply God Himself.

CHAPTER TWELVE

A FELLOWSHIP

Date: December 30, 1947
Place: Chanticleer Restaurant, Hong Kong
Speaker: Witness Lee

GRACE BEING THE UNIQUE REALITY

The Lord Jesus is the grace. John 1:17 says, "Grace and reality came through Jesus Christ." This chapter shows us that reality is something that can be seen, and grace is something that can be received. Grace is the unique reality in the universe. Other than grace, nothing is real. Even the heaven and the earth will pass away one day. This is why we say that the earth and everything that can be seen will not last forever, and they are therefore not real.

THE NEED FOR THE LIFE WITHIN TO GROW

The identifying death mentioned in Romans 6 can only be experienced and lived out in the Holy Spirit in chapter eight. Hence, it is useless to "reckon" alone. In the same way, the sin in Romans 5 is lived out in chapter seven. When a baby is born, sin is there already. But it is only when he grows up that sin is manifested. The same principle applies to God's life within us. When we are regenerated, we have life already. But this life needs to grow before its fullness is expressed.

Between 1938 and 1942, I saw this truth. In 1943, I was put into prison. One month after I came out of the prison, I became sick, and I was in bed for a whole year. During this period of time, this truth appeared clearer and clearer to me.

THE LORD'S DEATH AND HIS LIFE

Ephesians 1 and 2 cannot be separated from each other.

In fact, the end of chapter one is joined to the beginning of chapter two. Chapter two should not begin with a capital letter.

The death of the Lord Jesus contains two elements: death and life. The two combined together also give life. The Lord gives life to us out of His death. This can be likened to some medicine that kills germs, on one hand, and imparts life, on the other hand. Everything mentioned after chapter two confirms these two facts, that is, the fact of the Lord's death and the fact of His life. To sin, the world, human relationships, and the flesh, we are dead; whereas to God, we are living.

CHAPTER THIRTEEN

A TESTIMONY

Date: January 2, 1948
Place: Canton
Speaker: Witness Lee

The year before last, the Communists entered the city of Chefoo, but the brothers and sisters in the local church still continued to meet. We did not register ourselves with the government, nor did we hand ourselves over to them. The brothers and sisters continued to preach the gospel. The denominations used to be quite zealous in preaching the gospel, and they were critical of the local church, saying that we were narrow-minded and that we cared only for our own people and would not fellowship with others, nor would we preach the gospel in the rural villages. However, together with the brothers and sisters, we paid attention only to the matter of life and spiritual matters, and we were not affected by their criticisms. One day, when the time came, all the brothers and sisters rose up to preach the gospel, and we baptized one hundred two people. After that time, we had more baptisms. There were twelve or thirteen denominations in our city that met on Sunday, but their total number did not match the attendance of the local church. Three or four of these denominational churches could seat over a thousand people, yet their numbers were still less than ours.

CHAPTER FOURTEEN

GOD GAINING MAN

CONFERENCE (1)

Date: Evening, January 7, 1948
Place: Swatow, Kwangtung
Speaker: Witness Lee
Attendance: 200-300 people

GOD'S PRINCIPLE IN HIS WORK

In coming here this time, I do not expect to hold large conferences or to do any great works. My hope is to fellowship with the brothers and sisters, and especially with those who are involved with the Lord's service. We see that both in the Old Testament and the New Testament, God's principle in His work is the same, and that is to gain an individual or a few individuals from every place. When He gains an individual or a few individuals, He has a way to go on. Many people neglect this point. They like to stir up others and to rally others around them. But merely stirring people up and rallying them around oneself will not afford God a way. In every place, God needs to gain some people; without this God cannot do anything.

THE MEN GOD IS AFTER—
THOSE WHO ARE PURE, POOR IN SPIRIT, SIMPLE, TRANSPARENT, AND SINGLE-HEARTED TOWARD GOD

During the past twenty years, there were big conference meetings and big revival meetings everywhere. But God did not have a way because not many people were gained by the Lord. Today, we are not merely hoping to see many people saved and revived; what we hope to see is not that kind of work of the Holy Spirit. We only hope to see a small number of people rising up, those who are pure in heart, who are poor in spirit, and who can drop everything within them to seek after God single-heartedly.

Today, I hope that you will not be busy taking care of others, or waiting for others to come to this conference. I hope that we would go to the Lord in a quiet way. Please do not misunderstand what I am saying, but things such as your work, your church, the saving of souls, and so forth, have no place in my heart. I only wish to see us turning to the Lord in a pure, direct, and simple way, so that we can touch the Lord in a definite way and can know the way He wants to go on in us. Only one thing is crucial: to be taken hold of by the Lord. When that happens, God will have a way, and He will be able to flow out of us, and others will receive the blessing. Otherwise, we will not be able to render others any real blessing. We hope that we can meet God here, or that God can meet us and occupy us. Within us, we do not have to pray for others, or to pray for this meeting, and we do not have to pray for the Lord to bless this meeting. I do not expect the Lord to "bless" this meeting. I only hope that there will be a group of brothers and sisters who will fellowship with the Lord in a quiet, pure, unperturbed, and unencumbered way. I hope to see a group of brothers and sisters who are as transparent as glass. If there are such ones, we will see great blessings in this place.

We have to learn to turn to the Lord in a simple way. You do not have to pray for me, and I do not expect to see too many people here. Sometimes, when there are too many people, God does not have a way to go on. For example, Zaccheus was hindered from seeing Jesus because there were too many people. We have to be like Zaccheus, climbing higher than others. If we do this, we will see, and our lives will change. Too often people hinder us from seeing the Lord. Here we need to transcend, to rise above the crowd, and leave others under our feet. In the whole universe, there is only you and God; everything is under God. In this way, blessing will come. In Swatow, if there are two or three brothers who are touched by God in this way, He will have a broad and free way to go on. This is the only way to bring in a revival in Swatow.

Many people will advise you to fast or to pray without sleeping. But I say today: you do not need to pray that much. Of course, I am not saying that you should be lazy. What I mean is that your heart has to be pure and simple. We should not be unresponsive or passive. But neither should we be over-zealous or aggressive. Those who are not zealous will receive nothing, and those who are over-zealous will also receive nothing. Many times, God has no way to help the zealous ones, and He has no way to help the over-hungry ones.

During the past ten years or more, there were some very zealous ones in northern China. I have not seen another group of people more zealous than they were. They could fast for a few days, pray continuously for a few hours, or keep themselves awake a few nights without sleeping. When I met these people, I had no way to help them. I only wished that I could pull them back and have them sit down to rest. May the Lord be merciful to us. Here we do not have any excitement, and we do not have the flesh. We only hope to be simple, pure, and restful. In this way, we will touch God.

Many times, when we say we are turning to God, our turning does not cause us to obtain mercy. I see many people in the church who are like black chimneys; they are full of black smoke. No matter how strong the light is, a man cannot see anything through a cloud of black smoke. Many brothers and sisters cannot allow light to pass through them because of their flesh and their natural life. They are not transparent. A piece of glass is not like that; it is transparent, and light can pass through. Some people are too hungry, too unworldly, too much for the Lord, and too zealous. As a result, they become misguided. I am not saying this in a light way. We should pray before the Lord, and in our prayer we should ask the Lord to make us more simple and more clear. May the Lord be merciful to us.

A PRAYER

Prayer: Lord, we ask for mercy before You. We commit this word into Your hand. Cause us to be pure. Cleanse us, that we can meet You within us, and that our inner being can be turned to You in a real way. We need Your precious blood to cleanse us in many ways, so that our heart will not condemn us. May we turn to You from the depths of our being, and may we feel Your presence. May we come before You as coming before the throne. We pray this in the Lord's name, amen.

CHAPTER FIFTEEN

IMAGE AND THE TREE OF LIFE

CONFERENCE (2)

Date: January 8, 1948
Place: Swatow, Kwangtung
Speaker: Witness Lee
Scripture Reading: Gen. 1:27

IMAGE AND THE TREE OF LIFE

Genesis 1:27 mentions the word *image*. This word is very crucial. The Bible mentions image many times. The main thing this word reveals to us is the relationship between God and man. When many people think about salvation, they think about forgiveness of sins, the receiving of blessings, and so forth. But God did not create man just for him to receive blessings and to be forgiven of his sins. The first thought God has with man is that He wants man to be like Him. The first time the Bible mentions man and the creation of man, it mentions him having the image of God.

Genesis 2 mentions the tree of life and the tree of the knowledge of good and evil. The first chapter mentions image, and the second chapter mentions the tree of life. I hope that you will circle the words *image* and *the tree of life* with a red pen. Image is something outside, whereas life is something inside. First it speaks of the outside, and then it speaks of the inside. This is like saying that you have the image of a Chinese outside, and you have the life of a Chinese inside. Without having God's life inside him, man cannot have God's image. Life is the content, and in this life there is God's nature. When this life is expressed, we have God's image.

I want to ask the brothers and sisters a question: Why do you believe in Jesus? Many people answer that it is because they have sinned, or that they were poor and suffering, and they needed something to depend on. All of these are right answers, but this kind of understanding is too shallow and elementary. In God's creation, the earth is the center of the heavens, and the garden of Eden is the center of the earth. In the midst of the garden, there was the tree of life. God put man in the center of the center. He did not put man in the heavens, nor did He put man on the fringes. Rather, He put man in the center. In this center, there was man, and there were the two trees. Both trees speak of food. The tree of life is a matter of food, and the tree of the knowledge of good and evil is also a matter of food. We know that when food gets into a man, it becomes a part of him. I hope that tonight we will put aside matters such as heaven, hell, blessings, and sufferings. Let us set our hearts on two things: image and the tree of life.

THE TREE OF LIFE BRINGING IN LIFE, WHEREAS THE TREE OF KNOWLEDGE OF GOOD AND EVIL BRINGING IN DEATH

In Hebrew, the tree of the knowledge of good and evil is composed of three words: knowledge, good, and evil. Life is simply life; it is unique. But God cannot say that evil is good, or that good is evil. Other than knowledge, good, and evil, there is still another thing, which is death. Good and evil bring in death. Today, in order to gain God, we have to be pure. The meaning of being pure is to have one thing only. What we take into us is life, and what is lived out of us is the image. If it is life for us all the way from the beginning to the end and we have nothing besides life, we are being pure. When man joins himself to the knowledge of good and evil, he falls into death, and he becomes complicated. The tree of knowledge can be called the tree of good, and it can also be called the tree of evil. Humanly speaking, the tree of good and the tree of knowledge sound very nice, and the tree of evil and the tree of death sound very bad. But in the whole universe, nothing other than life is according to God's will. Everything outside of life is in the realm of knowledge, good, evil, and death. Today, man thinks that good is life, and evil is death. When man touches evil, he touches death. But when he touches good, does he not touch death also? When he touches knowledge, does he not touch death also? I have to shout loudly that the result of good and knowledge is also death. If someone hates you, or he is proud, this is to be evil. But if he loves you, and he is humble, this is to be good. On the one hand, the Bible teaches us to love our parents and our brothers and sisters. But on the other hand, Luke 14 tells us to hate our parents and our brothers and sisters. God's intention has nothing to do with good and evil; it has to do with life. God has no intention for us to do evil, and He has no intention for us to do good. You cannot please God by doing evil, and you cannot please God by doing good, because both good and evil come from the tree of knowledge of good and evil. Whether you are proud or humble, the source is the same, and the end is death.

GOD, THE DEVIL, AND MAN

What is life? John 1:4 says that in Him is life. First John says that he who has the Son has life (5:12). Whenever we come into contact with God, we have life. Life is versus death, in the same way that God is versus the devil. In the whole Bible, there are only these three things: God, the devil, and man. These three things stand as three separate entities. When man contacts God, there is life. When man contacts the devil, there is death. Everything with God is real, and nothing is false. Everything with Satan is unreal; he pretends to be good, and he pretends to give knowledge. A man may be touching something that he considers good, but within that something is death.

What did man touch in the garden of Eden? He touched the tree of the knowledge of good and evil. The result was that he received Satan into his being, and he became fallen. Satan is the evil one, the one who holds the power of death. The meaning of the fall is that Satan entered into man. The meaning of salvation is that Satan is driven out and God has entered in. Ephesians 2 says that within the unbelievers there is the operation of the evil spirits. Christ said once that we were of our father, and our father was Satan. This is why some people say that those who gamble are "gambling-demons," and those who take opium are "opium-demons." When a man sins many times, eventually the devil is lived out of that man. When you go into the casino, the people you see do not look like human beings; everyone looks like a devil. Before a man is saved, it is the devil that is living in him. Such ones may be honest on the outside, but they are deceitful on the inside. Who is inside of them? It is the devil who is inside of them. Many times, a person cannot control himself. This is because Satan is living within him. Man has been mingled with the devil.

Now man has become very complicated. Within us, it seems that there are three persons: God, Satan, and man. You are like a little garden of Eden, and you are standing before two trees. We are saying all these things to show you that today the garden of Eden is within you. These two trees are within you.

THREE KINDS OF LIVING

What is your attitude toward the knowledge of good and evil today? Christianity today has degraded. All that the ones there know is that evil is death; they do not know that good is also death. They do not know these two trees.

For example, a brother may become angry with his wife in the evening, and he may beat his wife. If you see this, you will say that he is an evil person. The next morning, he may become humble, and you will say that he is a good man. In the afternoon, he may fellowship with the Lord and live in His presence. When you see him, you will sense that he is neither an evil man nor a good man, but a God-man. Why do you have such a sense? It is because with him, there is the taste of God. This man has allowed God to rule over him and to live out of him.

I hate two kinds of people. The first is the proud ones, and the second is the falsely humble ones. Perhaps the second kind is worse than the first kind. Notwithstanding, whether a person is humble or proud, our question is this: Which tree is his source? In God's eyes, knowledge, good, and evil are all death. Very few people can discern this matter.

With some people, a person does not sense any good or evil in them. He only senses the taste of God in them. They are persons living in God. They do not know what is good and what is evil. They do not know what it is to be proud and what it is to be humble. They are people who live in life. Suppose you see a brother loving others, and you ask him why he loves. If he says that the Bible tells us to do so, it is wrong. If he says that God tells him to do so, it is right. The question today is whether we are living in God's tree of life, or in something else.

Prayer: May the Lord work into our being the words released tonight, so that we become enlightened within, and so that the eyes of our heart may be opened.

CHAPTER SIXTEEN

TWO TREES, TWO PRINCIPLES, AND TWO RESULTS

TALKS (1)

Date: Morning, January 9, 1948
Place: Swatow, Kwangtung
Speaker: Witness Lee

WHAT GOD WANTS BEING WORKS OF LIFE

The words of Confucius and Mencius are different from the words of life. We are not trying to make the cold brothers and sisters excited and the disorderly ones orderly. We are not doing a mortician's job here, improving men's outward appearance a little and eventually burying them in the ground. We have to ask what kind of work we are doing today. If we are merely putting some cosmetics on dead people, adding some plaster to thin cheeks and some color to pale faces, we are doing a work of death. What God wants is a work of life.

If we compare Genesis 1 and 2 with the last two chapters of Revelation, we will discover that at the end of Revelation there is no longer the tree of the knowledge of good and evil. The result of the tree of the knowledge of good and evil is death. Hence, the tree of the knowledge of good and evil eventually ends in the lake of fire. Satan is the constituent of death, whereas God is the source of life. Throughout the ages, God has been showing us one thing, which is that everything that has to do with the tree of the knowledge of good and evil eventually ends in death.

THE RIVER OF WATER AND THE RIVER OF FIRE

The Bible talks about the river of water and the river of fire. Daniel 7:10 mentions the stream of fire. Whenever we touch the tree of the knowledge of good and evil, fire comes. Genesis 3 mentions the flaming sword. Whenever we touch the tree of life, there is the river of life. Once the tree of life appeared, the river of life was produced. This river produced gold, bdellium, and onyx stone (Gen. 2:9-12). Gold signifies God's nature. Once this gold passes through you, you will be "plated" with gold. The bdellium is pearl, which is produced from a grain of sand. When the sand gets into an oyster, the secretion of the oyster produces the pearl. In the same way, when we believe in the Lord, we enter into Him. From that day on, God's nature is continually dispensed into us to turn us into pearls. This pearl in the end becomes the precious stones. Revelation 4 also mentions the precious stones. Precious stones refer to God's manifested glory. The New Jerusalem was constituted with gold, pearl, and precious stones. There the river refers to the Lord's life. Jeremiah 17:7 and 8 say that those who trust in the Lord are like a tree planted by the waters. Jeremiah 2:13 also says that when we forsake God, we are forsaking the fountain of living waters. Psalm 46:4 says that there is a river, the streams whereof shall make glad the city of God. Psalm 36:7 and 8 say that God makes us to drink of the river of His pleasures. On the one hand, we eat the fruit of the tree of life. On the other hand, we drink of the river of His pleasures. According to the footnote in Darby's Bible, the word *pleasures* here is of the same root as the word for Eden. Ezekiel 47 also mentions the river. This river is the river of life.

The river of fire signifies God's judgment. This river begins from the flaming sword in Genesis 3, and it flows all the way to the lake of fire at the end of Revelation. The lake of fire is the culmination of all the rivers of fire. When all the rivers of fire flow together, they become a lake.

TWO PRINCIPLES OF LIVING AND TWO RESULTS

Our burden is to show the brothers and sisters that to touch the tree of life is to touch God, and that to touch the tree of the knowledge of good and evil is to touch fire and death. Hence, in order to learn to serve God and to work for Him, a Christian must learn to stay away from the tree of the knowledge of good and evil. Suppose a brother or a sister is very meek, submissive to his or her parents, and full of all kinds of virtues. Outwardly speaking, these are very good things. Actually, they are all things that belong to the tree of the knowledge of good and evil. Of course, we do not want to see people fighting, sinning, or falling into the flesh. But neither do we like to see people remaining in the good of the tree of the knowledge of good and evil. For example, a couple may be arguing. Our natural concept is to exhort them to be reconciled with each other. But if we know the principle of the tree of life, we will not exhort them to be patient or humble. If we are clear about the principle of the tree of life, we will lead this couple into life. Only those who touch the tree of life will see their life and work remaining in the New Jerusalem. Those who are sinful will go into the lake of fire. Those who are moral will also go into the lake of fire. Today, we are not saying that we do not need love or humility. Within the tree of life, there is surely love and humility. But the love and humility that issue from the tree of the knowledge of good and evil will result in the lake of fire. Only the virtues that issue from the tree of life will last unto eternity.

CHAPTER SEVENTEEN

THE FOUR LAWS

CONFERENCE (3)

Date: Evening, January 9, 1948
Place: Swatow, Kwangtung
Speaker: Witness Lee

Scripture Reading: Rom. 7:21-25; 8:1-2
(Please note the words "law," "good," and "evil" in 7:21, the words "the law of God," "law of my mind," and "law of sin" in 7:22-23.
Verses 22 and 23 give a total of three laws in two verses.
Verse 24 is a groaning for deliverance from the body of this death.
Verse 25 says that the mind serves the law of God, while the flesh serves the law of sin.
8:1 and 2 again mention the law twice: "the law of the Spirit of life," and "the law of sin and of death.")

WHAT IS A LAW

Before I come to my subject tonight, I will first ask the brothers and sisters to forget everything that you have heard before and come as if you know nothing about God's word and you are starting all over from the beginning.

Tonight we will look at Romans 7 and 8. These two chapters mention many things concerning the laws. Last night we spoke of some basic matters. Tonight we will speak concerning an even more basic matter. This basic matter is the law. In order for a Christian to know God, he has to understand the laws. May the Lord open our eyes to see what a law is.

Paul mentioned a number of laws in Romans 7 and 8. When I was saved more than twenty years ago, I came across this passage, and I did not know what a law was. After more than ten years, I still did not understand what it was. Romans 7 and 8 mention the laws repeatedly. Bible students all agree that the book of Romans occupies a very important place in the Bible. It can be considered one of the most important books of the New Testament. In this book, the most important chapters are chapters five to eight. With chapters five to eight, the key word is "law." If a man does not know what a law is, his spiritual life will be confused.

A law is a natural force. For example, if I throw a book up in the air, it will surely fall down. I do not have to worry about whether or not it will fall down, and I do not have to help it fall down. There is a law that controls it and compels it to fall down. Every life has its natural ability. I dare not say that every law is a life, but I can say that every life is a law. If I plant a chrysanthemum seed in the ground, I do not have to pray, fast, or worry; what grows up will surely be a chrysanthemum flower. Are we breathing, speaking, and sleeping today? Breathing, speaking, and sleeping are the laws of the body. I do not have to exercise my will to breathe a certain number of times a minute, or to exercise my mind to consider if I have digested the food I have eaten. These things do not require the intervention of my mind and will. The more I exercise my will to digest, the more I become nervous, and the less I will be able to digest. Digestion is a law of life, a natural ability. If I hit you in the eye with my hand, your eyelids will spontaneously close; this is a law.

THE LAWS IN ROMANS 7 AND 8

The laws that we are speaking about are not the laws known to the lawyers. In Romans 7 there are three kinds of laws. In chapter eight there is another law, which makes four laws altogether.

A. The Law of God

First, there is the law of God. Everything that God created has its laws. For example, the rising and setting of the sun and the four seasons all have their specific laws. The farmers have to sow and reap according to these laws. God has also placed specific laws upon man. He forbids man to sin and teaches him to do good. If a man wants to live, he has to obey God's law. Once a man disobeys God's law, he will be condemned by it.

B. The Law of Good in the Mind

Second, there is the law of the mind. The outward visible part of a person is his body. The inward invisible part is his spirit. Between the body and the spirit, there is the soul. Man is divided into three parts, which are, from the inside to the outside: the spirit, the soul, and the body. The soul includes the personality, the mind, the emotion, and the will. After man fell, the mind became the biggest part of the soul. From Romans 7:23 we see that the law of the mind is good. There, the law of the members wars with the law of the mind. These two laws are against one another. If they are complementary to one another, they will only be companions. But if they are against one another, it proves that one is good and the other is evil. The law of the mind is good. God created man a good man, and, as such, his mind must be good. Sometimes we are not very accurate in our preaching of the gospel. We tell others that there is no good thing within man. A few years ago, I followed others to say the same thing. Later, I reconsidered and felt that this is not right, because even an unsaved person has good inclinations, such as honoring the parents, helping others, and doing good. The Chinese sages said that within every person there is a heart of sympathy. It is true that the Bible tells us that within our flesh nothing good dwells, but this does not mean that within my whole being there is absolutely no good whatsoever. If that were true, there could not have been the warring mentioned in these verses. There is warring because the body wants to sin, while the mind wants to do good, and in making up one's mind to do good, there is the conflict. The reasoning faculty is a part of the soul, and for the most part the reason chooses the good. Within man there is a natural law that urges man to do good. This is because man is created by God.

C. The Law of Sin in the Members

Third, there is the law in the members. The members here refer to the different parts of the body. The law of the members is the law of the body. This is not a good law. The law of sin in verse 25 is another name for the law in the members. According to the law of the mind, man wants to do good. But according to the law of the body, he feels that evil is present with him. Here it mentions "to will" (7:18), which is a question of the will. It also mentions to "delight" (7:22), which is a question of the emotion, and "to do the good" (7:21), which is a function of the mind. To will, to delight in, and to do good are all functions of the law of the soul. However, man is not strong enough to overcome. On the contrary, he is defeated and is carried away to obey the law of the members. This is why there is the sighing, "Wretched man that I am!" This man's mind, will, and emotion all desire to do good. But he fails, and he is not able to overcome the law of the body. Here, man discovers that within him there is present a law of evil.

Before man fell, there was the law of good, because at the time God created man, man was good and he was pure. After man ate of the fruit of the tree of the knowledge of good and evil, he took Satan into his body. The name of Satan is "the evil one." This word is the same in Greek as the word "evil" in Romans 7. Within every unbeliever, there are two laws, the law of good and the law of evil. The law of good is in man's mind, whereas the law of evil is in man's flesh. The Chinese have the so-called "conflict between reason and lust." The "reason" there is the law of good in the created life, and the "lust" there is the law of evil in the body. The conflict between reason and lust as described by the Chinese is similar to the conflict described in Romans 7.

For an opium smoker, his reason tells him that he should not take opium. Although he may make up his mind not to take any more opium, his body is addicted to it. Although his mind, emotion, and will agree that he should not take it, his body has been addicted to opium, and the addiction takes over his hands, feet, and his entire body, and it drags his body to the opium parlor. Although the law of the mind tells him not to take opium, once the opium-burner is lighted, he begins to take the opium again.

The same is true with losing our temper. The law of the mind tells a person not to lose his temper. But when the temper comes, a person cannot hold it down. His temper has taken him captive. Many times, after husbands lose their temper with their wives, they hit themselves in remorse. But then when they are stirred up again, their faces turn red, and they are led to do things against their will again. According to the law of the mind in their soul, they do not want to lose their temper. But when the law of evil in their body is activated, they lose their temper again, and the reason is once more overcome by the lust. In the end, they discover that their reason is weak, and their lust is strong.

D. The Law of the Spirit of Life

Fourth, there is the law of the Spirit of life. This law comes into us at the time we believe in the Lord. With which part do we receive the Lord? We receive Him with our spirit. Hence, the law of the Spirit of life is in our spirit. With every saved person, there is the law of good, the law of evil, and the law of life. The law of good is in the soul, and the law of evil is in the body, whereas the law of life is in the spirit. All the three parts of man, the spirit, the soul, and the body, have their own laws.

Suppose a brother becomes angry with his wife in the evening, and he begins to beat her. This is the operation of the law of evil in the body. The next morning his reason takes over, and he changes his attitude, and he becomes polite to his wife. This is the operation of the law of reason in his soul. In the afternoon when he fellowships with God and is filled with Him, he begins to bear a spiritual taste, and this is the operation of the law of the Spirit of life. The law of good in the soul desires to obey the law of God and to please Him. But the law of evil in the body frustrates it and causes a person to sin and to rebel against God's law, and to come under judgment. Thanks be to God. Here is the law of the Spirit of life to be man's salvation. It delivers man from the law of evil and good, and it causes man to transcend, to rise above good to satisfy God's law and to more than conquer all things.

THE NEED FOR A CHRISTIAN TO LIVE BY THE LAW OF THE SPIRIT OF LIFE

Today, we should not be a Christian according to the first, second, or third law. Rather, we should be a Christian according to the fourth law. If someone on the street hits you, why would you not hit him back? Some say that it is because the Bible tells us not to do so. If you say this, you are acting according to the first law. When a wife submits to her husband, and children submit to their parents, these submissions may be something according to the first law. To be a Christian in this way is wrong.

Perhaps some would say that they want to be a good man and that they have made up their mind to be good. This is to live according to the second law. Then there are those who say that if others hit them, they would surely retaliate, and they would retaliate in a stronger way than they were hit. This is to fall into the third law, the law of evil in the body. It is wrong to live according to the first, the second, or the third law. If I do not retaliate, it should be because my spirit feels not to retaliate, and because to retaliate would make me feel uncomfortable and cause my spirit to protest. If a wife submits to her husband, it should be because her spirit is telling her to submit. If we do this, we are living according to the fourth law. If we live according to the fourth law, we will be able to say, "Hallelujah!" Only by being this kind of Christian will we have peace, and only then will we be at ease.

In Shanghai someone asked me once, "Why can't I smoke?" I said, "If you can smoke in peace, go ahead and smoke more." If you can hit your wife in peace, and if by hitting her, you can be brought to God, go ahead and hit her some more. On the other hand, if by loving your wife you can gain the peace and can bring God into you, you should go ahead and love her more. If your love does not bring you peace, this kind of love is appalling. We should be fellowshipping with the Lord within us all the time. If we have peace to do something, we should go ahead and do it. If we do not have the peace, we should not do it. We should be a comfortable, peaceful, happy, and joyful Christian. We should not deceive ourselves or others. Only such Christians will meet God, and only they will see the blessing.

A PRAYER

Brother Weigh Kwang-hsi prayed: May the Lord lead men to God through His servant's words. May the words open man's understanding and enlighten man's inner being, so that the brothers and sisters would have a pure heart toward the Lord and would not become Christians who live according to morality or by resolutions, but would become Christians who live out their life in a spontaneous way. Grant Your children's conscience, spirit, and intuition to have sensitive responses. Amen.

CHAPTER EIGHTEEN

THE WORK OF THE HOLY SPIRIT AND MAN-MADE WORKS

TALKS (2)

Date: Morning, January 10, 1948
Place: Swatow, Kwangtung
Speaker: Witness Lee

Prayer: May the Lord deliver us from quick minds and curious thoughts. We admit that it is very difficult for the Lord's word to come into our heart. May the Lord cause the words that we hear to lead us to the presence of God.

MAN-MADE WORKS BEING COUNTERFEITS AND BEING ARTIFICIAL

In Christianity, preachers always try to impress others with the importance and goodness of a truth. At the end, they would point out how one can obtain such truth, what one should do first, and what he should do next. The listeners may be impressed and may try to practice accordingly when they go home. But in the end, they always find out that the teachings do not work. In the Bible, the apostles did not do this kind of work. Spiritual things do not come through our strivings, strugglings, or resolutions. They are a direct result of God's light. Saul on the way to Damascus did not hear any special message, but he saw the revelation of Christ. In preaching the Lord's word, we have to look to the work of the Holy Spirit, and our being has to go out with the release of the Lord's word. This is the way to put the word into others' being. Some preaching gives others the revelation, whereas other preaching only presents the methods in a clear way. In the latter case, the listeners may be touched, but when they try to practice the methods, their endeavors are but man-made works. Man-made works are counterfeit works.

When the Japanese occupied China, there was the so-called puppet government. The puppet government is a counterfeit government. Many so-called spiritual virtues are actually like artificial flowers. They are like the fruit on the Christmas trees, which do not grow out of the trees, but are put there by hand. Artificial goodness is man-made goodness. This kind of goodness is a result of the work of the preachers. A man can have any kind of outward performance; he can act like a seminary student, walking slowly with the Bible in his hands and with his eyes fixed to heaven. But this kind of acting accomplishes nothing. He can come to the meeting with bowed head and silent prayers, and he can nod his head continually while listening to the message. He can pray silently after the message to show that he is touched by the words. But after the meeting, on his way home his eyes will catch some attractive things, and his true self will be exposed again. No wonder there are so many hypocrites today.

DISTINGUISHING BETWEEN CONFUCIUS' TEACHING AND GOD'S TEACHING

It is good that the evangelists are helping people to be saved. Many of the truths passed on to such ones after their salvation are counterfeit teachings. What many so-called great pastors and evangelists are preaching is but Confucian teachings, or godly teachings. Man likes to hear these godly teachings. But ninety-nine percent of these teachings are on counterfeit goodness. Exhortations to be godly and to be just are things that a person uses to teach others; they are not things that a person lives out in his life. We have to forget about all these things. On the one hand, we should not be lawless. On the other hand, we should not bind ourselves; everything should be done in a spontaneous way. We would rather not do something than to do it in pretension. To do something in pretension damages a person more than not doing anything. If someone is somewhat loose, we should not feel sad. If someone is somewhat meek, we should not feel happy. Humanly speaking, to be meek is surely better than to be rough. But before God, there is not much difference between meekness and roughness. Spiritual matters are not accomplished through outward strivings. Paul received the light on the way to Damascus, not through his own pursuits or strivings, but through God's taking hold of him. You may say that if this is the case, we might as well give up. But while you may give up, God will not give up; He will take hold of you. The thing I fear the most is for a person to live by himself merely according to ethics. This kind of conduct is the work of producing artificial flowers. Of course, we have to admit that, humanly speaking, Confucius' teachings are good. The Chinese say that humility brings profit whereas arrogance brings loss. For thousands of years, we have upheld the Confucian teachings. Humanly speaking, they are good teachings. But the New Testament is not on human ethics, but on divine ethics. The New Testament says that we have to hate our parents, brothers and sisters, and children. It is not teaching us to be humanistic, but to live God and to follow Him. The teachings in Christianity tell people what to do, and the teachings in other religions also tell people what to do. But none of these teachings are of any value.

GOLD, SILVER, AND PRECIOUS STONES VERSUS WOOD, GRASS, AND STUBBLE

First Corinthians 3 says that with some people, their works will be burned up by fire. It does not mean that they have sinned or have lost their temper, and so forth. It means that the nature of their works will be tested, and their works will be found not to be built on the foundation of Christ. All works that originate from the self are wood, grass, and stubble; and everything that comes from God is gold, silver, and precious stones. Gold is versus wood. Gold signifies God's nature, whereas wood signifies the human nature. Silver signifies redemption, whereas grass signifies the flesh. Stubble is earthly, and it is versus the precious stones. The precious stones speak not only of God's image, but of the heavenly glory as well. What God wants to gain in us today is gold, silver, and precious stones, and not wood, grass, and stubble.

CHAPTER NINETEEN

THREE KINDS OF LIVES AND THREE KINDS OF LIVING

CONFERENCE (4)

Date: Evening, January 10, 1948
Place: Swatow, Kwangtung
Speaker: Witness Lee

THREE KINDS OF LIVES

Last night we saw the four laws in Romans 7 and 8. Tonight, we will go on to see the three kinds of histories that go on within a saved person. First, man is a created being. Later man fell, and he became a fallen being. After he is saved, he becomes a saved person. When man was created, he had the created life. After the fall, he inherited the satanic life. After he is saved, he received God's life.

The human life is created by God, and it is good. Hence, the law within man is good. After man fell, the life he inherited came from the evil one. Hence, the law that came with it is an evil law. After man is saved, the life he received came from God. As a result, the law that came with that life is also of God. Now, man has become a complicated mixture. If I ask who you are, it will be difficult for you to answer. If you ask who I am, it will be difficult for me to answer also. Within me there is God, there is the devil, and there is also man. Within man there are three elements: the element of God, the element of the devil, and the element of man.

THREE KINDS OF LIVING

When some hear us saying that within man is the devil, they do not feel comfortable. But I have to ask this: Is there hatred in man? If there is, this hatred is surely not created by God. Surely hatred comes from the devil. We know that it is not good to lose our temper, but we lose our temper involuntarily. What is sin? The sin mentioned in Romans 5 to 8 does not refer to the acts of sins, but to a living entity. There it says that sin dwells in man. A lifeless thing cannot dwell in man. It also says that sin reigns and takes hold of us to do what we do not want to do. What we do is not of our own will, but is done by the sin that dwells within us. This proves that sin is a living thing. When Satan entered into man's life, it became sin. In the Old Testament, after the Israelites were bitten by the fiery serpents, they became poisoned with the serpents' poison. In the same way, after man fell, he inherited Satan's life.

The question today is this: By which life are we going to live? Are we going to live by the original life, the satanic evil life, or the life of God? To be a Christian is not to be an evil person, nor to be a good person. The Christian standard is not good or evil. To take good and evil as the standard is to eat of the fruit of the tree of knowledge of good and evil.

THREE KINDS OF GOOD

The Bible mentions three kinds of good. The first kind is the good that was there when man was created. The life that man received at the time of creation was a good life. Hence, the law within that life is also good. The second kind of good is the good of the tree of knowledge of good and evil. The life that Satan put within man causes him to sin, on the one hand, and to do good, on the other hand. A fallen man can also be humble. A proud man offends God, but a humble man offends God even more. To honor one's parents is good, but Satan instigates man to oppose God and ignore God through his honoring of his parents. This good therefore comes from the satanic life. The third kind of good is that which is produced by the life of God. This kind of good transcends man's original good. Many people cannot distinguish between these three kinds of good in the New Testament. The good works described in Ephesians 2 are different from the good which one wills to do in Romans 7. The good in Romans 7 refers to the good that was there when we were created. The good works in Ephesians 2 refer to the good that is God's life living through the Christians.

LIVING BY THE TASTE OF GOD'S LIFE

A Christian should not take good itself as the standard. He has to take God's life as the standard. Whether a Christian should or should not do something is based upon whether or not that thing fits his taste. This is like whether or not a man drinks a certain kind of soup having nothing to do with whether or not he is glorifying God; it is a matter of his taste. We must not only exhort others not to beat their wives; we must also ask based on what does a man not beat his wife. A Christian does not smoke, not because smoking will not glorify God, but because smoking is contrary to his taste within. God's law is written in us, because God's life is within us. Whether or not we like something is based on the law of a taste within us. This law gives us a certain taste. A five-month-old baby cannot write or speak; his mind and reason are not fully developed. He cannot argue with you. But if you put ginger in his mouth, he will not swallow it. You do not have to teach him not to swallow it; it is not a question of mental knowledge, but a question of life-taste. When God created man, He put this law of life within the sense of life already. It is not up to the mind to decide whether a person wants something or not. It is up to the inner sense to decide it. If you put ginger in a baby's mouth, he will not swallow it. But if you put chocolate in his mouth, he will take it and will want more. He may not be able to speak with his mouth. He may not even be able to distinguish clearly with his eyes. But he can tell the difference between good food and food that is not good. This illustration is a most appropriate one.

Within every Christian, there is the life of God. We know how to reject everything that is contrary to the taste of God's life. In the New Testament, two passages tell us that a saved person can know God without others teaching him. These two passages are in Hebrews 8 and 1 John 2. We have to repeat a hundred times that a Christian who has life does not need others to teach him anything.

In Chefoo a brother once asked me at a dinner if he could do something. I pointed my finger at his heart and asked, "How does that part feel?" He said, "I know. I know." But soon after, he came and asked me again concerning another matter. I smiled and pointed my finger at his heart again, saying, "How does that part feel?" He said again, "I know. I know." I then responded, "If you know already, why do you come to ask me?" The third time he came and asked the same thing again, and I answered him the same way. Today, within us, all of us know. If you say that you do not know, you are lying. The real problem is not that we do not know, but that we are not willing to pay the price. If you have life, you will surely have the taste, and once you have the taste, you will surely have the feeling. Whether a thing smells good or bad is not determined by our teaching, but by our feeling.

Twenty-six years ago, I saw a child eating a rice dumpling. He should have added sugar to it, but someone added salt to it instead. Although the child could not distinguish between salt and sugar with his eyes, when he ate it, his taste told him the difference. Some food makes a person feel right, whereas other food makes a person feel wrong. Outwardly, things may look the same. But the taste tells the difference. This is the "law of the Spirit of life" spoken of in Romans 8 and referred to in Hebrews 8. This law has a taste. We reject anything that is contrary to this taste, and we accept anything that matches this taste. Every genuinely saved Christian has this taste. Unfortunately, many Christians neglect this inner taste. They live according to the outward standard of good and evil, and not according to the inner sense, taste, and law. What we need is not teachings, but the sense of life.

Eight or ten years ago, if you asked me some questions, I could give you many ways. But today, I will tell you that the answer to all the questions is found in the taste of our inner life.

There was a story in *The Christian* magazine which said that once, after Moody preached the gospel, a lady told him, "I am a Christian. But I am not like you. I have children, and I am married. My husband often takes me to the theater

THREE KINDS OF LIVES 105

to watch the plays. Should I go or not?" Moody asked the lady, "Have I ever mentioned in my pulpit anything about whether or not one can go to the theater?" The lady said, "No." Moody then said, "What I preach is all published in the newspapers. Can you find in any of the articles anything I have said about this matter?" The lady again answered, "No," but she added, "Although nothing was said, I imagine you would not like to see Christians going to the theater." One afternoon, the lady again went with her husband to watch a play. The minute she entered the theater, she did not have the peace within, and she left. The husband said, "You have become crazy through listening to Mr. Moody's preaching." She answered, "No. I am not crazy. The taste within me has changed. I do not have the taste for this any longer." Hence, we see that it is not a matter of outward teaching, but a matter of an inward taste of life.

CHAPTER TWENTY

GOD WORKING HIMSELF INTO MAN

THE LORD'S DAY MORNING MESSAGE (1)

Date: January 11, 1948
Place: Swatow, Kwangtung
Speaker: Witness Lee

Scripture Reading: Eph. 2:10; 3:17-20

GOD'S CENTRAL GOAL—
WORKING HIMSELF INTO MAN

Throughout the ages, God has only one work, and that is to work Himself into man. I hope that everyone sitting here can listen carefully to this. Why did God create the universe? Why did He create man? Why did He create you? What is God trying to accomplish? This is an important question. If God wants to do something, and you do not know about it, your Christian life is meaningless. You may think that God's intention is for you to have joy and peace. It is true that God wants you to have joy and peace, but these things are not God's center. God is not merely giving you peace, blessings, forgiveness, eternal life, and so forth; His central thought is to work Himself into man. What is the ultimate goal of God in the old creation as well as in the new? It is to work Himself into man. This is God's goal. God's redemption is for this goal. He created the universe in order to put man in it, and the purpose for Him to have man is to work Himself into him. I cannot tell you why God wants to do this. But I do know that this is His desire; He wants to work Himself into man.

A light bulb is very good to look at. But if you ask the designer who designed it, he will tell you that the bulb is not made just to be good to look at. It has one specific goal, and that is to transmit electricity. If electricity is not transmitted into it, all the electric wires and electric poles will be useless. What is the function of the electric wires and poles? They are there to transmit electricity to the light bulb. Everyone, whether male or female, young or old, honorable or lowly, exists for his three meals a day only. He eats so that he can work, and he works so that he can eat. Some say that they live for society or for their country. These are lies; they are but beautiful words. The best liars are the social reformers and the politicians. This world is a chaos; it has been put into disarray by the great politicians and by the so-called reformers. For a person to be a high officer or the head of a state will not necessarily bring blessing to humanity. Even if a man gains the whole world, what he ultimately gets is but a coffin. None of these are the meaning of human existence.

THE PURPOSE OF MAN—TO BE GOD'S VESSEL, CONTAINING GOD AND EXPRESSING HIM

Man is God's vessel. He is God's "bulb." God wants to put His life and light into man. He wants to live inside of man. What is the meaning of your existence? Is it for your family, children, or business? You have attended school for many years, and you have filled your mind with knowledge, but is this the meaning of your human life? Some people hope to have good children. But as their sons are growing up, the fathers themselves are dwindling down.

Other people say that they want to serve God and to keep His will; they want to please God, to work for Him, and to zealously do His will. Are these thoughts correct? Again there are those who hope to receive answers to prayers, to receive blessings, and to witness for God. Christianity today has been degraded by man to a pitiful level. To have blessings and peace is not the purpose of man. What then is the purpose of man?

Romans 9:20 and 21 say that man is a piece of clay. This piece of clay is not made to be God's servant or His maid. It is made to be a vessel. Any vessel, whether it is a cup or a bowl, exists for the purpose of containing something. A vessel is different from a tool. God has no intention to make you into a tool. It would be terrible if God were to make you into a tool. He has no intention to make you into a hammer and use you to hit others. He only wants to put Himself into you, so that His life can flow out of you. The real way to serve God, glorify Him, and keep His will is to put yourself in the hand of God and to allow Him to fill you up. In this way, God will shine out and flow out from within you. This is to serve God. It is not a matter of your working for the Lord, but of God's working Himself into you. It is a great blasphemy to think that a man can do anything for the Lord. God is the Creator. He does not need you to work for Him; He only needs you to allow Him to work in you. Ephesians 2 says that we are God's workmanship. We are not His workers. If the whole of Swatow would rise up to work, I can predict that soon these ones will argue one with another. But if here is a small group of people who would tell the Lord that they are not here to work for Him, but to be worked on by Him, God will have a way here. God does not need you to be His tool. He wants you to be His vessel to contain Him.

OUR LIVING AND WORKING
BEING FOR GOD TO WORK HIMSELF INTO US

The problem today is that no one is willing to contain God. Our eyes need to be opened. If there is such a group of people, God will have a way here in this place, and man will receive the blessing. God has no intention for you to love your wife or to hate your wife. God has no intention for the wife to submit to the husband or to rebel against the husband. God has only one intention, and that is to work Himself into man.

If Brother Chow keeps walking around, it will be difficult for me to pour water on his head. But if he sits down, it will be easy for me to pour water on him. It may seem that he is doing something for me when he walks around. Actually, I can do nothing with him.

If by hating your wife you can have more of God in you, you can go ahead and hate your wife as much as you like. In facing an issue, the question is how much of God will pass through you, and how much He will gain in you. Why did God give you parents, husbands, wives, and children? He gave you these things in order that He can work Himself into you through these things. If the more I speak, the more God is added into you, this will achieve God's goal. I did not come to Swatow to give teachings. I have come to have God worked into you. Why should the sisters manage their homes well? Is it to make better homes? No. It is to have more of God added into you. The more we manage our homes, the more God should be added into us. If you do this, after three or five years, you will have more of God. Your homes may still be the same, but God will have increased within you.

Some have asked me if they can quit their job to serve the Lord full-time. I told them bluntly that it does not mean anything for them to remain in their jobs, and it does not mean anything for them to quit their jobs and be a preacher. The question is not whether or not one should be a preacher, but whether or not one will allow the Lord to work in him. God's work in the old creation is outside of man. His work in the new creation is within man. One day, the work of the old creation will pass away. But the work of the new creation will remain until the New Jerusalem; it will never pass away but will have eternal value.

Every time we do something, we should not ask if that thing is right or wrong, or if it is according to God's will. In doing something, the question is this: Is it we who are doing it, or is it God? What we should ask is not what we do, but who is doing it.

GOD'S LEADING AND OVERSEEING BEING FOR THE PURPOSE OF WORKING HIMSELF INTO MAN

Today, many people talk about God's leading. The word *leading* has been much misused by men. You may say that God is leading you to preach the gospel today, or that He is leading you to take care of your home tomorrow. The issue is not this or that kind of leading. The question is this: In such leadings, what do you do? By whom are you doing these things? God has not asked you only to be a steward and to manage your household well. He has not asked you only to preach the gospel and to preach it well. God's goal is to go through you and be constituted in you. Some manage their homes well. But by doing so, God is put aside. The same is true in one's management of the church. Some are led to manage the church. But the question is this: By what way is this one managing the church? For him to be led to take up the management of the church is one thing, but the way he manages the church is another thing. With some sisters, the more they manage their homes, the worse their homes become. Yet all the while, God is worked into them. Before they try to manage their homes, they do not have God. But after they start managing them, they are filled with God, even though their homes are still not well-managed. God is managing them through their home management. In their managing of their homes, God passes through them. Some may ask, "If a person has God, will she not manage her home well?" Consider the world; it is true that the world is under God's management. But is the world good? Seemingly, the world is not managed very well. Out of this world, however, God gains a group of people that will allow Him to work Himself into them. This is God's goal. Even when you save the whole county, if God cannot be worked into you, His plan in man is still defeated. If God can only be preached to people, without being preached into people, His will is still not accomplished.

We have to remember all the time that the need today is for God to work Himself into us, rather than for us to work for God. All those who will only work for God without allowing God to work in them will eventually be rejected. Only those who allow God to work in them through various circumstances, people, matters, and events will be blessed by Him.

CHAPTER TWENTY-ONE

THE CENTER OF GOD'S TRUTH

TALKS (3)

Date: January 11 to 12, 1948
Place: Swatow, Kwangtung
Speaker: Witness Lee

TALK AFTER DINNER ON JANUARY 11

Brother Lee: Men beget children according to a law. As long as a person fulfills that law, he will beget children, whether or not the begetting is a legal one. In the same way, saving people through the gospel is a law. As long as there are those who preach the gospel, there are those who will be saved. This will happen spontaneously. But the question today is not one of being saved or not being saved. Rather, it is a question of the method we use, of whether or not the methods are up to the standard of God's desire.

Many of God's children have been spoiled by Christianity today. They are like a piece of material, which is best left alone to itself, because once it has been touched and has been made into some kind of vessel, one can never change it anymore. It is better to leave a piece of fabric alone than to cut it into something. Once it has been cut into something, nothing can any longer be done to it. The same is true with Christianity's work on some people.

TALK AFTER BREAKFAST ON JANUARY 12

God is going onward all the time; He never goes backward. In every age, He raised up men who would afford Him a way to go on, men like Abraham, Isaac, Jacob, David, and so forth. God's works are different for different people. God would never raise up another David, and He would never raise up another one like George Müller to do a similar work. Of course, these people can give us some principles of conduct. But this does not mean that we have to imitate them and be the same as they were. In northern China, a few people tried to imitate Madame Guyon. At the beginning I dared not say much, but in the end I realized that this would not work.

Brother Weigh Kwang-hsi asked: In 1934, Brother Nee spoke concerning Christ as the centrality of God. Brother Sparks also emphasized this same thing. Is this the same as what Brother Lee is speaking this time, that is, God working Himself into man, and man being filled with God? Or is what Brother Lee is speaking another aspect of God's centrality?

Brother Lee answered: There is no difference between these two things; they are the same thing. No other truth is more crucial than this truth today. Christ is God's centrality; this is the overall center. At the same time, the center of God's creation of man is His working Himself into man. This is for the purpose of establishing Christ as the centrality of all things. The Bible shows us this fact in a clear way.

Concerning the question of the Triune God, we can say that "God" is the personal name of the Triune God, that "Christ" is the official name of the Triune God, and that the "Holy Spirit" is the administrative name of the Triune God. It is better for us to say the Triune God than to say the Trinity. The end of Matthew mentions the name of the Father, the Son, and the Holy Spirit. This name is singular. The relationship between the Father, the Son, and the Holy Spirit can be illustrated by the sun, the sunlight, and the heat. It can also be illustrated by the water, the ice, and the vapor.

Sister Pearl Wang: Christ is the embodiment of God, whereas the Holy Spirit is the embodiment of Christ.

Brother Weigh Kwang-hsi: Brother Nee said before in Canton that the Holy Spirit is the second coming of Christ.

Brother Lee: Darby was a great teacher. But he did one thing wrong, and that was to excommunicate Newton. Newton believed that all believers will have to pass through the great tribulation before they will be raptured.

Two hundred years ago, the Brethren released many

biblical truths, but they did not touch the center. Instead, they only paid attention to the study of biblical teachings. In God's eyes, all His works are done in a corporate way. His salvation is a corporate salvation. In the Old Testament, salvation for Noah was directed toward his whole household. Salvation also came to the whole house of Israel. Although God's work in the church today has its individual aspects, it is all for the whole Body. God never saves people individually.

CHAPTER TWENTY-TWO

GOD WORKING HIMSELF INTO MAN

CONFERENCE (5)

Date: Evening, January 12, 1948
Place: Swatow, Kwangtung
Speaker: Witness Lee

Scripture Reading: Eph. 2:10; 3:16-19

Prayer: May the Lord cause the word to come out of us tonight, and may You cause others to receive these words into them. Although there is not much outward stimulation or excitement, may these words give others the freedom and the light as they enter into them. We admit our darkness and our foolishness. We admit that we have not given You the proper ground. We pray that You would have more ground in us tonight.

THE GOAL OF GOD'S WORK—
WORKING HIMSELF INTO MAN

Many people think that God's will is to make the proud person humble and the violent person meek. In other words, they think that God's will is to make the bad persons into good ones. But God's central work in man is not to do these things. He is not turning an evil man so that he becomes a good one. What is the goal of God's work? All the words and teachings will pass away. God has to open our eyes to see that throughout the ages, His work is to work Himself into man. Although this word is simple, most people have never thought of this matter before.

SALVATION BEING GOD WORKING HIMSELF INTO MAN

We will start from the very beginning. What is it to be saved? Before we answer this question, we have to ask why do men have to believe in Jesus? Men believe in Jesus because there are sufferings in the world and because they want to receive blessings. Man has sicknesses and sins, and this is why he needs Jesus. It is true that this is the gospel. But this is not the center of the gospel. I have to ask this: If man needs to believe in Jesus because he has sinned, would he need Jesus if he does not have sins?

One brother said that the gospel is for us to receive Christ. But why do we have to receive Christ? Today, many people can speak some spiritual terms, but they do not know what those terms mean. For example, to many people justification and sanctification are but terminologies only. What is it to receive Christ? To receive Christ is to receive Jesus. But what is the meaning of receiving Jesus? To receive Jesus is not merely for the purpose of being delivered from sin, suffering, and hell. It is right that a man is saved to receive Christ. Actually, salvation itself is simply Christ. For a man to be saved is for him to have Christ. Salvation is not merely for us to be delivered from sin and suffering. After a man has received the Lord, surely he will be delivered from these things. But God's work in man is to work Himself into man. Salvation is God entering into man. To receive Christ is to receive God Himself. Christ is God, and God is Christ. The Bible never tells us that there are three Gods. When He is in heaven, God is the Father. One day, when He came among men and was seen and touched by men, He was the Son. John 1 shows us that the Son is the Father manifested. The Father is the hidden God; He is the source. This is the meaning of the word father. One end of the Son is the Father, and the other end of the Father is the Son. When God is in heaven, He is the Father. When He walks on earth, He is the Son. One day, when He comes into man, He is the Holy Spirit. This is our God. He proceeds from the Father, passing through the Son, and becomes the Spirit. In John 14 the Lord Jesus said that His going is the Comforter's coming, and the Comforter's coming is His going. Not only was He dwelling among us; He wanted to dwell within us. The Son is the manifestation of God. His entry is the Holy Spirit. The Spirit is the entry of the Lord, God, and Christ. God was originally in heaven, and man was on earth; there was a great distance between the two. But through the Lord Jesus, man can now come to know God. However, although the Lord was among men, many did not know the Lord. This is why there is the need of the Holy Spirit. The Holy Spirit is the entry of the Lord. Through the Holy Spirit, man can now know the Lord.

When I was in Hong Kong, someone asked me where Christ has gone according to Matthew. If we take the Gospel of Matthew to a place where people have never heard the gospel, they will never say that Christ has ascended to heaven. It is because Matthew never says this. This is the result of the teaching in Christianity.

Matthew did not mention the ascension of Christ. If it had twenty-nine chapters, it would have said that Christ has entered into us. His name is Emmanuel, which means God with us. How is He being with us? He is with us by being in us. This is what the Chinese mean by "the shadow following the person all the way."

To be saved is not merely to be delivered from perdition and death, and to be forgiven of our sins. These are the necessary results of salvation, but they are not the center of salvation. The center of salvation is God working Himself into man. Salvation cannot be separated from the Savior. Suppose someone gives you a gift. It is wrong to accept the gift while rejecting the giver of the gift.

GRACE BEING GOD GAINED AND EXPERIENCED BY US

Many people talk much about God's grace. They think that making a fortune, having good children, and being free from calamities is God's grace. But the Gospel of John tells us that grace comes from Jesus. What did Jesus give to us? Did He give us money, houses, or palaces? The apostle Paul counted these things as dung. If you give dung to me, I will consider this an insult to me. God has given us Christ. Grace and truth are simply God Himself. If one day your son has died, or you have gone bankrupt in your business, yet you have an unspeakable power within you to allow you to say "hallelujah," that is God's grace. A man experiences grace in sufferings. It is not while we possess riches and houses that the Lord's grace is sufficient for us. It is while we suffer losses and are sick that the Lord's grace is sufficient for us. Health and children are not grace. Grace is when we experience and gain the Lord in adverse circumstances.

SPIRITUAL WORK BEING THE TRANSFORMATION OF GOD'S LIFE WITHIN MAN

A few years ago, I heard others speaking about the smooth stones David used in his fight with Goliath. They said that God's intention is for us to be the smooth stones. I have heard this kind of message before, and I have even preached such messages myself. But today, I have to say that this kind of teaching is nonsense. God has no intention for us to be smooth stones. His intention is to transform us. Suppose a few people meet together in a new place. At the beginning they are all hot in their tempers, and they often rub against each other. Gradually, as time goes on, they become "smooth." After a few years, when they meet together, they may still say things that offend one another. But they do not argue any longer. When the time comes for them to express their views, they may even agree fully with their mouths. But this is just to be outwardly refined. God has no intention for us to be "smooth." His intention is to work Himself into us. He is only doing one thing. He does not correct your mistakes, and He is not taking away your temper; He is only adding Himself into you.

Four or five years ago, I suffered great trials. For about two and a half years I had to lie on my bed to rest. At the beginning I thought that I had done something wrong, and I began to confess my sins in a thorough way. I thought that after I had confessed all my sins, God would heal me. I held to God's word in Psalm 103:3, which says, "Who forgiveth all thine iniquities; who healeth all thy diseases." I thought it was first the forgiving of the iniquities, and then the healing of my sickness, and for that reason I did my best to confess my sins. But the more I confessed, the more serious my illness became. Up to a point, I became tired of confession; yet I felt bad if I did not confess. After a long period of time, I gradually came to realize that God does not punish our

GOD WORKING HIMSELF INTO MAN 121

mistakes with chastisements. Although I did not have much wrong, neither did I have much God. During those two years, God showed me that His purpose is to work Himself into me. Suppose an opium smoker comes to us. How should we exhort him to believe in the Lord? Should we first ask him to stop taking opium before he can believe in the Lord? Surely we do not do this. We would surely exhort him first to believe in the Lord Jesus, and then the opium will automatically leave him. His problem is not the presence of opium, but the absence of God. When a man has God, he has life, and the law of life will chase out the opium. To exhort men to rid themselves of opium is the work of the anti-opium societies. Our work is to put God into people. If someone asks you if he can drink the water from the gutter, you do not have to tell him whether he can drink it. You only need to tell him to taste it a little. True spiritual work is not outward improvements, but an inward change in life. The work of life is a work of metabolism. God is not removing your sharp corners from within you, nor is He trying to make you a smooth stone; He is changing the stones into pearls.

Brother Mak can put on all kinds of clothing. He can put on a beggar's clothing, or he can put on a very nice suit. But Brother Mak is still Brother Mak; he does not change merely by changing his outward clothing. You may lose your temper at home, or you may be smiling and rejoicing at home. You may improve a little or worsen a little. But you are still you. Basically, your person has not changed, and your nature has not changed.

Once a man had a dream. In his dream he saw a worker of the Lord cutting hair for others. After he woke up from the dream, he interpreted his own dream and told others that his dream is a picture of the preachers' work today. Their work is to cut others' hair and shave others' faces. If someone is getting married, they would exhort the wife to be submissive and the husband to love. This kind of outward work is like cutting people's hair. After they cut it once, the hair will grow back after a while. This kind of preaching is doomed to fail.

No matter how much you grind a stone, it will still be a

stone; its elements will not change. God's work is to produce an organic process in the stone, so that not only are the corners removed, but its nature is changed, and the stone is changed to pearl.

God has no intention that you merely preach the gospel or manage a church. God's intention is to work Himself into you through your preaching of the gospel and your managing of the church. His intention is to make Himself your inward elements. God is wise. By doing this, He kills two birds with one stone. On the one hand, He can accomplish the work, spread the gospel, and take care of the church through you. At the same time, through these works, He can have Himself added into you. God has no intention to correct your mistakes. His only intention is to work Himself into you and to fill you up, so that day by day and year by year He would become ripened within you.

I hope that you will not take my words as a mere teaching. I am showing you something here. I am pointing out to you a way. I do not expect these words to give you some excitement or stimulation. I only hope that those who have a heart for the Lord would receive the blessing here.

Prayer: Lord, we look to You from the depths of our being. Be merciful to us, that we would touch You from our depths. Work in man's heart, and accomplish what man cannot accomplish. We cannot enter into man's heart. Only You can enter man's heart and accomplish what You are after.

CHAPTER TWENTY-THREE

THE TESTIMONY OF THE CHURCH

TALKS (4)

Date: Morning, January 13, 1948
Place: Swatow, Kwangtung
Speaker: Witness Lee

REMOVING THE VEIL AND HAVING A PURE HEART

The veil mentioned in 2 Corinthians 3 refers to anything that hinders us from seeing the glory of the Lord. Anything that frustrates us from beholding the glory of the Lord is in principle a veil. Our husbands, wives, children, fame, the world, and riches can all become veils. Anything that causes us not to see the Lord's glory is a veil. To turn our hearts to the Lord means to have a pure heart for the Lord; only people with such a heart do not have veils. The Lord says that the pure in heart are blessed, for they shall see God (Matt. 5:8).

THE WORK OF LIFE

The Christian living and work issue from life. An artificial flower looks much the same as a real flower. But the artificial flower cannot withstand the scorching of the sun or the beating down of the rain, whereas a real flower can withstand them. If a Christian's living and work do not issue from life, they are like artificial flowers and will not be of much use.

THE TESTIMONY OF THE CHURCH

There are four categories of work in Shanghai. The first is the gospel work, the second is the children's work, the third is migration, and the fourth is the work of visitation.

Brother Sparks emphasizes a personal ministry today. But our work today is to maintain a testimony of the church, which is why we have to build up everything at the same time.

The co-workers should do their best to transfer the work to the local brothers and sisters. Our work should produce more apprentices, instead of just producing the products.

In the coming days, we need to put out three kinds of hymnals. The first is the general hymnal, which only Brother Nee himself can be responsible for. The second is the gospel songs, which I will be responsible for. The third is the children's songs, which Sister Ruth Lee and others will be responsible for.

There is one kind of work which only Brother Nee can do, and for which no other person can substitute for him.

In the future, the work in central China and southern China should have more fellowship.

CHAPTER TWENTY-FOUR

GOD'S CENTRAL WORK

CONFERENCE (6)

Date: Evening, January 13, 1948
Place: Swatow, Kwangtung
Speaker: Witness Lee

Scripture Reading: Eph. 3:19b, 20

Prayer: May the Lord prevent anyone from having a wrong understanding of these messages. If anyone is to understand these messages, may their understanding be correct. For this we need the revelation of the Holy Spirit.

GOD'S CENTRAL WORK—
WORKING HIMSELF INTO MAN

Ephesians 3:19 speaks of the fullness of God. This fullness is the content. God's intention is to fill us with this content. Verse 20 shows us how God accomplishes this, that is, how He fills us with His fullness. The main work of God today is to work Himself into man. Unless our living, our walk, and our work are linked up with God's center, they will all pass away. Even the so-called blessings and peace will pass away. The only thing that will remain is God's work within us. I know that many will think that I am saying the wrong thing, and I know that many will misunderstand my words. But if a man loves the Lord with a pure heart, he will see the revelation.

GOD'S WORK IN TIME
BEING TO WORK HIMSELF INTO MAN

Everything that does not belong to God Himself, even if it has been created by Him, will all pass away. The heavens, the earth, and all things, even we ourselves, will all pass away, because the heavens, the earth, and all things, including ourselves, are not God Himself. That is why they will all pass away. No matter how good you are, and how nice and how clean you look, all these things will pass away. Of course, humanly speaking, it is always better to do good than to do evil. But the good and evil that come from the tree of the knowledge of good and evil are the same before God. Everything that is not of God will pass away. The Chinese have a saying, "Humility brings profit, while arrogance brings loss." But both of these things will also pass away. Today, we are not evaluating matters from a temporary point of view. Rather, we are evaluating matters from an eternal point of view. Many things may appear to be good in time, but they cannot endure for eternity. Good is something that exists in time; it cannot be brought into eternity. To do good is the goal of those in the world, but a Christian's goal belongs to eternity. In eternity, there are only things that belong to God. Only God's things are eternal. It is true that God's things pass through time, yet they proceed from eternity and extend through eternity. Everything that God accomplishes in time and in the world is for the accomplishment of His eternal purpose, which is to work Himself into man. Only when God is worked into man can God's eternal purpose be fulfilled. God passes through time in order that He can work Himself into man, that is, in order for Him to mingle Himself into man.

For a man to do good apart from God is as worthless as it is for him to commit sin apart from God. Of course, within the span of time, all virtues are better than evil. But in eternity, both are worthless. Time is in God's hand, and God puts the man He gained into this "furnace" with the purpose of working Himself into man, so that man can be in God and God can be in man. A glazed vessel must go through the firing in a furnace before the flowers painted on it can become one with the vessel. After the vessel has been fired, the flowers and the vessel can never again be separated. If the vessel breaks, the flowers on it will also break. God's intention today is to fill our inclinations and our character with God's nature and character. In the end, God will become our content, and His fullness will be mingled with us. God's life will have a "chemical reaction" with our life. This is God's work all the way from the beginning to the end. His purpose is for man to be like Him. He has no intention to merely improve us a little. This is man's natural concept. The human ethical mind thinks that all a person needs to do is to change the wrongs and make them right. But God's thought is not concerning good and evil, but concerning His working Himself into us.

THE CHRISTIAN EXPERIENCE BEING GOD'S WORKING HIMSELF INTO US

A Christian should not think that as long as something is good, he can do it, and that as long as something is not good, he should not do it. God does not care for right or wrong. What He cares for is to work Himself into us through the things that we encounter.

We can consider the experience of Jacob. He passed through many experiences from his youth to his old age. He did many evil things; he deceived his father, his father-in-law, his brother, and his wives. After so much experience and so many dealings from the Lord, we can say that there were not many things in his life that he had done right. Nearly everything he did was wrong. But the one precious thing is that God had worked Himself into Jacob. This is why in his old age his name was changed to Israel. By that time, he was no longer a man only, but a man filled with God. He became the prince of God, God's Israel. Maturity is not to change from being an evil man to being a good man. It is to be filled with God through His many and prolonged dealings.

Today the material, the method, the goal, and the power of our work is simply God Himself. If a carpenter makes a table and it is short of a leg, he would not use his own leg to be the material. But when God created man, He used Himself as the material. When God gives you power, He is actually giving you Himself. Power is simply God Himself. The material with which God works is simply God Himself. Suppose you do not have love, and you ask God for love. He does not give you a bag of love. Rather, He gives you Himself. Many people pray to God like beggars begging money from a rich man. When they have the money, they turn away from the giver. Many people think that once they have the love and the power, they can put God aside. We have to realize that love, humility, patience, and holiness are all God Himself. Anyone who does not allow God to work in him will not have lasting humility. Perhaps he has a temporal humility, but it is not an eternal humility. All the spiritual virtues, such as faith, love, and holiness, are simply God Himself. The same is true with prayer. Only when a man allows God to work Himself into him will he have real prayers. All the virtues, love, and goodness are not individual items of things. When God comes in and comes out of a man, that is love, that is goodness, and that is virtue. What is faith? Some say that faith is just to believe in God's word and His promises. But I have to tell you that faith is simply God Himself. When God comes in and out of you, that is faith. What is patience? When God comes in and out of you, that is patience. What is prayer? Many people say that prayer is to talk to God. But the real prayer is for God to come in and out of us. Our real prayer is one that allows God to pass through us. All those who do not allow God to pass through them do not have genuine, worthwhile prayer. What then is real prayer? Real prayer is simply God praying to God. Andrew Murray said that real prayer is the Christ in us praying to the Christ on the throne. This means that the God in you prays to the God in the heavens. Real spiritual power is a matter of God passing through us. His passing through is the power. The wife's submission, the husband's love, and all other virtues are a matter of God passing through us. This passing through will fill us with God's fullness, and in the end God will become our content.

Brothers and sisters, I can tell you that there are many people who know the Bible and who understand its teachings. But there are few people who have God's fullness in their mind, their character, and their nature. The way many people understand the teachings of the Bible is like wearing gold rings on their fingers without having gold in their heart. You may be serving God, building up churches, helping the brothers and sisters, and bearing some responsibilities in the church. But the key to all these works is to allow God to work Himself into you. When a man builds a chapel, he needs to use many kinds of materials, such as bricks, stone, and iron. Today, we are building the church of God. As such, the material must be God Himself. Many times we hear people say, "So-and-so is a good brother. He loves his wife, and he is never angry with her." I would say, "Oh, no! I am afraid that this brother has never allowed God to pass through his love toward his wife. He may never have lost his temper with his wife, but God's element has not increased in him either." After a brother has been saved for five years, if he grows spiritually, it would be like building a wall two feet high. If he continues to allow God to pass through him, the wall will become four feet high. But if he only exercises himself to be a good man, it would be like adding more mud beside the two-foot wall. The wall will become thicker, but it will not become higher.

THE WORK OF LIFE

After a brother is saved, he may become clearer concerning all kinds of scriptural knowledge from Genesis to Revelation. He may be able to compose better prayers, and his prayers may begin to sound very nice. Actually, these are all mud; they are all put onto the side of the wall and are not added on top of the wall. These are works of men. Because of this, after five years, the wall will remain two feet high, and God's life will not have grown in that brother.

On the other hand, suppose this brother beats his wife at home. What should we say to him? When many pastors, elders, and workers hear this, they will probably pray for this brother in private, and they will discuss how they should help him to read Ephesians 5. After this they may pray together, saying, "Lord, we are going to visit this brother. Please go with us, and make this brother open to our exhortations." Later they may go to this brother's house, and they may say, "You are wrong as a husband." They may also say to the wife, "You are also wrong as a wife." After much speaking, the brother may confess that he is wrong, and he may agree that he will no longer lose his temper with his wife. The preacher may go on, praying, "Thank the Lord. This brother is now open to our exhortation. We now commit him to the Lord's hand, and we pray that the Lord will cause him not to lose his temper anymore." Outwardly speaking, this way seems to work. But actually, what they are doing is but the work of a barber. They may cut a person's hair today, but soon afterward, that person's hair will grow back, and they will have to give him another haircut. This is the work of Confucius' disciples. This kind of teaching is the teaching of the Chinese ethical classics. No wonder when Christianity came to China, the disciples of Confucius said that Confucius' teachings are much better than those of this foreign religion. Therefore, if we take the Bible as a means for teaching others or improving others, we are taking the Bible as mere teachings only.

A wife once came to me and said, "My husband beats me. Don't you know that he is your brother? Your brother always loses his temper at home." She went on with tears, "Yesterday he beat me again." What should I do? Ordinarily, when a man hears such a word, he would go to exhort the husband, with the hope that the husband would change his ways. You may say, "If I do not exhort him to change his ways, what should I ask him to do?" You can only do such a thing because you are a person who is given to exhorting others and helping others to improve themselves. This is all you can do. If you do not do this, you will be out of a job. Please do not misunderstand me. Although I will pray for such a husband, my prayer will be different from your prayer. If this brother comes to me, I will say to him, "How do you feel when you beat your wife?" He may say, "After I beat my wife, I feel terrible inside for a week." I will then tell him, "If you feel that you will feel comfortable inside by beating your wife, you can go ahead and beat her some more." I will not tell him not to beat his wife. Instead, I will ask him how he feels inside. If this brother is touched by God, he will feel deep within that he has offended God.

You can teach others from the Bible, and you can exhort others with your theology. But if you do this, you are not the disciple of Christ; you are the disciple of Confucius instead.

By so doing, you will never convey God's life to people. This is a pitiful work.

If you buy a pen and a piece of paper, you can draw a beautiful chrysanthemum flower. But if I take a chrysanthemum seed, plant it in the ground, water it regularly, and then go to sleep, soon what the chrysanthemum seed produces will be more beautiful than what I draw on the paper. Today, our work is not to teach others according to the Bible, but to plant God's life contained in the Bible into others. The material, goal, and design of God's work are simply God Himself, and this work is to work God into us.

GOD AND MAN MINGLED AS ONE

Do you want to know how to be a real husband or wife? The way to be a real husband is not to be a husband. The real way to be a wife is not to be a wife. Do not think that loving your husband means to do many things for him. To love your husband does not mean that you buy some fabric and make some clothing for him. The real love is for you not to do anything and for God to do everything. God is not doing many things for man; He is working Himself into man. The reason God was incarnated was to put Himself into man. This is real love. The real love is for you not to be yourself, but to be the other party. The highest point of God's love is for Him to lay aside Himself; He would no longer be God. Instead, He would be a man and be the same as man.

Today we have to pray, "God, although I am a man, I would give up being a man. Hallelujah! I will accept You and allow You to work Yourself into me." This is the sweetest thought. In eternity God will say, "O man, you have God's nature," while you can say, "O God, the majestic God, You also have our nature, the human nature." This is the picture in eternity. Christ bears our human nature. In heaven He is God, yet He still bears our human nature. What is His work today? It is to work Himself into man. One day, when eternity comes, man will say joyfully, "God is like man," and God will say joyfully, "Man is like God."

In Shanghai I met a couple who had been married for many years. The two were similar in their minds and in the way they thought and acted. They had loved each other for many years. As a result, the male was like the female, and the female was like the male. Why were they so similar? It is because the male no longer lived as the male, and the female no longer lived as the female. The male lived as the female, and the female lived as the male. In the end, the two had become more or less the same. This is the relationship between God and man. God is our spiritual Husband. Because He loves us, He lives in the likeness of a man. If we love God, we should also live in the likeness of God. In the end, God will be in man, and man will be in God.

CHAPTER TWENTY-FIVE

HOW TO FOLLOW THE INNER LEADING

CONFERENCE (7)

Date: Evening, January 14, 1948
Place: Swatow, Kwangtung
Speaker: Witness Lee

Scripture Reading: Rom. 8:6; 1 John 3:19-21; 2 Cor. 3:16; Matt. 5:8; 6:21-23

Prayer: May the Lord give us the light not only while we are listening, but may the light be as the dawning of the day that shines more and more unto the perfect day. Raise up a group of people who would be touched by You in a genuine way, and whose hearts are genuinely opened up by You. Amen.

WALKING ACCORDING TO THE SENSE IN THE SPIRIT

Tonight we want to consider how we can follow the inner leading. This way appears to be a simple one. In our experience we all know that the Lord lives in us. The result of our going along with the operation of the Spirit of life is surely peace. Romans 8:6 tells us that to walk according to spirit is life and peace. If you ask me what it is to walk according to spirit, I will tell you that to walk according to spirit is to follow the peace within. If you have peace, you can go on, and if you do not have peace, you should stop. If you truly love the Lord and are willing to cooperate with Him, you have to take care of the peace within. When you feel peaceful inside, you can go on. When you do not feel peaceful inside, you should stop.

To be a Christian is not a question of mental exercise and analyzing in the mind; it is a question of the peace within and of the sense in our spirit. This is to follow the Lord. If we want to follow the Lord, we have to follow the sense He gives to us in our spirit.

A co-worker sister once went to a fabric store to buy some fabric. She saw some bargain items in the store. On the one hand, she felt within her that she should not buy the fabric. But on the other hand, she felt that the bargain was too good to miss. She went along with her mind and bought the fabric. When she returned home, she was bothered within and could not fellowship with the Lord, nor read the Bible or pray properly. Later, a brother needed that piece of fabric, and the sister sold it to him and spent the money. Her peace then came back. Hence, we should not analyze with our mind. Only the sense in our spirit is trustworthy.

Once a child dipped his rice dumpling into salt instead of sugar. His eyes may not have been very discerning, but when he took the dumpling, his feeling within told him that it was salt. We should walk according to the operation of the Lord's life within us. The mind expresses itself in analyzing, reasoning, and studying. A Christian who is in his mind is one who remains in the tree of the knowledge of good and evil. The sense in our spirit is very sensitive, and we have to walk according to this inner sense. The source of this inner sense is the tree of life. The tree of life is very simple; it does not require us to think or to analyze. Nothing can be more simple than the tree of life.

GOD'S WILL NOT BEING DETERMINED
BY SUCCESS OR FAILURE,
GOOD OR BAD ENVIRONMENTS

The result of following the Lord's leading may not be success in our work. God's work in us will not necessarily cause us to succeed in what we do. What He is doing is to work Himself into us through the many things. In order to work Himself into us, He may cause us to suffer many blows and to encounter many hardships. When these things come upon us, they may cause us to doubt Him. But God leads us this way in order that we would submit to Him.

When a piece of porcelain is being fired in the furnace, if it could speak, it would surely say that it is in the wrong place. Actually, to be in the furnace is the porcelain's fate. God does not necessarily lead believers into successes. Of course, He has no intention to lead them to failures either. What He is doing is to work Himself into them through all kinds of environments.

Suppose a brother and a sister are preparing to be engaged. The more they pray, the more they are clear that they should be engaged. When they do become engaged, they feel strongly that they have the Lord's leading to do it. Later they are married. After their marriage, they begin to find out many shortcomings in each other. By that time, they may think that their initial leading was wrong. But we have to realize that God's leading is to cause us to gain God, not to gain a wife. One day, when the brother learns this lesson, he will praise God when he looks at his wife, not because his wife is good, but because he will have gained God.

A brother may feel led to start a business. While he is praying, he may feel the Lord's leading in the matter. But when he is engaged in the business, he may suffer great loss. By that time, he may think that his initial leading was wrong. Man considers something as God's will or not God's will by the success of that matter. But God's intention is to work Himself into us. In the first two centuries, it cost a person much to be a Christian; there was no outward peace. But the Christians at that time did not count it a loss to sacrifice their lives. When we read church history, we realize that some people even prayed for an opportunity to be martyred.

Many people cannot be clear about God's leading because they take their own self as the goal. If we take God as our goal, He will surely give us the proper leading. Many people walk according to their inner sense, but they end up encountering failures. They may think that the leading they have received is wrong. But as long as our walking according to the inner sense draws us closer to God and to love Him more, our sense is right. God's leading is to give us peace. Although outwardly there may be sufferings and darkness, these do not mean that we are not walking according to God's leading. All successes, failures, sweet experiences, and bitter experiences are for the accomplishment of God's goal, which is to work Himself into us.

GUARDING AGAINST COUNTERFEIT PEACE IN THE MIND

In order for us to be a Christian who lives according to the peace within, we have to realize that the greatest enemy is our mind. Suppose something ought not to be done. But in order to go ahead and do it in peace, we give all kinds of explanations and reasonings. This kind of peace is not a natural one. When a Bible is laid flat on the table, it is level. When a person puts something under it, it will still remain level and will not fall. But this is not a natural peace. Rather, it is an artificial peace. The minute we fall into our mind, we will lose our fellowship with God. We can go against anything, but we can never afford to be cut off from our fellowship with God. Many sisters' dresses give them no peace. However, they find many excuses in their mind. This kind of peace is man-made. When is God glorified in us? It is when God is expressed from us that He is glorified. Anything great or small, as long as we do not have the peace within, we should not do it. Before the Lord, we should only walk according to the inner sense. If we do this, day by day God's content and His fullness will fill us up, and we will have God's nature within and His image without. If we do not have peace within, we should not do anything, however good or beneficial such a thing may be. A Christian is a person who has forsaken the world. He is one who has forsaken any kind of profit as his goal and has taken up Christ as his goal. He should be one who seeks after Christ Himself.

DEALING WITH THE CONSCIENCE

The growth of a Christian depends on his dealing with his conscience. In one's pursuit of the Lord, if he does not take care of his conscience, he will never grow.

A man may have been saved last night. He may be sitting on a chair today. If half of the money that went into the purchase of that chair was stolen from others, this person will surely not have peace. This means that after a person is saved, he will be enlightened, and his conscience will show him that what he did before was wrong and unrighteous. His conscience will require him to return that half of the money to others. We have to learn to deal with our conscience to the extent that our conscience becomes blameless. If a person has not taken care of his conscience to such an extent, he may be reading his Bible, meeting, and praying all year round, yet he will not grow.

Today, there are many saved ones, but there are few grown-up ones. The reason for this is that among the saved ones, very few are willing to deal with their conscience. It is true that after we have believed in the Lord, the blood cleanses us from our sins, and the Lord's grace is sufficient for us. But if we want to know the Lord's way within us, we must take care of our conscience. Otherwise, we will not grow before the Lord. We must not do anything that the conscience condemns. Anything that should be dropped must be dropped. If a man does not deal with his conscience, it is useless to talk to such a one about spiritual matters. Although the dealing with the conscience cannot be considered as something directly spiritual, it is a bridge to the spiritual matters. Brothers and sisters, has your conscience been examined? Today, many people hush their conscience and suppress it. They come to listen to messages, to act like Christians, to read the Bible, and to pray, but they are the same all year round. We must allow our conscience to condemn us, to speak to us. Only those who go along with their conscience will receive the blessing. If we do not deal with the things which our conscience condemns us of, we will lose all spiritual light.

If a man wants to pursue the Lord, he has to deal with his conscience in a serious way. After I was saved, for a period of three to four years the Lord was teaching me this lesson, and I had to deal severely with my conscience. Once I was staying in a room with another brother. While I was washing my face, a drop of water fell on his bed, and my conscience was bothered. When that brother returned home, I made a confession to him. He told me that it was all right. Not long after this, I stepped on his sheet with my feet, and I had to make another confession to him. Still some time afterwards, I dropped his pencil on the floor, and I had to make another confession. Within one day, I found myself confessing to him quite a few times.

Perhaps you will think that these are small things and that they do not matter much. But to my conscience, they were great matters. I really wished that I did not have to stay in the same room that he did. But both of us were guests there, and there was no way that we could stay in separate rooms. Later, that brother realized that it was too troublesome for me to make confessions to him all the time, and he said, "The worst kind of people do not confess their mistakes. The best kind of people have no mistakes to confess. Those who are neither good nor bad make confessions all the time." At that time, I thought that I would never be the worst kind, and I could not be the best kind; I always made mistakes, and therefore I had to make confessions all the time. Now I can laugh at what I did. But at that time, I could not laugh.

Many people's consciences are like the soles of those who walk around barefoot; their soles have become thickened and have lost all feelings. Although their consciences have not died, they have lost all feelings. A good Christian and one who is really growing is one who takes care of his conscience. I am afraid many people cannot withstand the examination of their conscience today. Can you say that your conscience is blameless before God and men? Can you say that your bank account, your houses, your clothing, and everything in your houses are clean and righteous? I am afraid that many things are unrighteous in nature. It is true that your record of sin before God has been erased by the precious blood of Christ. But in your home you may still have many evidences of sins. It is like a man who has committed a murder; his case may have been cleared in the court, but the corpse may still be at his house. No other way is as serious and clear as the way of following the Lord. The question is whether or not we are willing to pay the price. Zeal is useless, and listening to messages and attending services are useless. The question is whether or not we are willing to pay the price to follow the Lord.

In Chefoo some criticized my speaking. I told the criticizing ones that unless every dollar of theirs has been measured by God, they are not qualified to criticize me. I know what I am speaking about. In the first fall, man fell from God's direct rule to the conscience's rule. Later he fell from the conscience's rule to the human rule. It was because the conscience could no longer rule over the people that they needed others to rule over them. Before man fell, God ruled over man. After the fall, the conscience ruled over man. Still later, the conscience could no longer rule over man, and others had to rule over him. Today, if a Christian needs the government, the court, any institution, school, or his family to rule over him, it proves that he is still deep in the fall. If a wife or a son needs someone else to rule over him or her, it proves that he or she is deep in the fall. The conscience can no longer rule over such a one, and God can no longer rule over such a one. This is why there is the need for someone else to rule over them. The steps of man's fall are these: from God's rule to the conscience's rule, and from the conscience's rule to man's rule. Finally, it becomes self-rule. If a place does not have any law or police, that place will surely be full of robbers and criminals. We should find our way back to God through the recovery of the feeling in our conscience.

THE HEART TURNING TO THE LORD

Let me ask the brothers and sisters: Is the light within you bright today? Whether or not the light within us is bright depends on whether or not we love the Lord. Second Corinthians 3 says that whenever our hearts are turned to the Lord, the veil is taken away. Those whose hearts are for the Lord and who desire the Lord will see the light. If a man does not have light, it is because his heart is not turned to the Lord. Matthew says that the pure in heart are blessed, for they shall see God. Only those who are after the Lord with a single heart will see Him. God is light. Matthew 6 says that where our treasure is, there our heart is also. Whatever our hearts are inclined toward, that is where our hearts will be. If our hearts are right, we will see the light. Do you love the Lord? If you love the Lord and your heart is turned to Him, you will surely have light within, and you will surely be clear. Whenever a feeling comes along to urge you to deal with something, you will surely do it. As a result, you will be able to live in the Lord.

CHAPTER TWENTY-SIX

GOD'S ULTIMATE GOAL AND HIS PRESENT NEED

TALKS (5)

Date: Morning, January 15, 1948
Place: Swatow, Kwangtung
Speaker: Witness Lee

Prayer: May the Lord cause us to speak the things that we ought to speak, and may You cause the listeners to hear what they ought to hear. We confess that we are not godly enough and do not have the adequate knowledge. We need You to open up our eyes within. Every time we come together, we need Your precious blood to cleanse us.

THE BASIC PROBLEM

We may be a proper Christian, and we may manage a church well, but this is not enough to meet the need of this age. We need to understand our basic problem before we can consider the question of methodology. What God wants to do is to work Himself into us. There is no problem with God in this matter. But with man there is a big problem.

If we want to put water into a bottle, we can do it any time. We do not have to preach to the bottle or have the bottle's consent. But man is not so simple; he is living. I do not know how many people there are who are willing to be filled with God as a result of these few evenings' meetings.

THE ULTIMATE GOAL OF GOD'S SALVATION— WORKING HIMSELF INTO MAN

The man whom God wants to gain is a person fully endowed with a free will. God's mind is higher than man's mind. But man's mind is nevertheless very complicated. In addition, he is full of emotion. For this reason, if man wants to be filled, his will must first be put under subjection. It is hard to chop a piece of wood with uneven grain because it is too complicated. Only wood with even grain is good for chopping. God picked up us, the complicated pieces of wood, for the purpose of manifesting His power. He is able to clear up and to subdue our will and emotion. Although God has redeemed us, has given us eternal life and the forgiveness of sins, and has lived inside of us, His ultimate purpose is to work Himself into us. God's ultimate work is to have the New Jerusalem. The New Jerusalem is made of gold, precious stones, and pearls. In it are the throne of God, His light, and the river of water of life with the tree of life, and so forth. Gold signifies the divine nature, and pearl signifies the result of the transformation of God's life within man. The precious stones speak of the glory as a result of the work of God. The tree of life, the water of life, and the fruit of life all refer to God Himself. God's masterpiece is the New Jerusalem. The New Jerusalem is God with man. Everything else will pass away, and the heavens and the earth will be burned. Everything apart from God cannot be joined to God. Only that which comes out of God can be joined to God. Our eyes need to be opened, and we need a deliverance. Once we see this matter, we will no longer do what we did before.

EVERYTHING NOT OF GOD'S LIFE BEING BURNED

Genesis 2 is a picture. There we see the river of life. In chapter three we see the river of fire. The flame signifies God's holiness, and the sword signifies God's righteousness. As far as God's holiness and righteousness are concerned, we should die. All those who will not allow the river of life to flow through them will have the river of fire flowing through them. Everything that will not give way to the flow of the river of life will eventually pass through the burning of the river of fire. A Christian's life, work, family, and business must all be put under the river of life. In the Bible, many places mention fire. Some people have told us that when the atomic bomb was dropped in Hiroshima, Japan, even the iron and steel were melted. Today, God's river of fire of judgment will melt away anything that is not of Himself. Only by allowing the river of life to flow through us will there be the gold, the pearl, and the precious stones. Otherwise, everything else is wood, grass, stubble, and dung. Not only will our work pass away; even God's own heaven and earth will be burned one day. Of course, our own work, those things that do not belong to God, will be burned away also. Only God's life will remain forever. Everything that is not of life will be burned. Although these things may be created by God, they do not have the life of God. As such, they will be burned away also.

A carpenter takes a piece of wood and makes a beautiful table out of it. The table is placed in the sitting room, and the remaining chaff and odd pieces are taken to the stove in the kitchen. The stove represents the lake of fire. At the end of Revelation, on the one hand, there is the city of water. On the other hand, there is the lake of fire. The city of water signifies God's life and His holiness. The lake of fire signifies God's righteousness. God's glory speaks of God Himself, whereas God's holiness tells us that everything not of God and not according to His nature will be thrown into the lake of fire. This is our basic problem. We may do the right things and may manage the church well. But these things are not the gold, the pearl, and the precious stones, because God's life has not passed through these things. The fire does not remove defilements; it only removes that which is not holy, and that which does not belong to God.

God's fire not only burns away everything bad; it also burns away everything that is not according to God's nature. In man's mind, there is only good and bad. When a house is burned, no matter how beautiful the wood outside looks, it will all be burned away. The only thing that will be left will be the steel and the concrete. The fire separates and tests things out. Everything that is not of God, no matter how good it is, will be burned away. Wood is very good, but it will be burned away. I do not know if you can take my words. If you can take them, your whole being will be turned, and you will not dare to walk according to your own will any longer.

Suppose I am about to visit a person. I should not ask if this is God's will and if I should do it. Rather, I should ask if God is going with me. What we are afraid of is not doing the wrong thing, but doing things apart from God. If we have God with us, not only will we do the right thing, but God will pass through us. Formerly, our only fear was that we would do the wrong thing. Today, our fear is that we would do things by ourselves. Even if what we do is right outwardly, as long as there is the self-element, we will not please God. The real work is one in which God works alongside of us. Everything that comes out of the mind and the will are rejected by God. God only wants something that comes out of Himself.

Today, between the river of water and the river of fire, there is still a river of blood. What should have been consumed by the river of fire is merged into the river of water by passing through the river of blood. We have the river of blood to take care of everything that is of ourselves. On the one hand, we need to examine ourselves. On the other hand, after we have examined ourselves, we need to trust in the blood of the Lord. In this way, we will be saved from the river of fire into the river of water.

THREE PERIODS OF THE CHURCH OF CHRIST IN CHINA

Christianity has been in China for over a hundred years. Of course, before that time there were the Nestorians in the Tang Dynasty, which cannot be considered as part of God's work. In the Ming Dynasty, the Catholics were here also, which also cannot be considered as part of God's work. The coming of Protestantism began with Robert Morrison, which began only a little over a hundred years ago. During these one hundred years or so, Christianity in China can be divided into three periods.

A. The Period of the Gospel

The first period is the period of the gospel, which lasted from the Ching Dynasty to the beginning of the Chinese Republic. During this period, the Western missionaries could only do some rudimentary works in China, such as running elementary schools in the villages. What they preached was at most Jesus as the Savior, and heaven and hell.

B. The Period of Revival

From the beginning of the Chinese Republic to the end of the Second World War, there was a period of twenty to thirty years. This was the revival period. The change from the previous period to this one can be likened to a change from an elementary school to a high school. Not only was there the gospel, but there were the revivals also. Many people began to live for the Lord and to be zealous for the gospel. In both northern and southern China, many people were raised up to work for the Lord. During this period, there were Dora Yu, Ding Li-mei, John Sung, and others. These revival meetings were widely publicized. From 1922 to 1941, many people lived for the Lord and consecrated themselves. Sister Pearl Wang, who is sitting among us today, was also an evangelist in 1925. All these were God's works. But the work of revival ceased by 1941.

Sister Pearl Wang interrupted: During 1940, I was working in Southeast Asia, and I felt something was wrong; I felt empty inside. All my past works became history behind me. Many places invited me to go at that time, but I felt that I could not meet the need. I had no assurance how I should help the believers, and I felt that I could not meet God's demand in this age.

C. The Period of Life

Brother Lee continued: The third period is the period of life. God's work during this period is to deal with all the human elements and to remove them from our heart through the cross. Mrs. Penn-Lewis once said that spiritual experience is of three levels. The first is the level of salvation, the second is the level of revival, and the third is the level of the way of the cross. In principle, this corresponds to the three periods of the church in China. Of course, the third period includes the things covered in the first two periods, in the same way that the university includes the things covered in the elementary school and the high school. But the elementary school and the high school are not the goal; they are there to prepare a person to get into the goal, which is the university. We are not saying that we do not need the elementary school or even the kindergarten. But it is wrong to be running a kindergarten all the time. If a student remains in the kindergarten all the time, even up to twenty or thirty years of age, there is something wrong. Today, the revival movement is no longer so prevailing. Many revivalists have been put aside, or they have died. Throughout the ages, God never repeats His own work. It does not mean that the former works were not good; it merely means that they cannot meet the demand of this age.

GOD'S PRESENT NEED—A BODY TESTIMONY

Today's need can no longer be met by revivals. Man's need today speaks of God's need. If all I have been speaking during the past seven nights were but revival messages, I believe the speaking would not satisfy men.

What is needed today is the work of a university. Of course, the elementary school and the high school are preparatory institutions. These preparatory institutions are there to prepare a person for the university. The so-called seminaries and revival conferences are but "crash courses"; it is difficult for those who graduate from "crash courses" to get into the universities. A high school is there only to meet the need of society; it is not the goal. Today, we do not preach the gospel to bring people to heaven. The gospel preaching is for a higher goal. As long as a man can breathe, he has to be a proper person. As long as he is a proper person, he has to love the Lord. But if a person only loves the Lord without living in life, this will not meet God's need. Today, God wants us to go into the university. The standard of this university is quite high. Although it is not the graduate school, its standard is still very high.

We must never despise God's spiritual blessings to China. Other than China and England, I am afraid there is no other country which has experienced so much of God's blessings. Even places like America and Denmark have to admit that God is blessing these two countries. May the Lord be merciful to us, that our work will match God's need in this age. I feel that the most shameful thing is to send a group of people to

America to study in the seminaries and then through them to raise some funds for China. What China needs is not the U. S. dollars. What China needs is every drop of our spiritual blood. Today, we will never barter men's souls for U. S. dollars. During 1926 and 1927, there was a strong anti-Christian and anti-foreigner movement. Since that time, Chinese [indigenous] churches began to appear in China. They did a better work than the Western missionaries did. I am afraid that the influence of the U. S. dollars is a frustration to the work in China.

Today, in the third period, God does not need spiritual giants any longer. What He needs is the Body testimony. Today, we only need to be the members. A small member is a member, and a big member is also a member. No member can be the whole Body. When the whole church rises up to preach the gospel, others will only say it is the church that has saved them; they will not say that it is Dr. So-and-so who has saved them. Today, whether it is the gospel, the revival, or life, everything is for this goal. Today is not the time for the co-workers to serve the Lord by themselves, but the time for the whole church to rise up to serve Him together.

FREE FELLOWSHIP ON THE AFTERNOON OF JANUARY 15— FOUR KINDS OF WORKERS

Today there are four kinds of workers. The first are the co-workers who match the need of the ministry of God in the present age. This is a small group of people who have been dealt with by the Lord and who are in one accord. The second kind are the younger co-workers. They are willing to receive the direction and to come under the coordination of the older co-workers, and they are willing to follow and to learn in humility. The third kind are those who are unwilling to submit to the senior co-workers, who do not belong to the denominations, yet who are happy to remain in fellowship with us. The fourth kind are the preachers and free evangelists among the denominations. What we need today are the first and the second kind of co-workers.

When a co-worker is in a certain place, he has to cooperate

with the local church in that place. The work and the church cannot be separated one from the other. When a co-worker is working in a certain place, he is at the same time one of the local brothers. When the church assigns work to the saints, the co-workers should stand on the same ground as the local brothers and should accept assignments in the same way.

Concerning the third and the fourth kind of co-workers, we can only let them choose their own pathway. With some people, God has not assigned them to take the same way as we do, and we dare not say anything to them. Whatever the situation may be, we are here to do the work that God has committed to us. We cannot interfere with others' work, and we are not here tearing down others' work.

CHAPTER TWENTY-SEVEN

CONCERNING THE WAY OF LIFE

OPEN TALKS

Date: Evening, January 15, 1948
Place: Swatow, Kwangtung
Speaker: Witness Lee

Tonight, first of all, we will make an announcement regarding the nature of this meeting. In this meeting, we hope to discuss the problems we face in the way of life. On the one hand, we do not want to be loose; on the other hand, we do not want to be restricted. We will only talk about problems related to the way of life. Anything apart from the way of life will not be discussed here.

THE LEADING OF THE HOLY SPIRIT AND THE PROVISION IN THE ENVIRONMENT

Question: I know that as long as I have the peace within, I can proceed with what I want to do. But do I also have to wait for the proper provision in the environment?

Brother Lee answered: Terms such as "provision in the environment" and the "leading of the Holy Spirit" have all been used in a loose way in Christianity. For this reason, we do not like to use these terms. Those who truly know God will not question about provisions in the environment. If there is a leading within them to do something, they can ignore all favorable or unfavorable environments. Sometimes a favorable environment will turn out to be a frustration to God's work. In the Bible, you find very few cases of people getting clear about God's will through going along with environmental provisions. The most important thing is the heart, and not the environment. God's leadings for Christians are all in the spirit. If a person is right before the Lord, almost everything he does is right.

From Paul's life we can see that his environments were mostly contradicting ones. In Acts 16, we see that he wanted to go to a certain place, but the Holy Spirit forbade him to do so. In his spirit he realized that it was God's forbidding. He did not act according to the provision in the environment, but according to the leading of the Holy Spirit. Do not think that God's leading will direct us to success. He is not for our being successful or failing. The main thing He is doing is to testify of Himself.

Sometimes we do not have to be too clear about anything. When we are too clear, we may end up being wrong. There was a brother who told me once that he had prayed and was clear that God wanted him to go home and give his wife a good beating. This kind of leading is not reliable.

The relationship between the leading of the Holy Spirit and the provision in the environment can be illustrated by the riding of a bicycle. On the one hand, we need to tread the pedal. On the other hand, we need the brake. We need to aggressively follow the leading of the Holy Spirit, but at the same time we also need to accept the limitations in the environment.

PAYING THE PRICE TO DEAL WITH THE CONSCIENCE

With some people, right after they are saved, they begin to deal with their conscience before God in a thorough way. I was saved in 1925. From 1932 to 1935, I learned to deal with my conscience in a severe way. During those few years, it seemed as if I learned no other lesson except to deal with my conscience. By 1935, I could say that my conscience was clean. If a man wants to go to a place by train, he has to buy his ticket at the station, and he has to board the train. If he does not buy his ticket and does not board the train, but instead walks day and night in the countryside, it will be difficult for him to arrive at his destination. In the same way, if a man wants to go on in God's way, he must obey the Lord. A person can preach the gospel, work, manage a church, and study the Bible, but if he does not obey the Lord, he has not taken a single step forward in God's way. If a person truly obeys the Lord, the Lord will give him feelings within.

Once he deals with one feeling, a second feeling will come. What we need to find today is the way, and not the doctrine. Let me ask if there are any among us here who have thoroughly dealt with their conscience. If there are, please raise up your hand. Today, there are many preachers, evangelists, and students of the Bible. But there are very few people who seriously deal with their conscience. Many Christians act according to the way their mind analyzes matters. If a thing suits their taste, they will accept it. If it does not suit their taste, they will reject it. But we have to learn to be a person who walks according to the inner feeling and the peace within. Only this kind of person will know God. Today, we have to be delivered from man's rule into God's rule. Ephesians 4:19 says that some have cast off all feelings. We cannot cast off our feelings. You can give me two billion dollars. But if my conscience will not give me peace about it, I would rather not take it.

A little chicken does not need us to help it to come out of its shell. If we try to help it, the little chicken will surely not survive well. Only those chickens that come out by themselves will be strong. Today, in order to follow the Lord we have to pay the price. It is difficult for those who will not pay the price to know God. What is it to pay the price? The real price is to cut off our heads. It does not take much of a price to listen to a message. The real price demands that we have our heads taken off. Today, we cannot know God with our head; we have to know Him with our heart. Suppose a child sits in the snow with no clothes on. Others may criticize and study how to clothe the child. But when the mother of the child sees the situation, she will run over and cover him with her own clothing. This is the difference between studying in the mind and paying the price in a real way.

GOD'S CENTRAL WORK

Today, we have to see what God's work is, and we have to know what is God's central work in man. We must be led to see the way to receive God's life. After we receive this life, we should know how to live in this life, so that God can have a way among us. This is God's central work.

Many people today like to be the peanut shells. Some are worse; they cannot even be compared to the peanut leaves. May the Lord be merciful to us that many of us would be raised up to be the peanut seeds who supply life to others. Only the peanut seeds will grow peanuts when they are planted in the earth. If a person plants the shell or the leaves in the earth, they will never bear peanuts. What we need today is not peripheral works, but God's central work.

CHAPTER TWENTY-EIGHT

GOSPEL, REVIVAL, AND LIFE

TALKS (6)

Date: Morning, January 16, 1948
Place: Swatow, Kwangtung
Speaker: Witness Lee

Prayer: May the Lord cause all of us to realize that spiritual matters are not loose or vague. May the Lord's word not only be spoken through man, but may every one of the words spoken be filled with light, and may they shine within man.

THE WORK GOD IS AFTER TODAY

Our need today is to do only the work that God wants us to do. This work includes three things: first is the preaching of the gospel, second is to lead the new believers, in particular, the young people, to love the Lord, and the third is to usher the saints into God's life and into the riches of His life. These three things need to be developed in a balanced way, and neither of the three should be given less emphasis than the others.

A. The Preaching of the Gospel

1. Doing Our Best to Preach

Concerning the preaching of the gospel, we have to do it frequently, do it well, do it in a widespread way, and do it in a weighty manner. If a church does not increase in number, it is because it has slackened in the matter of the preaching of the gospel. If the whole population in China does not produce any children in fifty years, we will not need foreigners to come in with the cannons and the gunboats to conquer us; we can give up our whole country that way. In the same way, if no new ones are added into the church in thirty years, the church can close its doors. The Lord's command is that we go to the whole world to preach the gospel. Many people want to imitate Madame Guyon, but they all end up being barren. Wherever there are "Madame Guyons," there must be the accompanying preaching of the gospel. If some are saved and they begin to love the Lord, we have to encourage them, and especially the young ones among them, to rise up to preach the gospel. Every church should saturate the city where it is with the gospel and should distribute gospel tracts to every household, every street, and every lane. It should send out gospel teams to spread the gospel in the open air and to put up gospel posters. All the schools, homes, and institutions should be filled with gospel posters, and we should all beget many spiritual children. It seems to me that Swatow has not come up with any spiritually distinguished ones yet. The brothers and sisters have all become set in their ways. Some have been cared for by others for ten years already, but they are still the same today as before. Today we should realize that the young ones have great potential. We have to encourage the young ones to rise up to preach the gospel. The more they beget, the better it is. Even if some new ones appear to be false ones, it is still all right. It is like a factory manufacturing goods; some products are of the top grade, whereas others are of a poorer grade. When the number of saved ones increases, some among them would surely not be that much up-to-standard. This is all right. It is always better for a family to beget children than to be barren. I myself had ten children. Three of them died, and seven are still left. Of course, in preaching the gospel and in begetting spiritual children, it is better that none die. But whatever a person does, if a church continues to have only a few dozen people meeting year after year for decades and there are no spiritual children produced, no matter how good its teachings are, it is not a normal church.

2. The Secret Being to Be Thick-skinned

The secret to preaching the gospel is to be thick-skinned. In preaching the gospel, all we have to do is to go. There is no need to worry about whether or not we are in the flesh. If a sister would pass out tracts on the street, and while she is doing that, if she would kneel down on the sidewalk to pray, surely some will repent. A gospel preacher must be one who is full of emotion, who can cry, laugh, and jump. Dr. John Sung was a good example. Lot's daughters committed incest with their father and produced Moab and Ammon. Of course, this is a shameful thing. But we have to realize that even the flesh of the Lord Jesus has Moabite blood in it. Therefore, in preaching the gospel we do not have to analyze too much.

3. Not Being Selective about Whom to Preach To

Once a person asked D. L. Moody if all saved ones were predestinated by God. Moody answered yes. That man then asked what would he do if a person who was not predestinated by God became saved through his preaching. Moody answered, "Dear brother, it does not matter. If a person is saved, surely he was predestinated by God already. All you have to do is to preach, and the predestinated ones will spontaneously be saved."

If a person is fleshly, he will be fleshly whether or not he preaches the gospel. If that is the case, it is better for him to preach than not to preach. If he preaches, at least God can use such a one to bring some to salvation. If among a thousand people who are saved, four hundred go back to their sins, still we have six hundred people left. The other four hundred may fall into sin, but they are at least saved. At any rate, if you do not save them, they would have been in their sins anyway. For this reason, we should not limit the gospel. In preaching the gospel, there is no need to exercise discernment; you only need to preach blindly. The management of the church, the care of business affairs, and the receiving of believers—all these require the proper discernment. But in preaching the gospel, all we have to do is to preach. If a person casts his net into the sea and the fish come, all he has to do is to draw the net. A gospel preacher does not have to worry about too many things, and he cannot exercise too much discernment. Leave the discerning to the ones who are sorting the fish; the ones who are drawing the net do not need to exercise any discernment. Only the ones sorting the fish need to have the concern; the ones drawing the net need not have any concern.

4. The Testimony in Chefoo of the Church Preaching the Gospel

In 1941, our number in Chefoo doubled within half a year. Every month some people were baptized. Of course, not every one of them was good, but we can say that most of them were good. In April, we had only about a hundred people. By the end of the year, we had about six hundred people. We printed two hundred thousand gospel tracts for the two hundred thousand people living in Chefoo. On every street we put up large posters. The brothers' and sisters' homes were filled with more posters. Some even rented wall spaces to put up posters. In the evening, some went out with lanterns, others with accordions in their arms, to preach the gospel in coordination. Some would sing, while others would pass out gospel tracts. Some even knelt by the sidewalk to preach the gospel. During the last few days of the Chinese calendar year, the whole church would fast and pray. In 1943, within a few days twelve hundred people were saved. All the brothers and sisters offered up their possessions, houses, and even land deeds. From January 1, the whole church rose up to preach the gospel, and at least eighty percent of the saints were mobilized. None of them would celebrate the New Year. Some would pray, while others would go out to invite friends. Every year, we had at least a few hundred saved this way, and among them at least a hundred would be baptized. After baptism we would distribute the names of the new ones to the brothers and sisters and ask them to go to visit these new ones. After the visitations, the saints would come back and report to us about the new ones' conditions. Every year we sowed the seed at the beginning of the year, after which we began to reap, and the reaping continued until the fall season. The Chinese celebrate their New Year by having fellowship with demons; during the New Year, they put out idols and worship them. When we preached the gospel during the New Year, we had to fight a spiritual battle with the devil. The people in the world indulged themselves in eating and drinking during the New Year, but our brothers and sisters only took simple meals. Later, after the Communists took over Chefoo, our brothers and sisters were still bold to preach the gospel just as before.

The gospel preaching in Chefoo in 1943 experienced the greatest blessing from the Lord. During that time, I only preached twenty minutes. While everyone was singing the song "Vanity, vanity," the Holy Spirit was already working, and when the call was made for all the ones who wanted to believe to stand up, the whole congregation stood up.

One lady in high-heeled shoes came to listen to the preaching. At random, I pointed my finger to her and said, "Your husband did not have much money, but you still wanted him to buy you this and that." After that meeting, that lady asked a sister, "How come Mr. Lee knows so much about me? I was just the kind of person he was talking about." Later she believed in the Lord.

Another time when we were preaching the gospel, again at random I pointed my finger to a young boy, and I said, "You have stolen a piece of chalk from the school, and you have taken it home to draw circles." That boy happened to have stolen a piece of chalk from his school and was indeed using it to draw circles at home. He said in his heart, "What does it matter?" Immediately after that, I said on the platform, "You are still saying in your heart, 'What does it matter?'" When the boy heard it, right away he believed in the Lord. During that period of time, every time I went up to the platform I was filled by the Lord, and people were saved.

Once I was preaching the gospel in a place which was a hall with an adjoining small room. During the meeting, both the hall and the adjoining room were filled with people. But the strange thing was that every time I preached, some from the hall would be saved, but no one from the small room would be saved. During one meeting, I purposely directed my speaking to the small room, but still no one stood up there. I then said, "This room has demons in it. We have to pull these demons out." Soon after that, a mother and her daughter came to the meeting and sat in the small room. The daughter held back the mother and would not allow her to stand up to accept the Lord. I then pointed my finger at them and said, "Today, there are demons here trying to stop people from believing in the Lord." The daughter became afraid and dared not stop her mother any longer. Later both the mother and the daughter were saved.

The more we preach the gospel, the more new ones will be added to us. Once new ones are added to us, the old ones will come alive.

B. Revival

The second thing is the work of revival. After people have believed, we have to lead them, old and young, to love the Lord and to have concrete expressions of love. Our money, time, and energy should all be used for the Lord. The few years when we were in Chefoo, the number of saved ones increased, and we began to have many home meetings. The brothers and sisters paid much attention to the work of visitation. Later when the revival came, all the brothers and sisters offered up everything they had and gave up their material possessions, to the extent that this kind of consecration went on from morning until midnight. Even the offering boxes became too small to take care of the offerings. After the revival in 1943, over a hundred people migrated to northwest China for the spread of the gospel. We conducted revival meetings for over three and a half months. Up to a certain point, the brothers and sisters dared not even open up their chests in their homes, or touch their clothes in their closets. The minute they touched their possessions, a voice within would say, "Consecrate!" During that period of time, many miracles and wonderful things happened among us.

One sister was over thirty years old. Her husband's name was Wang, and he was a rich man in Chefoo. In the villages, they also owned many houses. But he was not zealous at all, and he did not come to the meetings often. During the first month that we conducted our revival meetings, the husband dropped in a few times. Once when he came, I purposely asked him to give a testimony. That day, we happened to be reading Isaiah 1 and Jeremiah 8, which say that the ass knows his owner, but that God's people do not know Him, and that the birds in the air know the season, but His people do not know the judgment of the Lord. I did not know that before the meeting this Brother Wang had already made an agreement with his wife and was about to offer up his land and house deeds to the Lord. The wife thought that I would not normally call out people to testify during the meetings, and she thought that if I would do that to her husband, it would prove that the consecration was of the Lord. The Lord's leading was wonderful. On that day, I invited her husband to testify.

Before the meeting that day one young brother was at home reading the same passages from Isaiah 1 and Jeremiah 8, and he felt the words quite meaningful that man would be worse than the ass and the birds. Later this brother came to the meeting hall and heard me speaking on these two passages, and he thought that I was directing my speaking to him.

If a church is not revived, all the teachings it has are dead. If we want to love the Lord and to consecrate ourselves to Him, we have to do it until it hurts. During that period in Chefoo, we met every day from ten in the morning until six at night, and time was still too short for us.

C. Entering the Life of God

The third part of the work is to know God's life. When we preach the gospel, we have to know where we are bringing people. We are bringing people into God's life. The gospel preaching is for the revival, and the revival is for ushering people into the life of God. If a man loves money or his career, he cannot be ushered into God's life. The way to be ushered into God's life is first through the gospel, and then through revivals. Revivals mainly cause a person to love the Lord, but there are many revivals that only stir up an exciting atmosphere. I have been a Christian for twenty-two years, and I have never seen a revival as strong as the one in Chefoo in 1943. During that period of time, many times in the meetings nothing was said, yet many were in tears, and many were convicted of keeping back the Lord's grace and of saying that they were living for the Lord while in reality loving themselves. Today we need to have the gospel, and we need to have revivals. Without the gospel and without the revivals, there is no way for us to be ushered into God's life.

CHAPTER TWENTY-NINE

CONFESSION AND FELLOWSHIP

TALKS (7)

Date: Evening, January 17, 1948
Place: Swatow, Kwangtung
Speaker: Witness Lee

CONFESSION

The Purpose of Confession

A Christian makes confession in order to keep his conscience in peace. This kind of confession has nothing to do with salvation and has nothing to do with the removal of sin before God. Confession is an acknowledgment before man. When a man believes in the Lord Jesus, his sins are forgiven before God, but these sins may not be forgiven before man. This is why there is the need for confession. The purpose of confession is to be reconciled with men; it is not a demand of God's law, but a step we take to clear our conscience of all blame and to have a good testimony before men. The Bible gives many examples of men bearing fruits of repentance after they have believed. Zaccheus is one such example. The Lord Jesus also tells us that when a man wants to make a sacrifice on the altar, and he remembers that his brother has wronged him, he should first go and be reconciled to his brother. Confession has to do with men, but the result of confession keeps us in good fellowship with God.

The Extent of Confession

The extent of our confession goes as far as the feeling of our conscience. The amount of light we receive determines the amount of confession we need to make. Today, we are not asking you to deal with your sins, but to have fellowship with the Lord. If you have fellowship with the Lord, God's life will work in you, and when the light comes, your conscience will be bothered, and it will urge you to deal with your sins. There is a difference between dealing with the conscience and dealing with sin. Dealing with the conscience depends on our fellowship with the Lord. The more the Lord enlightens us, the more we deal with our conscience. Dealing with sin is the result of dealing with the conscience. When our conscience points out our sins, we deal with them accordingly.

The Necessity of Confession

We have to know that our God is a God who means business with us. He is not loose. The teaching of confession can be covered easily. But once we are saved, God will bother us and trouble us within day by day. The more we love the Lord, the more trouble He will give to us. Man thinks that as long as he loves God, God will be lenient toward him. Actually, the more God loves us, the more He troubles us. God allows those who do not love Him to go their own ways. The ways of such ones are broad and the gates wide. But if a man loves the Lord, God will come to him and bother him.

In the matter of paying tax in Matthew 17, we see how the Lord bothers people. Strictly speaking, there was no need for the Lord to pay the tax. But since Peter made his proposal too quickly, the Lord wanted him to learn some lessons. Peter wanted to argue with the Lord and to find out from Him whether or not one should pay the tax. The Lord had a better way to deal with Peter; He asked him to walk a long distance to fish. This shows us that the more God wants to train us, the more He would bother us.

The Principle of Confession

Concerning the principle of confession, we have to realize that the conscience deals only with unrighteous things. In dealing with our conscience, we need God to give us the wisdom so that we take care of matters in a proper way. The principle of dealing with our conscience is that in our dealings God would gain the glory, others would receive the benefit, and we would be edified. We need wisdom especially in dealing with matters related to adultery. There are some things which cannot be dealt with, and we can only ask God for His forgiveness. We must not pursue peace in our conscience to the extent that it would cause damage to others. There are certain things that cannot be dealt with, and we should not try to deal with them. These matters are over once they have been put under the blood. It is true that we have to be faithful in dealing with the conscience. But sometimes we can go too far. When we realize that we have gone too far, we should stop. Sometimes, it is not God who is telling us to deal with the matters, but Satan who is telling us to do it. The principle of Satan is to hold us back initially and to keep us from advancing. When he cannot hold us back any longer, he will try to push us forward and make us go to the extreme. Sometimes, in the matter of confession, time is a big factor. With some matters, it is wrong to deal with them too early, and it is wrong to deal with them too late. In all these matters, we need the Lord to grant us the wisdom.

Confession Needed Especially for Our Speaking

One area that we have to make confessions in all the time is in the matter of speaking inaccurate words. This is particularly true with us who are speaking for the Lord. We do not know how many times we have to make confessions in this matter. We have to ask God to send His angels to guard our mouths. Psalm 19:14 says, "Let the words of my mouth, and the meditation of my heart, be acceptable in thy sight, O Lord." For a long time, this was my daily prayer.

BEING SENSITIVE IN OUR RESPONSE TO THE LORD

In order to maintain our fellowship with the Lord, we have to be sensitive to His calling. Sometimes the Lord calls us to fellowship with Him. If we do not come to Him, and if we wait until it is too late, we may find that the Lord has left. This kind of people will suffer the punishment of being cut off from the fellowship with the Lord. They have to suffer much punishment before they can come to Him again and meet Him once more. In the matter of fellowship, the Lord is not under our control. This is why we have to be sensitive in our response to Him.

The Lord shows us in the Gospel of John that He is never under man's control. In John 4, the Lord asked the disciples to buy food, but when the food came, He did not eat it. In chapter six, the Lord Jesus knew very well how to take care of the crowd, yet He asked the disciples what to do. In chapter seven, the Lord's brothers wanted to go to Jerusalem, but He would not go. After a while, He Himself went. In chapter eleven, Lazarus was sick, and Jesus remained in the same place for another two days. After Lazarus died, He went. When there was hope, He would not go. When the hope was gone, He went. In all these cases in John, the Lord's intention was to train the disciples to know that the Lord had His timings; He wanted the disciples to know His timings. In chapter eleven, when the Lord came late, although Martha did not blame Him, she did murmur. She did not realize that the Lord had His own timing. What the Lord wants us to learn is to accept His timing in all things, to allow Him to be the Lord, and to fellowship with Him. Even when something appears to be unreasonable outwardly, He wants us to submit to Him. Only by doing this will we be able to go on with the Lord.

CHAPTER THIRTY

GOD'S SPEAKING AND MAN'S SATISFACTION AND REST

THE LORD'S DAY MORNING MESSAGE (2)

Date: Morning, January 18, 1948
Place: Swatow, Kwangtung
Speaker: Witness Lee

Scripture Reading: S.S. 1:6-7; Psa. 27:8; Hosea 2:14; Rom. 8:6b

(In Psa. 27:8, the first part was the psalmist's heart speaking on God's behalf: "Seek ye my face," and the second part was the psalmist's reply in his heart: "Thy face, Lord, will I seek."

In Hosea 2:14, God will "speak comfortably unto her." This word is the Lord's word to our heart.)

Prayer: May we receive grace from God, and may the brothers and sisters meet You, and may the eyes of their hearts be opened. May the words we speak this morning be released, and may others receive the help from these words.

TWO KINDS OF GOD'S WORDS—
THE HOLY BIBLE AND THE HOLY SPIRIT

Today in fallen Christianity, men pay too much attention to God's word outside of them. Many people think that the words in the Bible are God's words. It is true that they are God's words, but we have to know that other than the words of the Bible, there is also the word spoken by the Holy Spirit within man. The words God speaks to us in the Holy Spirit are just as important as His words to us in the Bible. When the Israelites were in the wilderness, God led them by day and by night with the pillar of cloud and the pillar of fire. These two symbols are actually one thing. In the daytime, it is easy to see the pillar of cloud. In the night, a person cannot see the pillar of cloud, and there is the need for the pillar of fire. The pillar of cloud signifies the Holy Spirit, and the pillar of fire signifies the Holy Bible. Both are God's word, but the way they are manifested is different. The pillar of cloud is the Holy Spirit speaking to us, and the pillar of fire is the Holy Bible speaking to us.

When the Holy Spirit leads us in a clear and bright way, it is like the speaking of the pillar of cloud. But we are not that clear twenty-four hours of the day. Sometimes we will fall into darkness. All those who have been through spiritual experiences know this kind of story. Sometimes a person may have been clear the night before, but he becomes unclear after a night's sleep. You may think that you have become blind. Actually, it is not that you have become blind, but that the sun has gone down. The same is true with our spiritual experience. Sometimes we have the daytime, and sometimes we have the night. In the daytime, we need the pillar of cloud, whereas at night we need the pillar of fire. When we are clear, we follow the Holy Spirit. But when we are not clear, we follow the Holy Bible. During the day, the Israelites did not need the pillar of fire; they only needed it during the night. In the same way, when we are clear, we can trust in the Holy Spirit. But when we are not clear, we can trust in the Bible. The two are equally important. We need both the word within us and the word outside of us before we can become clear concerning God's voice.

God gives to us these two kinds of words. Outside of us, we have the Bible, and inside of us we have the Holy Spirit. In the wilderness, the pillar of cloud was there in the night also, but the Israelites did not see it. When they did not feel the presence of the pillar of cloud, they had to go on with the pillar of fire. If a man is not clear about the leading of the Holy Spirit, he should compare himself with the Bible. But if a man only walks according to the Bible, his living and working will be merely according to the letter; they will be lifeless and will not be worth much. We should fellowship with God in our spirit. When the Spirit of God speaks to us, we should act accordingly. On the other hand, God is afraid that man would make mistakes, and therefore He gave to man the Bible as the yardstick, so that man can compare himself with the Bible. In this way the leading he receives will be accurate. We must always learn to do one thing, which is to follow the leading of the Bible, on the one hand, and to learn to know God's speaking and to hear His voice within us, on the other hand.

THE SPEAKING OF THE HOLY SPIRIT WITHIN US BEING MORE PRECIOUS

One older brother has been a Christian ever since he was a student in school. But for all the years that he had been a Christian, he never knew that God could speak within man. One day he wanted to buy something, but a voice within him said, "Do not buy it." Later, he discovered that the thing he wanted to buy was booty stolen from others. Had he bought it, he would have trespassed the law. This brother told his pastor about this story and told the pastor that God was speaking within him. The pastor told him, "It is enough for God to speak to you from the Bible. There is no need for Him to speak again within you."

We have to know that God still speaks to man through the Holy Spirit today. The Holy Spirit is speaking on God's behalf within man. On the one hand, those who follow the Lord today cannot act contrary to the Bible or go beyond it. But the more precious fact is that God speaks to man within him. God's speaking within man will never be contrary to the Bible. If a man has never learned to follow God's speaking within him, his living and work will not be of much worth.

THE FEELING OF GOD SPEAKING WITHIN MAN

Thirst and Dissatisfaction Being God's Calling for Man to Fellowship with Him

What kind of feeling does God give to man when He speaks within man? The best proof of God's speaking is our feeling of dissatisfaction. If you ask others if they are satisfied, most people will tell you that they neither feel satisfied nor feel dissatisfied. Those who say this prove that they have not allowed God to work within them. If a man does not have

God's word within him, he will feel neither hungry nor satisfied. If a man feels thirsty and dissatisfied, as if he lacks something, it proves that God is working within such a person already. If a man feels empty and lacking in something, this lacking is God's speaking within him. It speaks of a need. It proves that God is working in him to empty him out. This is like when a man feels hungry, it is his stomach speaking on behalf of water and food.

Satisfaction Being the Result of Fellowship with God

If your meeting, praying, and study of the Bible do not satisfy you, it means that God is speaking to you and beckoning you to seek after Him and to have more fellowship with Him. Once you fellowship with God, you will be satisfied. You will be filled like a hungry man having taken a meal. When God speaks within man, man becomes hungry. When man meets God, he becomes satisfied. The Lord Jesus says that those who hunger and thirst after righteousness are blessed. Also He says that whoever thirsts can come to the Lord to drink. Only the thirsty ones will come to the Lord, and only the thirsty ones will be satisfied. If we receive grace to have fellowship with God, the result will surely be satisfaction. I ate last night, and this morning I am hungry again. This hunger is my stomach speaking for food. When a man is hungry, even if you give him gold and jewels, he will not be satisfied. On the contrary, it will increase his sufferings. There is only one way to solve man's hunger, and that is to bring him to the food. Only two kinds of people are not hungry, the dead ones and the critically ill ones. After a person has died, all year round he will not be hungry. If you do not have the sense of hunger within, I am afraid you have not been regenerated and have not been enlivened yet.

The Increase of Hunger and Thirst Being an Indicator of the Growth in Life

The more a person grows, the more hungry he becomes, and the more food he needs. A newborn babe only needs his mother's milk. But after he takes the milk, he becomes hungry very soon. As he grows, he will need more food; he will need to have the rice, the vegetables, and the meat before his hunger can be satisfied. When a man is first saved, he may think that the pastor's preaching is very good. But after three or five years, he will feel that the pastor's preaching does not satisfy his inner need any longer. This does not mean that the preacher's speaking is not good, or that it is wrong. It is the same pastor. But the growth in life within a man causes him to have higher and deeper needs. Hence, the hunger within man speaks of the degree of growth he has. Today, your need is God's need. Outwardly, it seems to be man's own need. But actually it is God's need. Man's need speaks of God's need. Man's dissatisfaction speaks of God's dissatisfaction. It is like the prodigal son having no rest away from home; it speaks of the father having no rest at home. Only when the father has rest will the son have rest. The rest the father has and the rest the son has are the same rest. The two rests are joined together and are related to one another. Frequently, we tell people that the Samaritan woman was thirsty. But the Lord was even more thirsty. The woman's food was the Lord, whereas the Lord's food was the woman. When the Savior meets the sinner, He is satisfied, and when the sinner meets the Savior, he is also satisfied.

Daily Hungry and Daily Satisfied—
the Normal Experience of One
Who Is in Fellowship with the Lord

The Christian experience is one where we are daily hungry and are daily satisfied. I had a meal this morning. But by this afternoon and this evening, I will be hungry again. This is like a person having fellowship with the Lord in the morning; he feels sweet and satisfied. But in the afternoon, he needs to come to Him again. This is God speaking in Him. Many Christians do not pay attention to this. They do not realize that every time they are hungry, they have to contact God. Every time we do not follow the Holy Spirit, we will lose the sense of hunger. This sense of hunger is the sense of life.

The Song of Songs says that God's leading directs us to

the place of peace and rest. If we do not have rest, this proves that God is speaking to us. In the Song of Songs we see a person working for God, yet one who did not fellowship with Him. She was busy with her work, yet she was hungry within. She asked where the Lord fed His flock, because she wanted to be satisfied, and she asked where the sheep could find rest. She asked these questions because she herself did not have rest. This sense of hunger and restlessness is God's speaking. The purpose of this speaking is to turn us to seek after the Lord. The result of the Lord's leading is to bring men to Him. At the end of chapter one of the Song of Songs, we see the result of the Lord's leading, which is the seeker sitting at the table with the Lord. In chapters two, three, and four she was repeatedly hungry and restless. Every time she was hungry and restless, it was God's speaking to her for the purpose of drawing her to the Lord. In this way, she was kept constantly in a state of seeking after God. There is no other way to take care of man's hunger and restlessness except by coming to the Lord.

ALL SPIRITUAL EXPERIENCES BEING
GOD PASSING THROUGH US

Some people study the Bible and pray, but they are not satisfied. The reason for this is that they need to have the sense of the Holy Spirit within them. When we pray, we cannot pray according to our mind or our memory; we have to pray according to our inner feeling. If we pray according to our inner feeling, the more we pray, the more we will touch God. This kind of prayer is like our eating; it satisfies us.

Some people pray according to their memory. They pray for their husbands, and they pray for their sons, from the first one to the last one, and ask God to protect them from car accidents. But the more such ones pray this kind of prayer, the emptier they become. After the prayer, when such ones see their children, they lose their temper again. What is the real prayer? The real prayer is the Christ within praying to the Christ in heaven. The real prayer is God passing through you and praying out of you. All spiritual experiences are a matter of God coming in and going out of you. The real prayer is not a matter of kneeling down or saying the right words, but of praying according to the inner feeling. If the Lord wants you to pray, you should pray. You should pray to the extent that you are filled with God and that God passes through you. This is the real prayer. It is right that we pray for the brothers and sisters, and sometimes God does give us the burden to pray for others; the more we pray that kind of prayer, the more burden we will have. But many times when others ask me to pray for them, I would not answer anything. It does not mean that it is wrong for others to ask me to pray for them. It means that I have to go before God and see what His mind is. We are not praying according to man's need, but according to the inner feeling. In other words, we pray according to God's need.

The same is true with our reading of the Bible. For example, when we read Matthew 1, we should not right away look up the meaning of the word Abraham. Rather, whenever we come to some words that we are touched with, we should immediately pray. In this way, our reading of the Word will cause us to touch God and be filled with Him.

Chapter Thirty-One

THE SERVICE IN THE BODY AND LISTENING TO OTHERS

TALKS (8)

Date: Morning, January 19, 1948
Place: Brother Cheng's home, Swatow, Kwangtung
Speaker: Witness Lee

TRUE KNOWLEDGE OF SPIRITUAL THINGS

Man always pays attention to methods and ways. Actually, a way is just a law. God has no intention for us to know the methods, but He intends for us to have the knowledge of the spiritual things. At present, our knowledge concerning spiritual matters, such as loving the Lord or consecration of material things, is not genuine enough. It is not sufficient for a person merely to know that there is air and light; he has to have a genuine realization of what air and light are. In the past seven or eight years, many times we have probed for ways; we hoped to find out the proper way to do things. But what God is after is our genuine knowledge concerning Him and concerning spiritual matters.

THE KNOWLEDGE OF THE BODY LIFE

Service is not an individual matter; it is a corporate matter. The Bible uses the body as an illustration of this matter (1 Cor. 12:12-27). Any time a member is isolated, it becomes useless. The minute we mention the members, we think of their functions. As far as our function is concerned, we are the members, not the sons, the workers, or the brothers and sisters. We can be God's workers individually, and we can be brothers and sisters or children of God individually. But we cannot be members individually. The

Bible mentions the Body in at least three places. They are 1 Corinthians 12, Romans 12, and Ephesians 4.

God's Will Being the Body of Christ

Romans 12 first mentions consecration (v. 1). Next, it speaks of knowing the will of God (v. 2). After this, it speaks of the Body (vv. 4-5). Today, many people talk about Romans 12, verses 1 and 2, but they separate these verses from the Body mentioned in the following verses. The period after verse 2 should be removed, because verse 3 is connected to verse 2. Verse 2 mentions the will of God, and in verse 4 we see that God's will is the Body of Christ. Chapters one through eight of Romans speak of God's work, and chapters nine through eleven speak of God's mercy and selection. Based on His work and selection, we should consecrate ourselves to Him, and the goal is the Body of Christ.

Coordination in the Body of Christ

First Corinthians 12 speaks of the coordination in the church. Here we do not see individual members; we see only the Body. Paul used many words to explain this fact.

Every Member Coordinated in the Body

Ephesians 4 also speaks of the Body. There we see that all the brothers and sisters need to coordinate together. For example, the mouth may be very useful, but it can only fulfill its function when it is coordinated in the body. A member is not the whole body. Some people may be "first-class" members, great members, but they are nevertheless members only. On the other hand, other people may be small members, but they can never be so small that they cease to be members. There is much that we can say about this. You can ask a medical doctor, and he will tell you that if the coordination in the body is out of order by a little, the body will be sick. Someone has once said that sickness is caused by the malfunction of the coordination in the body. Every member has to learn to coordinate with other members. This may cause one member to feel uncomfortable, or it may cause another member to feel uncomfortable. However, even if it involves bringing discomfort to ourselves, we must nevertheless not care only for ourselves. Almost all the mistakes committed by Christians are on this point. Once the Body is not comfortable, the supply will be gone. If we want to be coordinated together, we must ensure that the Body feels comfortable.

SUBMITTING TO THE AUTHORITY IN THE BODY OF CHRIST

Submission Bringing In Benefits

The first thing we have to see concerning coordination is God's arrangement in the church (see 1 Cor. 12). In 1 Corinthians 12, coordination is a Body matter. If you hit me with your hands, you are offending my head. For anyone to offend the Body of the Lord is to offend the Lord. We have to realize that those brothers and sisters ahead of us have their authority. We should know and realize this authority. If we know this, we will see that nothing is more serious than offending God's authorities on earth. A brother who causes such an offense can never serve the Lord. One member cannot become angry with another member or be separated from another member. If one member is separated from the other members, and if he refuses to receive the supply from others, he will become isolated. Some older brothers and sisters are ahead of us; they have much more knowledge concerning the Lord than we do. The other members should therefore receive their supply from these ones. But many people feel that to submit to them is very difficult. However, you have to realize that they are a help to you. They render you the supply and enable you to fulfill your ministry. The arm receives blood for the hand. The members ahead of us receive supply for the benefit of the other members. The work may be done by the hand, but the supply comes from the arm. The Body is not merely an illustration, but a fact. If the arm is gone, the hand cannot work even if it has the capacity to do so. The arms should not try to be the hands, and the hands should not try to be the arms. Here we see the Body in its many different levels, with each member having its own work that it ought to do. This is not an organization. Rather, this is something organic.

Submission Being without Any Choice of Your Own

If I hit you or kick you, who is it that is hitting or kicking you? Is it my members that are doing it, or am I the one who is doing it? For my members to do it is for my whole body to do it. Consider the action of sweeping the floor; it is not the work of one member, but the work of the whole body. The blood in my whole body supplies the member that is doing the work. The body is organic. When the hands, the feet, or the face is in motion, the blood in the whole body directs its supply to these working members. There is the need on the one hand to submit to authority, and on the other hand for others to submit to you. It is difficult to submit to authority. It is more difficult to have others submit to you. You must first be dealt with yourself, and you must first learn to listen to others, before others will listen to you and submit to you. Those who are rebellious cannot expect others to listen to them. I know one sister who has changed maids twelve times. Every time she changed maids, it was because she could not tolerate the maid. What this sister has done was a proof that she has never learned the lesson of listening to others. I am afraid that when such people come to serve in the church, they will cause problems. This is like your mother asking you to buy her some sugar and ginger, and you keep the sugar, while giving her only the ginger. This is the way many people obey God; their obedience is a selective obedience. If I receive the order to buy ginger, I only need to obey and to buy it.

Obedience and Listening to Others Bringing In Blessing

Let me ask you: if it is not enough that we listen only to the Lord's word, how then should we listen to man's word? Whose word should we listen to? Perhaps you will say that we should listen to those whom we trust and love. But this is wrong. We should not be selective in our listening.

If there is a group of people here who are willing to listen, this place will experience a big change; Swatow will see thousands of people saved. If the window is open, the sunshine will come in. There may be clouds today. But tomorrow or the day after, blessing will come. Here the older ones listen to the younger ones, and the younger ones listen to the older ones. To listen to others means to be related together in the Body. If we talk about mutuality day after day, yet never listen to others, the coordination of the Body will be but an empty term. We may not be fighting with one another, but neither are we coordinated together. Men on the streets do not fight with each other day after day, yet there is absolutely no coordination or relatedness among them. The book of Acts shows us that there is no such thing as serving the Lord alone. Service is something in the Body. In Acts Paul charged Timothy to come and go; he did not leave any ground for Timothy to pray or to seek for God's will. Many people are very capable in the church, yet this is not necessarily a good thing. In the coordination of the Body, we need to work by listening to others. If you want to open the window, you have to check first with the responsible brothers. If you want to close the window, you also have to check with the responsible brothers. A good work is one that is done through fellowship and in coordination.

In the church in Shanghai, we have an elders' meeting once a week. Everything is decided by the elders. I admit that during the past year, many things were first proposed by me. But when it comes to making a decision in one accord, I also put myself as one among those who are under orders. This is how we handle everything, including affairs such as the service office record-keeping, and the receiving of saints for fellowship. Here we see no dictatorship or usurpation of authority. All the brothers and sisters can put forth their views and suggestions, and all can go on in the Body.

LEARNING TO LISTEN TO OTHERS

Listening to Others Being the Requirement for Service

In the meeting hall in Chefoo, there is a fixed place for everything, including the rags, the toilet paper, the pencils, and the nails. Nothing can be placed at random. There is a person in charge of every matter and every article. After a person is finished using any article, there are definite rules as to where the article should go. Sometimes we change the arrangements a few times a month. The purpose of this is to train the brothers and sisters to listen to others. Today, many people have never learned to listen to others. If we want to serve together, we have to fulfill this requirement in service. Once we are loose, we become "Sunday-Christians." To serve the Lord is different from doing any other piece of work. If you want to be a proper brother or sister, you have to declare that we who serve the Lord are people who would listen. We cannot work according to our own ways. Our own ways must be dropped. They must be dropped absolutely. When a decision has been made by the elders concerning ushering, none of the brothers can act any longer according to his own wish. A brother cannot come for a week and not come for another week. Once, in a certain church some chairs were moved. When I heard about it, I asked who had moved them. The one who gave the order said that the chairs were in the wrong place. I said, "It is not a question of the right place or the wrong place, but a question of who is giving the order." Later, the matter was decided in the elders' meeting. If you can neither take orders nor give orders, then you can only be one that takes candies; you can only do what you like to do. I can testify that during the past year, I have been exercising myself in Shanghai in this way; I put myself under the direction of the "little" brothers and yield myself to the brothers' arrangement to take a turn to serve in the fifteen districts.

Listening to Others Being Listening to the Lord

The church is not a place of dictatorship. Here we all learn to listen to others. The Lord is the Word. Hence, for us to listen to others' words is actually for us to listen to the Lord. This is why we have to learn to listen to others' words. There should be some persons responsible for every item of service in the church. There are responsible ones for the cleaning service, the ushering service, and the visitation service. There should be someone in charge of every item of service. This will make things easy to handle. In this way, those who practice submission will experience the joy and presence of the Lord.

In the church in Chefoo, the floors are cleaned by the brothers and sisters themselves. While the brothers and sisters were cleaning, they would pray that those who put their feet on that floor would be saved. Those who clean the chairs would also pray that those who sit on those chairs would be saved. All the brothers and sisters have a heart for the church, and everything was done for the Lord. Every item of service in the church was carried out through love for the Lord. Once a man passed by the meeting hall on a bicycle. When he saw the posted time for the meeting, he stopped and prayed. Afterwards, he went away. Later when we asked people to sign up for baptism, he came and asked to be baptized. He testified that he came to believe because he noticed how responsible the brothers and sisters were toward the church, and how they did everything for the Lord. He was touched by this and consequently asked to be baptized.

There was another sister whose husband had an unbelieving friend. The friend once had a dream in which he saw this sister in the meeting telling him that if he wanted to go to heaven he should follow her, and that if he would not follow, he would go to hell. He also saw that this sister's husband was not in hell. Some time after that dream, the church had a gospel meeting, and this sister's husband invited this friend to go to the meeting. When the friend stepped into the meeting hall, what he saw was exactly the same as what he experienced in his dream. As a result of this, he came to believe in the Lord.

On the one hand, the elders have to put matters before the Lord and consider the way to make the decisions. On the other hand, they have to learn to stir up the brothers and sisters to participate in the services.

The Need for the Church to Be Filled with Men Who Would Listen

Some brothers have asked me, "What is the requirement for me to come to the church in Shanghai?" The requirement is to listen to others. If you are not told to say something, do not say it. It is not a question of whether or not a thing should be said, but a question of learning to listen to others. One brother by the name of Geh was a college student. He had had some experience of working for others. He stayed in Shanghai for a number of days, and the church assigned him some work to do. Every morning he had to come from ten o'clock until twelve o'clock to transcribe messages. He could not be even one minute late. This was an exercise and a restriction for him. None of us is an expert. It is through serving that we become skillful. There is the need for the church to be filled with people who would listen to others.

Listening to Others Saves Much Trouble

Whenever the different denominations in Chefoo came together, they would argue with each other. Among us, we did not have a large number at the beginning. After some trainings, the number increased to eight hundred or one thousand. Yet there was very little opinion or criticism, and we made very few mistakes. We must cultivate this atmosphere in the church. We do not like to see many people making proposals concerning a matter. The brothers have a lot to say; the sisters have even more to say. Sometimes the sisters would even persuade the brothers to agree with them that something ought not be done. If there is the talking, it is better that we do not do anything. If we are to do anything, it is better that we stop the talking and start listening. We have to learn to do the works without having the talking. No one in Chefoo can move the chairs around at will. It is not a matter of why, but a matter of who gives the orders. Everything must be done by first checking with others. This is not being troublesome. Rather, this saves trouble. In the baptismal service, once we baptized one hundred twenty people in one hour and twenty minutes. Another time in Shanghai, we baptized one hundred thirty people in a little over an hour; it took only one minute to baptize each one. It took each one only fifteen minutes for the whole procedure, including the time to change clothes; after fifteen minutes the baptized ones were back in their seats already.

THINGS THAT ELDERS SHOULD LEARN

The church is different from the home. What the responsible ones discuss in their meetings cannot be taken outside the meetings. If anyone wants to know anything, he should first ask the elders. Those in the world are used to meetings without discussions, and discussions without decisions, and decisions without actions. But the church should not be like this. Once there is a decision, we have to take action. After the elders make the decision, they should assign someone to execute the decision. Any decision that is made must not be announced independently. A brother cannot even tell his wife about the decision. After the meeting is over, the matter should not be discussed any further. Before an announcement is made, no one should pass on the news privately. One time, words about a decision went out to the brothers and sisters. When I tried to trace the person who spread the word, I found out that the source was a certain wife. When I asked the wife about it, she told me that a responsible brother had told her about it. Later I asked that responsible brother, and he admitted that he had said it through an oversight.

Exercising to Be Dealt With in the Flesh, Being in One Accord, Having the Lord as the Center

It is not a matter of doing the right thing, but a matter of having the proper exercise. If a person's flesh is not dealt with, he is not qualified to touch God's work. He can be a "pew-member" or a "Sunday-goer" in the church. He can even be a good brother. But he cannot be a member of the Body. In order for the church to be built up in every aspect, both the human affairs and the things of God as well have to be up to the standard. Here we need God to remove our presumptuousness and our looseness as well. When a brother or a sister moves to another locality, he or she should not go there to assume any headship or to disrupt the order of the church. Human organization is different from the church. A human organization works by voting and by the consensus of the majority. But spiritual oneness is something spontaneous. The secret to all the blessings in the church is to be in one accord and to take the Lord as the center in everything.

CHAPTER THIRTY-TWO

SERVING BY THE WHOLE BODY

CONFERENCE (8)

Date: Evening, January 19, 1948
Place: Swatow, Kwangtung
Speaker: Witness Lee

Scripture Reading: Phil. 1

PREACHING THE GOSPEL IN COORDINATION, WITH EVERYONE FUNCTIONING

Gospel preaching is not an individual matter, but a corporate matter. It is quite a demanding work, and we cannot consider it lightly. I can testify that before every gospel meeting, I have to speak to the brothers and sisters at least twice, to let every one enter the burden of the gospel before we actually preach to the outsiders. Today the gospel is preached by the church, and everyone has a part in it; everyone can give themselves to this work. Of course, this does not mean that everyone can deliver a message on the podium. Yet in the work of gospel preaching, the delivering of the message occupies only a small part of the various responsibilities. The other responsibilities rest with the brothers and sisters. This kind of gospel preaching will not put the burden on the shoulders of one person only.

There is a big difference between a gospel preaching that is done in coordination and one that is done individually. Every time, before I deliver a gospel message, all the brothers and sisters first do their part in inviting their friends and making all the preparations. I am like one who sits on a sedan chair; there is no need for me to do much. After the message, everything is handled by the brothers and sisters also. I can go home and rest. This kind of coordination does not put the burden on the shoulders of one person alone. Instead, it becomes the church preaching the gospel.

THE CHURCH PREACHING THE GOSPEL IN ONE ACCORD

In Chefoo, during the New Year, none of the brothers and sisters would celebrate the festival. Everyone prepares only simple meals. Some brothers and sisters only cook once in the morning and eat leftovers for lunch and dinner. Some who come from distant localities bring their own food with them, while the church provides only water and tea for them. Other brothers and sisters would invite gospel friends to eat at their homes. The Chinese New Year festival is very much related to superstitious practices and idol worshipping. In addition, during the New Year season, all the illegal and sinful things are done in the open. In this demonic festival, theatrical groups would be set up in front of the idol temples and would sing to the idols. In spite of all these activities, every time we preach the gospel, we gain many people.

In preaching the gospel, as long as we are one, we will see many people saved. In Tsingtao, our number was originally quite small, about one hundred thirty brothers and sisters. After I worked there for two months, from April 15 to June 15, we had an increase of two hundred people. Originally we did not have a baptistry. Later a baptistry was built in a brother's home, and the church began baptizing people every month.

Here in Swatow, you have about three hundred brothers and sisters. If you are in one accord, by the end of this year you should have one thousand saints. But if you argue with one another and divide yourselves into five or six groups, the number will surely decrease.

I have a burden in my heart, which is that the church here should preach the gospel in one accord. In the matter of gospel preaching, I hope that the church would learn to mobilize everyone. The main emphasis is not merely the saving of the sinners, but the oneness among the saints. If you do this, the number of saved ones will increase all the time.

A CHURCH LIFE IN WHICH EVERYONE SERVES

Passing On the Burden to Every Brother and Sister

When a co-worker goes out to work and to build up a church, he should pass on all his work to the brothers and sisters. In the beginning he may come with a burden. But gradually, the burden should be passed on to the shoulders of the brothers and sisters. Suppose here is a brother. First, you would hold his hand and work together with him. Gradually, you would pass on your work to him, while you stand beside him to help him. Up to a certain point, you can let go completely and transfer everything to his hand. If you do this, when you leave, you will not need to go through any transfer procedure, for all the things will have been passed on to him already. In 1943, on April 12, I became ill. Immediately, I conferred with the responsible brothers and made arrangements for the Lord's Day meeting. After this, I lay down on my bed and began to rest. All the services were taken over by the brothers and sisters immediately. The church at that time had many areas of service. Offerings alone were classified under seven or eight categories. There were many other kinds of work besides. At that time, we had about a thousand brothers and sisters, and business affairs were complicated. Yet all the saints divided up the work and proceeded in an orderly way. This lasts until today. A few years have elapsed, but today the brothers and sisters are still serving in the same way as they did then.

The Example of the Church in Chefoo

Here is how we divided up the services among the brothers and sisters in the church in Chefoo: one brother who was a postman was responsible for mopping the floor. He would come every Saturday to mop the floor, and he would find out in detail from the responsible brothers how to mop it. After he had found out the way from the responsible brothers, he would go about doing his work quietly. When he completed his work, he would leave. In the same way, all the brothers and sisters learned to listen and to work without talking.

This is the best kind of service. One brother who worked in an insurance company was assigned to clean the windows. At home, he had his own maid, and at work, he had people working for him. But when he came to the meeting hall, he did everything with his own hands. We have to learn to start with the small chores. At the beginning, I washed the toilets. Later, other brothers and sisters joined me. One sister was responsible just for putting clean rags in a bin. Every Saturday, some serving ones would come and pick up the rags for cleaning. After they finished their service, this sister would pick up the rags and bring them to be washed. Some sisters in Shanghai are doing the same thing with the hospitality linens.

Not Replacing, but Perfecting the Saints

When I first came to Nanking, some brothers and sisters thought that I came to "run" the church. I told them that I did not come to "run" the church. Instead, I came to give them trouble. I came to generate work for them. It is true that I came with a burden, but this burden had to be passed on to the brothers and sisters. Do not think that because Brother Lee has come, everyone is now free. The same is true in the church in Shanghai. This time, when I left Shanghai, I did it in such a way that I do not have to go back anymore, because all the responsibilities have been transferred over to the local saints. When the western missionaries came to China, they came to "run" churches. They monopolized everything. They even solicited foreign money for them to "run" their churches. This is not our way. We are here to help the brothers and sisters to fulfill their functions.

No More "Pew-members" and Nominal Christians

We should not have the concept of coming on Sunday to a so-called service. When the brothers and sisters come together on the Lord's Day, they do not come for a "service"; rather, they come with their hearts prepared to hear the Lord's word. In the afternoon, they should go out to preach the gospel. It is not a matter of listening to a sermon, but a matter of striving together in oneness for the gospel. In the evening, they should come together to remember the Lord, to fellowship with Him and to worship Him. The prayer meeting is the time when we bring our problems and needs to the Lord. If we do all these, we will receive the Lord's blessing. We should never be "Sunday-service Christians." If you want to be a "Sunday-service Christian," you should go to the denominations. If you think that this is not the right place for you, you can go to some other place, some Christian organization. If we are merely "running" churches, organizing Sunday services, and producing "pew-members," we might as well close our doors.

Concerning the Ushering Service

Concerning the ushering service, the ushering brothers and sisters should stand in an orderly way in the meeting hall before the meeting begins. Once the meeting has begun, they should not move around or make gestures anymore. This will frustrate the brother giving the message. The late ones should find their own seats. If the ushers stand up again, then you have one more person moving around. The ushers should also help the saints to take up the front rows first, and every row should have some brothers and sisters, so that new ones can be cared for.

Everyone Serving in Oneness, Submitting to One Another

If the brothers and sisters would take up all the services in oneness, they will realize the sweetness in serving the Lord. The church belongs to everyone; it does not belong to the preachers. Hence, in serving the Lord we need grace on both sides, on the side of the brothers and sisters, and on the side of the responsible ones, the elders. The co-workers and the elders should always be concerned that the number of serving ones would not be too few. They have to do their best to invite others to join the service. At the same time, all the brothers and sisters should learn to listen to others and to submit to one another.

In degraded Christianity, a person "runs" a church; a

pastor is hired, a Sunday service is held, and everyone comes to listen to a sermon and attend a service. But this is not our way. When we come together, everyone puts in his portion, and we all serve the Lord together. This is what the Lord is after today.

CHAPTER THIRTY-THREE

THE WAY TO PERFECT A PERSON

TALKS (9)

Date: Morning, January 20, 1948
Place: Swatow, Kwangtung
Speaker: Witness Lee

Prayer: Lord, we are gathered here before You. Enlighten us concerning Your word, and may we touch You from deep within. Lord, show us that Your word is life.

GOD CARING FOR THE PERSON MORE THAN FOR THE THINGS

In the church the most important thing is the person. The importance of the person far exceeds that of any work. In the world it is just the opposite; there, the work is more important than the person. But for us the person is more important. Time stands between the two eternities; both creation and redemption are within the span of time. During the span of time, God does many works. God's main goal, however, is not the works, but to gain persons through the works. God does not work for the sake of working, but for the sake of gaining men through His works. God is not here merely to accomplish a work, but to use His work to gain some people. Hence, our views have to be changed.

The Heart Being Proper toward God

God pays much attention to man's heart. The Lord told the Israelites once that "this people draws near with their mouth, and with their lips they honor Me, yet they remove their heart far from Me" (Isa. 29:13). From this, we see that what God cares for is man's heart. Although many words about the heart are from the Old Testament, we find the

Lord quoting them in the New Testament: "You shall love the Lord your God with all your heart and with all your soul and with all your mind" (Matt. 22:37). "Blessed are the pure in heart, for they shall see God" (Matt. 5:8). "For where your treasure is, there will your heart be also" (Matt. 6:21). "But whenever their heart turns to the Lord, the veil is taken away" (2 Cor. 3:16). For this reason, a man's heart must be right and proper toward God.

It is of course right that we love the brothers. But if we do this without having our hearts aimed at God, such love is not proper. When the Gentiles do the right things, they are right only with respect to the things themselves; they are not right with respect to God. Matthew 7 describes a group of people who have done many things for God, but their hearts are not right toward God. For that reason, they are considered lawless ones (v. 23). If you ask how it could be that a person whose heart is not right can cast out demons, I will tell you that it is indeed possible. Even the Gentiles can cast out demons. As long as a person fulfills the natural law, he can get the expected result. If a man opens the window, air will naturally come in. If a man and a woman are married, naturally they will bear children. Even Lot's daughters who committed incest with their father were able to bear children. If a man is not right in his heart, he can still preach and can still perform miracles. As long as he goes along with the law, it will work. Hence, we cannot judge anything by its outward results. The important thing is where the heart is.

The Heart Being Attached to God

Sometimes, troubles arise among the brothers and sisters because some have an improper heart. Some people are caused to stumble because their hearts are not right. Some people become disappointed because their hearts are not right. Among a thousand brothers and sisters, it is difficult to find one or two whose hearts are near to God. If you suffer loss in your business, and your heart is attached to your business, you will be hurt. Out of the heart are the issues of life (Prov. 4:23). Man's heart is like sticky paper; it attaches itself to whatever it touches. A person who loves the Lord will not be moved by anything good or bad, or by any changes in the human life, because his heart is attached to God. Those who have a proper heart will not put blame on others; they will not condemn others. They will not treat others well when others treat them well, and treat others in an evil way when others treat them in an evil way. We are all hard-to-deal-with people. If someone is a proper person, he will not be overly subjective toward many things.

A Heart after God's Will

A person who has learned the lessons is one who is always fearful of God and who always fears Him in everything. Whether or not a man fears God depends mainly on whether or not he does things by himself or by the life of God. To love God is a matter of the heart. To fear God is a matter of life. If the heart is right before God, it is all right even if the things are done a little bit off. Sometimes I hear people say that we should pray more about such-and-such a thing. When I hear this, I do not feel at peace about it. It does not mean that the words are wrong, but the person who says the words is not a proper person. Solomon said that it is ugly to put a golden ring on the nose of a pig (Prov. 11:22). The golden ring is surely good, but some people are like the nose of the pig; their hearts are not right, and they do not have a proper kind of life. Can a person love a pig just because it has a golden ring on it? If you take away the ring, nobody will want the pig any longer. As long as a person is after God's will, this person is a right person. A handsome person is handsome even if he puts on pig's skin. Many people talk about God's will, but they are not proper persons. Such persons can never really know God's will. God can never reveal His will to an improper person. To have the blessing is one thing. To have the blessing does not mean that you are a proper person. Our God is not stingy. God blesses even those whose hearts are not right. Our hearts must be calibrated on God, in the same way that the needle of a meter should be calibrated to the scale.

First a Proper Heart, Then a Proper Person

If a person's heart is right, that person is right. Even if he does the wrong things, he will not veer off very much. Even when he makes a mistake, he will not go too far off. Whether or not you can become a blessing to others depends on your heart. If you are a proper person, wherever you go, you will become a blessing there. If a person's heart is not right, even if he were to accomplish monumental works, others will still not receive the blessing. Some people have become a problem to us, not because of what they have done, but because of their person. With the conscience, it is a question of righteousness. With the heart, it is different; the heart only deals with the question of being for God or not for God. The heart must be set on God, instead of set on the works. Many things in the church life, such as the persons, the things, the events, the relationships one with another, the love toward the church and the brothers and sisters—all these can turn man's heart away from the Lord. A sinner is saved by turning his heart to God. He is not saved through having something to do with any person, things, or events.

If a robber comes to you and tells you that he will treat you well, you should not believe in him. The reason for this is that the person himself is not a proper one. One story goes that a yellow fox was once paying a New Year's visit to a chicken. The heart of the fox was not right, for after the visit he intended to swallow the chicken down into his stomach. The chicken would not believe in the fox, because the fox's heart was not right. In serving the Lord, we have to pay attention to the person, and not merely to doing the right things.

OUR WORK BEING TO PERFECT OTHERS

Producing Apprentices and Developing Talents

Our work does not depend on the achieving of the job, but on the perfecting of men. We have to produce apprentices and develop the personnel. In order for a company to expand, it must discover the talents. During the past few years, our church life did experience some shortages. In all the churches, the attendance is high, and those who come to listen to messages are many, but you cannot find the suitable persons. To do a work is easy, but to produce some apprentices is hard. If we are to preach the gospel and save sinners, we have to do it in such a way that some men are perfected in our work before God. For someone to be able to do something himself is not so extraordinary. To be extraordinary, a person has to be able to cause others to do the same thing that he is doing, and even to do it better than he does. A person does not have to be a scholar himself, but he has to be able to produce an apprentice who is a scholar. In the same way, a person does not have to be a performer himself, but he has to be able to train others to become performers. Some can only do a good job if they are to do it themselves. This is like some people who cannot tolerate having an amah, a servant, not because they are ill-tempered or they are unkind, but because they always think that they alone can do the job well; nobody else can. To them, no amah is suitable. They have to make their own dumplings. If the amah were to make the dumplings for them, they would think that the dumplings are not right. Actually, they may be making dumplings that are clumsy and ugly. Yet they still think that they are the only ones who can do it, and that no one else can do it. There is a fallen concept within man; people always think that what they do is better than what others can do. Actually, if you are truly good at doing something, you can pass on the skill to others and can help others to become just as good. If others do not do it right, you can ask them to do it again, until they become as good as you are. If you would do this, it shows that you are one who has learned the lessons and has been dealt with by the Lord.

Allowing Everyone to Have the Full Opportunity to Serve the Lord

One responsible brother once assigned some sisters to make some tablecloths. After the sisters tried for a few times, the brother was still not satisfied. In the end, when he asked other sisters to help, no one dared to try it anymore. Yet this brother could not do the work himself. His disposition was too strong, and he had frightened others away. If he would repent of his way, he may be able to gain one or two hundred brothers and sisters. The Lord has been very much restricted by us. We have offended the Lord within us. We should afford all the brothers and sisters full opportunity to serve the Lord, to offer up their possessions, and to give up everything they have for the Lord. Everything should be consecrated, whether it is the person or the things. If we do this, the church will become the Lord's blessing to others.

If you assign a brother to do something, you have to first pray and consider much. Moreover, when you speak concerning it, your words have to be accurate. The matter should first be discussed among a few people, and then presented to the brothers. In helping a brother, you should try your best to utilize his strong points. To perfect a person, we have to do it slowly.

Hong Kong is a gold mine, not in the literal sense, but as far as talents are concerned. If someone would work there diligently, it would affect the whole of southern China. We should pray that the Lord would use us. Shanghai is the center of the whole of China. Swatow is the center for Singapore and Ceylon. Hong Kong is the international center. Our work today cannot be like that of traditional Christianity; we cannot have a pastor to take over everything any longer. Instead, we should have every brother and sister rising up to work and to preach the gospel.

Perfecting Men for the Migration

Concerning migration, the brothers and sisters in Hong Kong can migrate to Southeast Asia. In the church in Chefoo, once over sixty people migrated west from Chefoo to Inner Mongolia and the Ningsia regions. Their traveling expenses were all taken care of by the church. May the Lord change our view so that we can see clearly the things of God. At the same time, if we are not proper ourselves, there is no way that we can perfect others. If some have passed through some serious dealings in the basic matters, the work ahead will have a free course. Some works experience periodic revivals. But after the revivals, everything subsides again. Time and time again there are consecrations, but no essential personnel are produced. If we do not produce fresh recruits, mere revivals are useless. From this, you can see the crucial need of perfecting others.

OUR ATTITUDE TOWARD THE DENOMINATIONS

We left the denominations not only because they are wrong, but because they have not come up to God's standard. If there were the possibility of joining or uniting with them, there would not have been the need for another group. There is an absolute difference, rather than a relative difference, between them and us. Some have asked if we can help the denominations. My answer is that we are like a shopkeeper. If others ask the shopkeeper for help, he would say that he does not have the time. He works every day from eight in the morning until night. Brothers and sisters, we do not need to ask how the elders should deal with the denominations. Those who help others to work do so because they have no work of their own. Our work today is not a scattered work. The question is not whether or not we can cooperate with others or help others. The question is whether or not we know what we are doing. A person who does a scattered work is one who does not know what kind of ground he stands on or what work he is doing. Those who are engaged in serious work will not walk into another's office asking for help, for they know that others are busy also.

You may say that the work of sweeping the streets and hauling fertilizer is low, but some people are doing this work also. I would not criticize others' work, nor would I oppose others' labor. However, I know what my own responsibility is. There are always people who will sweep the streets, and there are always people who will pick up the trash. Today I cannot do something merely because it is a good thing to do. Others may say that this is good and that is good. It is true that street-sweeping is good and that hauling fertilizer is not bad. There is the need for both. But the question is this: what does God want you to do? Already I do not have enough time to speak what the Lord wants me to speak. How can I find the time to oppose others' work? It is not a question of opposing or cooperating, but a question of what we are doing here.

CONCERNING THE APPOINTING OF ELDERS

The elders are produced mainly not through appointment but through manifestation. It is a matter of the growth in life. If a person can do many things only after he has been appointed to be an elder and will not do anything if he is not appointed, something is wrong. Can I appoint Mrs. Chow to be the mother of her four sons? And can I remove her from being a mother after a while? If you appoint her, she is a mother. If you do not appoint her, she is still a mother. Her being a mother is not due to your appointment, but to her relationship in life. Who is an elderly person? This is something relative. If a certain brother is the most elderly among us and another person comes along who is thirteen years older than this one, naturally this second one is the more elderly one. There is no question about this. The same is true with respect to spiritual maturity. If you have maturity, you have it, and maturity will manifest itself. It is best for the work of appointing the elders to be done by the co-workers. The same is true with the appointment of the deacons. To serve the Lord is not a question of a profession. The main thing is that we put ourselves in the church. The most necessary thing for a servant of the Lord to have is absoluteness.

ON BEING A GENUINE PERSON IN ORDER TO SERVE THE LORD

I know people in the same way that Brother Cheng knows his trade—silk embroidery. The minute he touches a fabric, he knows what kind of material it is made of. We have to be a genuine person. You may have a hot temper, or a bad disposition. But even if you oppose and criticize, you have to be genuine. We must be a genuine person if we are to serve the Lord.

Chapter Thirty-Four

MIGRATION

TALKS (10)

Date: January 21, 1948
Place: Swatow, Kwangtung
Speaker: Witness Lee

Prayer: Lord, do not allow us to walk in darkness. Give us the light, and make our light shine as the dawning of the day until midday. Lord, we believe that our prayers will be heard and answered. Lord, make us healthy within and without. When we preach the gospel tonight, may others receive mercy through seeing the love that the brothers and sisters express toward You. Lord, may our future be clear, and may all those who grope in darkness see the light. Forgive us for limiting Your ways.

THE WHOLE BODY
VOLUNTARILY RISING UP TO SERVE

It is a difficult thing to help the brothers and sisters to become useful before the Lord. It is easy for us to go to various places to preach the gospel and to give a few messages. But to remain in a place to serve the Lord properly, be coordinated together, and fulfill the function of each one, is a very difficult thing. This is something that the co-workers must pay attention to in the future. If this matter is carried out properly, God will have an oracle and a mouthpiece here. It is not right for the co-workers to see results only when they themselves are working, but not to see results when they are not working. A local church must be something organic; it must be on the move all the time. The co-workers must have an adequate amount of spiritual life, and they must have a proper view to promote this matter. When the elders and the co-workers are not there, the brothers and sisters should still continue to work. When that happens, the co-workers are free to go to work in another place. A built-up church is one that mobilizes by itself and that functions by itself.

WORKING IN ONE ACCORD, SETTING THE MIND ON THE THINGS OF THE LORD

We should not consider our own house more than we consider God's house. Rather, we should set our minds on the things of the Lord. We are not here to do a scattered work. Today, we have to work in one accord. Only then will the Lord have a way among us. The co-workers and the elders have to help one another, for the co-workers may be away from a locality at times, and the elders have to fill in the gap at those times.

LEARNING TO BE A PROPER PERSON THROUGH DOING THE WORK

We have to learn to be a proper person. In serving the Lord, the main thing is not our work, but to learn to be a proper person through doing the work. One of the basic trainings in serving the Lord is to learn to be a proper person through doing the work.

CONCERNING MIGRATION

Question: What is God doing in China today? What should be our emphasis? What are the steps we have to take? It seems that these matters are not so clear to us yet.

Brother Lee answered: In the past, we have laid quite a foundation for our work already. But the way to go on is indeed a problem. First, let us consider the question of migration.

God's People Being Sojourners on Earth

God's spiritual people are a group of people who are constantly on the move on earth. This was the way with the Israelites in the Old Testament. They were not settled in a fixed place. Rather, they moved around. We are a people who are called by a heavenly calling (Heb. 3:1, 9); we do not belong to the earth. Today, God has called us. We are but sojourners on the earth. The Bible says that we are the heavenly citizens. Our commonwealth exists in the heavens (Phil. 3:20). In the Old Testament, Abraham was called to leave Ur of Chaldea to go to the place that God had prepared for him and to serve Him there. He moved from one place to another, and he was a sojourner on earth (Heb. 11:8-9). A sojourner is a person whose heart is always on the move; he has no heart to settle down. This is like the co-workers who travel and work in various places; everywhere they go, they may be served with good food, comfortable lodging, and warm hospitality. Yet after they stay in a place for a while, they have to leave. This is how Christians should be—they should be like the Israelites.

The Calling, the Beginning, and the Revival of the Church

The word "church" is *ekklesia* in the original language. It should be translated "assembly." The "assembly" is a group of people who have received a heavenly calling. They are but sojourners on earth. At the beginning, both the apostles and the saints as well were moving people. In Acts, the scattered saints went everywhere to preach the gospel. Not only were the co-workers moving; the saints were also moving (Acts 8:4). The way of the gospel is composed of the going out of the apostles and the going out of the saints. Before Acts 13, there was the going out of the saints. After Acts 13, there was the going out of the apostles. Later, both lines ceased. Two hundred years ago, there was the great Moravian revival in Bohemia. As a result of that revival, many people went out from that place to North America, the Pacific regions, and the Atlantic regions. This move was lost when the church became degraded. When the church is revived, the gospel goes out, and many workers go out also.

The Christian Way Being to "Go"

Today, however, how many saints are going? What God wants us to do is something that has not been done before, and that is migration. For people to move because of the war is something they did against their will. During our war with the Japanese, many people moved to Kunming, but after the Japanese were defeated, these people moved back to their original places. This should not be the case with those who are moving for the gospel. The Bible shows us that we "come" to receive grace, and we "go" to serve. In the Bible, there are many "comings." Many of us should circle these "comings" with a red pen. But the Bible also speaks of "going." The last chapter of Matthew speaks of "going." The first chapter of Acts also speaks of "going." By Acts 28, the "going" had only gone as far as Rome; it was not completed yet. Acts is an unfinished book. In heaven, there may be two hundred chapters to Acts by now. The gospel went from Rome to Europe, then across the Pacific, and finally to the east coast of China.

Although the gospel has come to the East, it was difficult for the Westerners to spread the gospel to the interior of China. The Chinese do not like to move, and hence the gospel stopped at the east coast of China. This is the case with the church and the saints today. Man likes to settle in a place. Some families have been living here in Swatow for over a century. Their living revolves around this place. Their children are born here, they die here, and they are buried here. Everything is set. I hope that some would go to Tibet for the Lord's sake. When we "come," we drop the earth. When we "go," we take up heaven. This is the way of the Christian.

The Testimony of Migration in Chefoo

During the revival in Chefoo, of the eight hundred or more brothers and sisters, almost ninety percent of them consecrated everything. The Holy Spirit was working, and everyone was enlightened to repent in tears and to vow that they would never hold back the gospel again. Many of the saints consecrated their families, their jobs, and everything they had to the Lord. When we met together, there was a time when we had only tears before the Lord. During those days, no one preached much, and it is hard to describe the atmosphere of the meetings. Once a person stepped into the meeting, he would feel the Lord's presence. The brothers and sisters consecrated all that they had. Some saints dared not open up their closets when they went home, for when they did, a voice within would say, "Consecrate!"

One brother who was a judge observed the consecration of the brothers and sisters, and he remarked that what happened then was even more than what happened at Pentecost. What he said may be too much, but this brother did not say things lightly. He could say such a word because God's work was really prevailing then. At that time, there was a brother in his fifties who at one time saw the Lord Himself standing on the podium. When the brother was giving the message, the Lord was standing beside him. What he saw was something real, not an illusion.

During one of the meetings, I lifted up my hands to pray for about half an hour. The words just kept coming unceasingly. There was no need for me to think about what to pray; the words flowed out spontaneously. If you ask me to repeat what I prayed then, I cannot do it. At the end, when I lifted up my two arms, one brother sitting in front of me lifted his hands also to hold up my arms. After this, two groups of brothers and sisters migrated out. The first group consisted of over seventy people, among whom over sixty of them had their traveling expenses taken care of by the church. Later another thirty or more saints migrated to Manchuria. Today, the Lord is still blessing them.

From that time on, many people began to pay attention to us. But we did not know what power it was that was upholding us. At that time, our meeting on Fourth Street became the subject of conversation for many people, and some rumored that we had a sack of gold. After the Japanese came, they spent two and a half months to investigate me.

After the first group migrated out, we were going to send out the second group; the second group consisted of professionals, such as doctors and merchants. Not long after that, the Japanese arrested me. I was put into prison for a month. When I came out, I contracted a serious illness. After a year, I left Chefoo and have not returned since. The ones who migrated went to Inner Mongolia, Sinkiang, and Ningsia.

Migration Being to Live for the Gospel

There is some problem about settling in a place for too long. Some people were poor at the beginning. After they believed in the Lord, they took care of their businesses well and made profits from them. As a result, they offer more. But although they offer larger amounts, the percentage of offering compared with their profits becomes less and less. For example, they may have made a thousand dollars in the first year, and they spent only a few hundred dollars. The offering was fifty percent of their profit. After their business grew to a few hundreds of thousands of dollars, or tens of millions of dollars, they began to keep more for their own use, and they offer less percentage-wise. Although they are clear in their prayer, they become confused in practice. When others come around and persuade them, they invest in real estate again or start more partnerships. When opportunity comes and other businesses relocate elsewhere, they would buy the others' properties. In this way, they become settled, and the heavenly people become rooted on the earth. Their roots embrace the earth, and they have "colonized" themselves on the earth. All the churches begin to take root this way. In the meetings, everyone agrees that we should not love the world. But in practice, it becomes entirely different. When material wealth increases, offerings in the church increase, but so do the luxuries in the saints' homes. Without realizing it, the church has become worldly and secular. Migration is an uprooting in which a person sells all he has and moves to another place to live for the gospel.

One doctor by the name of Wu once talked with me, and I told him that if he sold everything he had and moved to a certain place, he could practice medicine during the week, preach the gospel on the Lord's Day morning, and have a Bible study in the afternoon. His wife could be a "sister-preacher." In a year's time, he could very well bring a hundred people to the Lord. If he would do this, after a few years, he could move to another place and do the same thing again. After a year in the second place, if he could not save a hundred people again, he could come to see me. If you sell all you have and get only three billion dollars for a five billion dollar business, outwardly it seems that you have lost two billion dollars. Actually, you have gained your soul. In Acts 1, after the Lord's resurrection, the disciples were interested in the question of the kingdom; they were not enthusiastic about going out. In the end, the Lord had to send a fire to burn Jerusalem and force them out in that way (Acts 8:1-4). The Lord's word says that the gospel would be preached from Jerusalem, through Judea, unto the remotest part of the earth.

The Need for a Revived Living

God's children should be a "moving" people; they should not be a "staying" people. They should go to the frontier lands. Man cares for human relationships, and he is reluctant to move. But God wants man to move. In the past God has gained some good vessels in China. If we will not do this for the Lord, who else will do it? In order to practice this, first we must recover the preaching of the gospel, and we must have a revived living. After this, we should migrate out. The Japanese may have been defeated, but something else may come. In Chefoo, we had the blessing because we sent people out. At present, there are over thirty places with the Lord's table in Sui-yuan province already. These brothers moved out from Chang-chia-kou, station after station, and went all the way from Chefoo to Sui-yuan province.

Migration Being Likened to a Relay Race

At present, over a hundred brothers and sisters in Shanghai have signed up already. Whenever the Lord gives us the leading, and whenever there is the opportunity, these ones would migrate out. Today, we need a group of pioneers. When a person moves out, he is really dropping everything. In Shanghai we have about a thousand brothers and sisters. We should have over fifty million dollars in offerings every month. In Chefoo, the more the saints migrated, the more people we saw added to the church. In preaching the gospel, there is the need of stations. This is like a relay race. The Westerners have sent the gospel to the coastal regions of

China. Today, we have to carry the gospel from the coastal regions to the interior regions. The Westerners cannot open the door of the gospel in the interior regions. Today, however, God will open this door through us.

CHAPTER THIRTY-FIVE

LIVING BY THE LORD

TALKS (11)

Date: January 22, 1948
Place: Swatow, Kwangtung
Speaker: Witness Lee

Prayer: Lord, what we need is not some passing excitement, stirring up, or exhortation, but the remaining work of the Holy Spirit within us. We do not want to be ahead of You, nor do we want to be behind You. May we be filled with You within.

LIVING BY THE LORD'S LIFE

What we need today is not merely that we do not live for ourselves, but that we do not live ourselves. We have to work not by ourselves, but by the Lord who lives within us. If we do not realize this, we will still trust in our own strength, and we will work according to our own preference. All works should be initiated by the Lord. No human efforts are of the Lord. After we are saved, the Lord's love revives us and causes us to live for the Lord and to consecrate ourselves to Him. This is the beginning of our spiritual revival. Ultimately, however, what the Spirit does is to lead us to know the life within us and to live by this life. On the one hand, our hearts must love the Lord, and we must be in fellowship with Him. On the other hand, we should act promptly according to the sense we have within. We should not work according to outward circumstances. Rather, we should work according to the inner sense we have received from God. After we are revived, we will surely take God's work as our center. But God must work on us to the extent that we realize that it is not enough to do the right thing. We must also ask by what strength we are doing the work and whether or not God's life is our strength. After a man is revived and sees God's work and His needs, he will try to do something hastily. However, God must eventually bring him to a place where he works by God alone. Outwardly, there does not seem to be very much difference between the two things, but only those who do not know God would think that the difference is an insignificant one.

THE KEY TO MINISTERING TO OTHERS BEING TO HELP THEM TO KNOW AND EXPERIENCE LIFE

In matters concerning God's life, there is a question of degree of depth. Experientially, a person can go through three stages: (1) salvation, (2) revival, and (3) life. Only those who have passed through these three stages of experiences can help others in these areas. The basis of the help we render to others is our experience. We must work according to our experience. Only when we are taking the lead in the front will others follow us at the back. Many like to hear teaching concerning revival, but few like to hear the teaching concerning life. In the past, many people thought that the teaching of life is the teaching of revival. Most likely, these people know about the knowledge and experience of life in terminology only. Most people think that what God wants is excitement. What God did in China in the past was mainly gospel work and revival work. There is a world of difference between revival and life; this difference is greater than the difference between high school and college. Revival is only a means; it is not the goal. It is only the procedure; the goal is life. The more we fellowship with the Lord, live according to the sense of life, and go along with this sense, the more we will be initiated into God's life. The help we render to others all revolves around these three things. If others ask, "How should such-and-such a passage of the Scriptures be expounded?" you should answer, "If you want to know about Bible exposition, go to the seminaries." If others ask about such things as baptism and head covering, you should return the question to them by asking if they have believed in the Lord, and if they have been fellowshipping with the Lord. You should ask if they are under any authority, and if they have the sense of life. If others ask whether this meeting is better or that meeting is better, you should tell them that everything depends on whether or not a person can meet God in a meeting, and whether or not a meeting can satisfy a person's inner need. What we care for is how many people are living by the Lord.

KNOWING NOTHING BUT LIFE

Brother Mak, if others oppose you or criticize you, you do not need to require them to come to you and explain to you what they are doing. Do not be carried away by others' questions. You have to take the initiative, and you should never be passive. There are thousands of ways to answer a question, but I know only one thing, and that is to turn back to life. Helping others to know life is like a doctor feeling the pulse of a patient; as soon as a person comes to you, you should be able to give a diagnosis and to discern the spiritual condition of that person. You can only minister to others what you have. Life is not knowledge. When a person comes to us to ask all sorts of questions, we should not give him answers to the questions. Instead, we should give him the Lord's life. When others come to you, you should not give him many ways to work. You should only give him the Lord. Do not carry him away into work. In the case of those who criticize you, you should try to turn them to life. You do not need to ask the reason for their criticisms, nor do you need to give explanations for yourself. Much less do you need to bring someone else along to vindicate or justify yourself. You only need to check the spiritual condition of such a one and ask him to pray with you. If you do this, you will see that you do not have to do anything; the Lord has done everything for you already. Such a person will say, "Thank you. You are truly a messenger from heaven." You do not know anything on the earth. You do not know any misunderstanding, any criticisms, or any agreement or disagreement. You only know life. There is nothing but life.

In Galatians 6:15, Paul told the Galatians that it was not a question of circumcision or uncircumcision, but a question of being a new creation. Following that, he said, "As many as walk by this rule, peace be upon them and mercy" (Gal. 6:16). If we practice this, all the blessings will follow.

BEING MINGLED WITH THE LORD AND WITH THE SAINTS

A. The Need to Deal with the Peculiar Characteristics

We have to mingle ourselves with the Lord. All the peculiar characteristics, the unaccommodating attitudes, and the odd dispositions have to be broken. If we do not do this, we will not be able to mingle with other Christians, and we will only be an individual Christian. Some people are like a drop of oil in water. Among the brothers and sisters, they are a drop of oil, whereas others are like a glass of water. Such a one cannot mingle himself with the others. When a drop of water falls into a glass of water, immediately it becomes one with the water in the glass. This should be the way with us as Christians.

B. The Need to Deal with Individualism

Cement, water, and stones are the elements that make up concrete. The Holy Spirit is like the water, the Lord is like the cement, and we are like the stones. In order for the three things to be mingled together, the stones must first be cleaned. If the stones are not clean, even if there is water and cement, the three will not mix together. The stones must first be cleaned. When they are clean, they can be mingled together with other stones in the water and the cement. Many people can serve God, but they cannot serve men. They can love God, but they cannot love the brothers and sisters. They can submit to God's authority, but they cannot submit to men's authority. They can confess their sins before God, but they cannot confess their sins before men. They can fellowship with God alone, but they cannot fellowship with the brothers and sisters. These people are like individual stones; they cannot come together with the other stones.

For some people, some part of their skin is too old and is not functioning properly. There is the need to remove the old skin and to graft in new skin. When the new skin is grafted in, what is grafted in must be fresh and new. In the process of grafting, such a one must endure pain for the old skin to be removed and the new skin to grow together with the other parts. Many brothers and sisters are too old. They have to experience some cutting before they can be joined together with others. Are you able to withstand such cutting? This is where the crux of the matter lies.

THE PERFECTING OF ALL THE SAINTS

In our serving together with the brothers and sisters, we have to spend time with them to learn together and to practice together with them. Moreover, we have to learn to pass on everything to the saints in a systematic way. We should be a person who is living before the Lord, and we should produce men instead of merely producing works. The church is like a hospital; not only should the sick ones receive treatment there, but the hospital itself should perfect the doctors and nurses. The church is also like a school, where not only students receive their education, but teachers are perfected. The church is also like a factory. Not only does it manufacture goods, but it produces apprentices as well. Again, the church is like a family. Under the love of the family, the children are nurtured, taught, and caused to grow. In this way, the saints are raised up and educated in the church, and eventually they will graduate to become "doctors" to take care of others. By that time, when God gives the leading and the direction, some will be able to go to migrate for the gospel's sake. This will put everything and everyone into use. Since we are clear about the Lord's way, we should go on faithfully today.

THE INNER SENSE

Concerning the inner sense, what we have to pay attention to is not the sense itself, but to have our hearts turn to the Lord, to love Him, and to look to Him. Whatever the first feeling is, we should go along with it and should not analyze. When I talk with others, I am bothered when their eyeballs begin to turn. This means that such a person is turning things around in his mind. Do not analyze the feelings. If you consciously try to remember which foot you should put forward first when you walk, you will never walk. God's life is living. We need to reject all outside voices and the so-called lights, and we should pay attention to the inner feeling and the anointing.

MINISTRY AND GIFT

We have to be clear concerning the difference between ministry and gift. Ministry is the result of life, and gift is something that the Holy Spirit gives spontaneously. First Corinthians speaks of the service that comes by the gifts, whereas 2 Corinthians speaks of the service that comes by the ministry of life. The gospel, revival, and life—all these three things are for the producing of the ministry. George Müller, Mrs. Penn-Lewis, and many others have an obvious portion of supply. Hence, they have the ministry.

Our work is the result of our fellowship with the Lord. If we experience life, we will produce the works. There is only one life of Christ, but its expressions are varied. There is only one life in the body, but there are the eyes, the ears, and the different organs. There is only one circulation of blood in the body, but when this same blood flows to all the different members, the functions manifested in the members are different. Today, it seems that God is no longer raising up spiritual giants. Instead, He is raising up every brother and sister to do the work. During the past years, among us the number of full-time serving ones has not increased. On the contrary, some have dropped out. At the same time that this is happening, we see many saints serving the Lord faithfully in their jobs. This is like building a house; in order to build a house, there is the need, on the one hand, for foremen and architects, and there is the need, on the other hand, for all kinds of materials to be assembled together.

If I pass on these things to you as mere teachings, I would be very pitiful indeed. What I am doing here is to show you a way. To those who want to go on in this way, this is reality. To those who do not want to go on, this is dead teaching.

NOT LEAVING THE FIRST LOVE

One of the most serious things mentioned in the seven epistles in Revelation is the leaving of the first love. This was the starting point of the church's degradation. When we come to the last church, the Lord was shut outside its door. Between these two points, many things took place; the main lesson they teach us is that the church's attention was drawn to the things and the works instead of to the Lord. Among the many things, some involved errors in doctrines, whereas others involved sins. But the real failure underlying all these things is that the heart has departed from the Lord.

FOLLOWING THE FLOW OF THE SPIRIT

God's way is forever onward. Although men may frustrate Him, they will not be able to stop Him from going on. In every age, He does a unique work that is not repeated in other ages. He is always going on. There can be only one George Müller in history, and there can be only one D. L. Moody. Even if others try to imitate what these ones did, they cannot do it.

TOUCHING THE FOUNTAIN OF LIVING WATER

What we need to do today is to touch the living fountain. Once we touch the fountain, we will never exhaust our speaking. I used to love to read writings of men from the past. But when I took their sermons and repeated them, it took only a few times before I would exhaust the subject. Later I was connected to the fountain of life. From then on, my speaking became exhaustless. The teachings of many Western missionaries are like the sofa chair; they are comfortable to sit on, but they are too soft. Some brothers are like a concrete wall; when you meet them, they make you feel uncomfortable, yet they render much help to you.

CHAPTER THIRTY-SIX

HOW TO BUILD UP THE SERVICES

TALKS (12)

Date: January 23, 1948
Place: Brother Chia's home, Swatow, Kwangtung
Speaker: Witness Lee

MAN COOPERATING WITH GOD, ALLOWING GOD TO HAVE A WAY IN THE CHURCH

Today, man must give God adequate cooperation before He can have a way in the church. The channels must be cut deep before the water can flow to all the places. In the same way, a person must pass through deep digging before God's grace can have the opportunity to flow into the church.

ARRANGEMENTS IN THE SERVICES

First Learning, Then Making Careful Arrangements

Concerning assignments for the work in the church, we should allow the brothers and sisters to begin by first learning to serve in one or two specific areas of service, such as gospel preaching. After this, three or four elders can discuss among themselves to see which of the saints are more worthy of trust. These ones should then be invited to a fellowship. If they have some proper suggestions, they should be taken. Once a person has been invited to take up some assignment, we should not easily remove him. There is no need for everyone to answer to everyone else. Once the way is made clear to all, everyone can concentrate on his own work.

Sister Pearl Wang: For example, in the church in Shanghai, every aspect of the hospitality service has its specific assignments. There are people responsible for the linens, people responsible for the laundry, for patching, for the storage, and for the housekeeping. Everyone has his own duty, and there is no confusion.

Brother Lee: In the matter of service, we are not afraid of being slow. The only thing we want to avoid is confusion. We are not afraid of being not aggressive. We only want to avoid being too hasty. Once we are confused and hasty, we will not do a good job. At least a year will be needed before the various areas of services in the church in Swatow will have some direction. Other than the work that absolutely requires hiring someone to do it, all the rest should be done by the brothers and sisters themselves.

In the Matter of Service,
Learning to Touch God from Within

Of course, the most basic thing in the service is to learn to know God and to touch Him from within.

Not Considering the Saints' Outward Condition

Surely there are some difficulties in selecting the right persons to serve. Some who are so-called unpromising should not necessarily be rejected, and some who are promising should not necessarily be taken. To be weak or to be strong does not mean much.

The Elders First Working Alongside the Saints,
Then Entrusting the Work to Them Completely

If a work is assigned to an inexperienced one, the elders should first work with such a one alongside him. Up to a certain point, they can entrust the work completely to such a one and allow him to do it on his own.

CHAPTER THIRTY-SEVEN

ON BEING A PRACTICAL CHRISTIAN

TALKS (13)

Date: Evening, January 24, 1948
Place: Swatow, Kwangtung
Speaker: Witness Lee

VAIN DOCTRINES AND PRACTICAL WAYS

Today, what many people receive is but doctrines. These doctrines do not render much benefit to the practical Christian living. Many spiritual terminologies are but terms only. For example, to say that a certain person is fleshly or spiritual is but empty spiritual terms to some people. The foreigners spread the gospel to the East, but what many of them preached was but doctrines. In the end, the ones who preached gave nothing but doctrines, and the ones who listened heard nothing but doctrines, and neither knew what the words spoken meant. This is like some people who have never seen snow, yet they keep talking about snow. The pastors in Christianity study in the seminaries and pick up a lot of doctrines. For example, one pastor has a wonderful plan; he has prepared fifty-two sermons, one for each week of the year. With this preparation, he has no fear of running out of sermons. This serves well for his congregation also, who think that by doing this, they will not be out of food or lacking in sermons all year round. But this kind of listening will only make a person big in his head. Today, many people know only the terms and have no idea what they really mean. The reason for this is that they have never properly experienced the things themselves.

What is to love the Lord? What is to be humble? What is to follow the Lord? What is it for God to be glorified? What is to be led? And what is to love the brothers? I am not here trying to give you a hard time. I am not asking if you understand these doctrines. It is easy to understand the doctrine of love. As long as a person takes a cross-reference Bible, he can prepare a message on loving the Lord. But he does not necessarily have the thing "love" itself. This is the condition of Christianity today. In Christianity everybody says what everybody else is saying, and men only pay attention to the study of doctrines and the attendance of Sunday worship services.

What is humility? Is it to hold the Bible in your arm and to walk slowly, looking at heaven every few steps? Is this humility? This kind of behavior is false humility. When people who behave this way lose their temper, they will yell and bang on the tables. We should not merely be those who come to attend worship services or to listen to sermons. We need to have fellowship with the brothers and sisters. Today the flavor of Christianity is too strong among us. When someone comes to our city, we hope to receive some help, and we expect the visitor to come with an abundance of grace. But I can hardly believe that a person can receive any help under such circumstances. If you receive any help, it is some other kind of help; what you have received is but beautiful thoughts. Some Christians have large heads, small bodies, and almost no legs. Some saints are experts in criticizing others. They are good at listening to messages. They are good at reading books, and they like to listen to famous speakers. They are like the professional opera-goers. This kind of people is terrible. Sooner or later, they will become tired of listening to messages or of attending services. I am speaking contrary words today. I do not expect you to understand my words. On the contrary, I expect you not to understand my words. Today it is not a question of understanding or not understanding. Today it is a question of whether or not we are willing to be a practical Christian.

Christianity today is filled with fallen conditions. Here we need a real revolution, a revolution that revolutionizes a person. In a group of seven or eight hundred people, how many are there who are serious about going on? Many people like to attend revival meetings. But the question is this: Will these meetings help a person to go on in the way of following the Lord? I do not like people coming to me telling me that they have received help from me. I do not know you that well. If I did, I would ask you, "What kind of help have you received? Did you receive help from me in expounding the Bible? Or did you receive help from me in knowing the doctrines?" Doctrines will only give people something to talk about. There is a difference between doctrine and a way. A way affords a person a path to follow, whereas doctrines can only afford a person something to listen to and to talk about. I am not here helping you to know more about doctrines or to have a bigger head. Do not ask me how a portion of the Scripture should be interpreted. We need to be a practical person, living a practical life. In Shanghai some young people came to me and asked me about the second coming of Christ. I told them that whether or not the Lord will come soon is not their concern. What they have to do is to preach the gospel and to learn to love the Lord more.

THE PRACTICAL LIVING OF A CHRISTIAN

A. Concerning the Reading of the Bible

Today I will ask you some practical questions. Are you a Christian in a practical way? Is your reading of the Bible a practical one? You may say that you do read the Bible. But I have to ask you, how much of the Bible have you read? I will ask the sisters if they have read the Gospel of Matthew once. What do Matthew 2, 3, and 4 talk about? Can you tell me the main points in each chapter? The young people should familiarize themselves with every chapter of the New Testament and should be able to tell others the main points in each chapter. How many chapters are there in each book of the New Testament? Some brothers and sisters cannot answer me right away. If I were to ask how many coats they have at home, or how many buttons on their dress, they would be able to tell me right away. One brother has been a believer for three years already. When I asked him what is the first book of the New Testament, he first said that it is the Gospel of John and then corrected himself and said that it is the

Gospel of Matthew. I asked him, "Brother, do you ever get confused about your surname? If you can remember your surname, you should know what the first book of the New Testament is."

I know that I am giving you a hard time here tonight. I am doing this to revolutionize you. If you can answer my question, I will pray for you. If you cannot answer my question, I will not pray for you. Even if I were to pray for you, my prayer would be useless. Some people are too muddled. If you tell them that there are twenty-three chapters in the Gospel of John, they will say, "That is right." If you tell them that hell is in heaven, they will readily believe it. Such people are too muddled. In order for you to understand the things of God, first you have to study the Bible well. You do not have to try to understand, and you do not have to look up the reference books. All you have to do is to study thoroughly. One elderly brother does not know how many books there are in the Old Testament. He has been a Christian for many years, but still does not know the number of books in the Old Testament. This is really a shame. If a man does not want to study the Bible properly, but desires only to be zealous and to listen to messages, whatever he does will be useless.

Tomorrow I will leave Swatow. You do not have to go to see me off. If you do not know the Bible well, everything else is useless. The Lord willing, I will come back again. When I come back again, the first thing I will ask you is how many times you have read through the Bible. I will not ask if you understand what you are reading. I will ask how many times you have read through the Bible. Perhaps I will write to Brother Mak and ask him how many times have the brothers and sisters read through the Bible. Perhaps I will ask one of you brothers to write me a letter three months from now and tell me how you are doing in your reading of the Bible. I can pay for the stamps. If you do not write to me, I will write to Brother Mak. I do not want to offend you, and that is why I am talking to you in a smiling way. Actually, my words are like a knife sticking into you. What I am saying to you is very polite already. In Tsingtao I was not so polite when I spoke with the brothers and sisters. I could speak to them in not so polite a way because they were begotten of me, and I treated them as my own children. Today we have to be a practical person. We cannot be lazy, and we cannot gloss over matters. Otherwise, we can listen to message after message, and it still will do us no good.

B. Concerning the Dealing with Our Conscience

Has our conscience been thoroughly dealt with? Some brothers answered that they have not thoroughly dealt with their conscience. If we have not thoroughly dealt with our conscience, what is the use of coming and listening to more messages? Do you know God's will? I am not here giving you some beautiful thoughts; rather, I am here giving you "hot ginger soup." I am your brother. That is why I am talking to you like talking to the family. Please do not be angry with me. I am giving you such a hard time in order that you may gain the pearl. When the Lord comes back, He will ask you the same questions. By that time, it will be a greater suffering and a greater loss of face to you. If you need to repent, it is better for you to repent today.

C. Concerning the Preaching of the Gospel

Are we serious about the preaching of the gospel? In Swatow you have three hundred people meeting here. If everyone would bring one person to the Lord per year, in ten years there will be one hundred fifty thousand people saved. This means that in ten years the whole of Swatow will be saved. Our gospel work is wrong today. We need the Lord's mercy. It is difficult for an old tree to bear new fruit. The older a tree becomes, the thicker its bark is. But a young tree can bear much fruit. Among us, the new ones grow much faster than the old ones. This exposes our unfaithfulness. How many gospel tracts have we passed out today? How many people have you invited to the gospel meetings? In the matter of gospel preaching, we cannot be a person who only talks but who does not do anything.

You may say that you have preached the gospel. But how many times have you passed out gospel tracts? How many times have you posted gospel posters, and how many times have you preached in the open? How many times have you given books away to people? How many times have you written letters to others exhorting them to believe in the Lord? Do not say that you are concerned about having false believers. Even if they believe in a false way, you can still bring them in. We have to have a love for the sinners. Only this love is the real love.

Once Moody was standing in the rain without an umbrella. Others thought that he was crazy, but he told them, "I am doing this to show you something. You say that I am foolish. Actually you are more foolish than I am. One day when God's judgment comes, the fire from heaven will shower down. If you do not believe in the Lord, one day you will suffer punishment." Moody also told others that he preached to at least one person a day. One night, he was in his bed already and remembered that he had not preached to anyone that day. Immediately, he got up and went out to the street. There he met a policeman, and he preached to him. The next day the policeman asked around and found out that the one who was preaching to him was Moody. Later he visited Moody and was saved through him. Today we have to drive out fallen Christianity, and we have to chase away the dead pulpits. The real work today is one that revolutionizes a person.

D. Concerning Material Offerings

How much have we done with respect to the matter of material offerings? Do we offer according to a budget? What is our budget every week? If you walk on the street today, you can see many advertisements, but you do not find one gospel advertisement. The reason for this is that men have not offered up themselves thoroughly enough. When a person comes to the meeting hall, he comes only to attend a service, and there is no real consecration.

E. Concerning Supplications

In the matter of making supplications for others, how many times have you dealt seriously with the Lord? How many of your prayers have been answered? How many times have you prayed for the servants of God? How many times have you visited the sick? How many poor brothers have received your help?

F. Concerning the Services

In the matter of the services, have we taken them up in a serious way. Have you ever mopped the floor of the meeting hall? Have you ever cleaned the windows, the doors, and the chairs of the meeting hall? You cannot expect the angels to come and do these things for you. Many jobs require the brothers and sisters to do them together. Do not be so spiritual. We have to learn the proper lessons in the practical services before we can learn the lessons in the spiritual matters. I wish that we did not have any hired laborers here, and that every work would be taken up by the brothers and sisters themselves. This is more precious in the eyes of the Lord. The brothers and sisters in Chefoo all gave themselves to serve this way.

G. Concerning Knowing the Brothers and Sisters

Do we have a definite understanding about the condition of the brothers and sisters? Do the brothers and sisters know each other? One brother has been in the church for two months, but this Brother Cheng, who has been in the church for three years, still does not know that one's first name; he only knows that his surname is Chen. We are saying that brothers and sisters should have fellowship one with another. But if we do not even know the names of one another, how can we have fellowship? Can you tell me twelve names of brothers and sisters who are here? Paul could remember so many names in Romans 16. I do not mean that you have to know everything about the brothers and sisters, but at least you have to know their names. If you do not know their names, it is too vague to say that you are practicing the brotherly love.

Today I have no message to give to you. I have come to bother you. If you want me to give you messages, I can give them to you every day for three months, and I will still not exhaust the messages. However, what I am doing here today is not giving you messages.

H. Concerning Our Testimony in Our Daily Life

Do we have a real testimony at home? Have we lost our temper at home? Have we preached to the members of our own family? Have we prayed for them? Have you ever prayed with a few brothers in private for others, for your colleagues, your classmates? If you have not done these things, you are not living a solid Christian life. Let me ask you: Do you agree with what I am saying?

EXPERIENCING THE LORD IN A PRACTICAL WAY, AND BEING A PRACTICAL CHRISTIAN

If we want to follow the Lord, we have to be a practical Christian. Only by experiencing the Lord in such a practical way will we know what humility is and what it is to serve the Lord. Our message meetings in the future do not need too much doctrine. We only need to check if others are willing to go on. May the Lord be merciful to us and give us a thorough repentance, so that we would no more be just a Chinese, but be another kind of person, one with a pure heart and clean hands.

[Editor's note: After Brother Lee's words, the brothers and sisters prayed a little. Then everyone sang "Just as I Am," the last two stanzas. Four or five more prayed. Brother Mak wept, and other sisters wept. After this, the brothers and sisters all agreed that Brother Lee should speak ten or even one hundred times more severely than he did, and everyone raised their hands to show that they would take these words.]

CONCLUDING PRAYER

Concluding prayer at 11 p.m.: Lord, be merciful to us. For many years we have had only the outward works and zeal. Others may have thought that we were quite good, and we ourselves have thought that we were quite good. But this time you have enlightened us, and now we realize that we have nothing. All our works are wood, grass, and stubble, and they cannot stand the fire. We confess that we love the world, that we indulge ourselves in the flesh, that we do not have love, and that we have sinned much. O Lord, wash us with the precious blood of Jesus Christ. Preserve us and strengthen us in the days ahead. In the name of the Lord Jesus, we pray. Amen.

FELLOWSHIP WITH BROTHER WEIGH KWANG-HSI

[Editor's note: conversation between Brother Lee and Brother Weigh after the meeting.]

Brother Lee: It is hard for you to handle the work in Hong Kong, Canton, and Swatow, all by yourself.

Brother Weigh: It would be best if some co-workers can come from Shanghai and work in these three places, which can serve as stations. When these three stations are strengthened, there can be further spreading out.

Brother Lee: When I was in Shanghai, I talked with Brother Yu concerning the matter of the inner life, and we both have the same feelings. Sometimes even the examples are similar. In the future, the way to build up the church is by the three things: the gospel, the revival, and life. All three things have to go on at the same time. Concerning this, everyone feels the same. I thought that I was the only one to use the term "migration," but I found out that Brother Nee also used this term.

Brother Weigh: Concerning Brother Nee, he felt that there are some things that are hard for him to do. He has received no commission to do what you are doing now, but neither can his burden be released among the ordinary brothers and sisters. This time when you go to Amoy and Foochow, perhaps you can have more talks with the brothers and sisters who are really for the Lord. Hopefully, there can be more fellowship with the co-workers and the elders.

Brother Lee: At present, there is practically no testimony in Canton. Outwardly things look good, but inwardly it is empty. These few places need some serious work done in them. May the Lord be merciful. God has no intention for us to keep His will in an outward way. This time in Swatow, I have not expected others to understand my words. I only hope that some would receive light before the Lord in a genuine way.

[The fellowship lasted until midnight.]

CHAPTER THIRTY-EIGHT

THE SERVICE OF THE PRIESTHOOD

CHURCH CONFERENCE (1)

Date: 7:30 p.m., Friday, April 9, 1948
Place: Hardoon Road, Shanghai
Speaker: Witness Lee

Scripture Reading: 1 Pet. 2:5; Rom. 12:1, 11; Luke 19:11-17

ALL THE SAVED ONES BEING THE PRIESTS, AND BEING THOSE WHO SHOULD SERVE GOD

I have not been standing on this platform for over four months. What I will speak to you tonight will not be related to anything spoken before or afterwards. The first thing I would like to speak to you is that every redeemed person is part of a holy priesthood (1 Pet. 2:5). Here in 1 Peter it does not say a clean priesthood, but a holy priesthood. To be holy means to be separated, to be set apart.

Second, the spiritual sacrifice mentioned in Romans 12 refers to our bodies. The first thing that the priests have to offer is their bodies. Such a sacrifice is reasonable. Not only is it a reasonable sacrifice, but it is one that makes you feel comfortable. The life that a person receives from his mother's womb, the first life, has its needs. When a person eats, drinks, or exercises, he feels happy. In the same way, the life that a person receives at regeneration, the second life, also has its definite needs. It needs to serve the Lord. If a person has to mop the floor, the mopping nevertheless makes him feel happy within. Even if he is to clean the toilet, he would do it happily. Any service that would make a person feel happy is definitely a reasonable service.

UNDERSTANDING THE MEANING OF THE SERVICE

Among all the spiritual things that the Holy Spirit has

led us to know, do we know this one particular thing—the service? We have been taught concerning how to save souls and how to help others to be delivered from sins. But do we know what is the meaning of service?

Being Priestly in Nature

The service in the church is not prophetic in nature, but priestly in nature. If the service in the church is prophetic in nature, then all the brothers and sisters would have to be prophets. In the Old Testament, the service of the priests consisted of putting forth the showbread, lighting and dressing the lamps, burning the incense, and slaughtering the bulls and goats for others. Today's service in the church consists of living before God, speaking for Him, and ministering unto Him in the many small and miscellaneous affairs. In the denominations, only the pastor gives the message. The janitors are only the menial laborers. But the service in the church is composed of the speakers, plus the piano players, plus the janitors, plus the window cleaners, and so forth. Our work today is to bring in the church service. The church service is not prophetic in nature, but priestly in nature. The speaking occupies only a small portion of the work, and the speaker is but one of the members.

The service of the priests included the emptying out of the animal refuse. In principle, it includes cooking for others, doing the laundry, and so forth. All these are the work of the priests. The priestly services have to do with miscellaneous works.

Consecrating Oneself to Be a Living Sacrifice for the Satisfaction of Both God and Man

To offer up sacrifices is to offer up food for God. What is God's food? God needs to eat and to drink; He has His food in this universe. In every age, God desires to gain some men who would consecrate themselves to Him. If no one would consecrate himself to God, God would be hungry. If no one would pour Himself out to God, God would be thirsty and unsatisfied. Many revival meetings use Romans 12:1 to exhort people to offer up themselves, and at the end of the exhortation they would add the words, "Be a preacher!" But after a person has become a preacher, God may be even more hungry and thirsty. Only sacrifices satisfy God. The demand within us is God's demand; our inner man represents God. When we serve God, we are satisfying God. What is the meaning of a living sacrifice? A sacrifice should be one that is dead, but a living sacrifice means sacrifices that are offered up to do some works. While you serve and work, your spirit will become enlivened through your working.

Our service to the Lord is expressed in the smallest matters. The Lord asked Peter to fish. This was a small matter, but the principle involved is the same, and that is to satisfy man. The Lord turned the water into wine and fed the five thousand with loaves, both of which are small matters. The goal of these works is not to satisfy the physical life, but to satisfy man's spirit. If a man is hungry, he can eat later. Even if he does not eat, it is still all right. The question is not one of outward eating, but one of the Lord's being satisfied and man's being satisfied through the small matters. This is the principle of service. In itself, service is a small matter, but it satisfies both God and man.

CHAPTER THIRTY-NINE

THE WAY OF OUR SERVICE TODAY AND ITS CRUCIAL POINTS

CO-WORKERS' MEETING (1)

Date: 3:00 p.m., April 9, 1948
Place: Hardoon Road, Shanghai
Speaker: Watchman Nee

Brother Witness Lee: How should we go on in the Lord's service in the coming days? What are the crucial points? What are the things that we should pay attention to in this age?

UNDERSTANDING THE TWO ASPECTS OF THE CONDITION OF THE CHURCH

Brother Watchman Nee: First we have to see the condition of the church in this age. Concerning this matter, there are generally two schools of opinion. One group says that the church is always advancing. In every age, there are different recoveries of the truths, such as the truth concerning justification by faith, the truth of sanctification. The other group, represented by brothers such as J. N. Darby, says that the present church is in a state of desolation. If you consider the church life of the first century, the absolute consecration seen in Acts 2 and 4, the keeping of the apostles' teaching, and the perfecting of the saints unto the fullness of the Body of Christ in Ephesians 4, and compare such conditions with the condition of the church today, there is undoubtedly a vast difference between the two pictures. Once when I was in England, I was invited by Brother T. Austin-Sparks to have afternoon tea at his house. He asked me my opinion concerning Ephesians 4 and when this chapter would be fulfilled. Humanly speaking, the condition of the church today is too far from that described in Ephesians 4.

If we read the final epistles of Paul, we will see that the church had degraded at that time. In 2 Timothy, he said that "all who are in Asia turned away from me" (2 Tim. 1:15). Peter's description in 2 Peter of the situation at his time was the same. In the end, the apostle John also declared that Antichrist has come, and he warned the believers to be watchful (1 John 2:18; 4:3).

CATCHING UP WITH GOD'S PRESENT WORK TO MAINTAIN THE TESTIMONY OF THE BODY

Both of these views are true, and they are based on facts. However, what God wants today is to gain a group of people who will stand on God's side under these two contradictory conditions, who will maintain God's testimony, and who will uphold such a testimony of overcomers together with God. In every age, God has His work, and the purpose of such work is to maintain His testimony.

The book of Kings says that at the time Solomon's temple was being built, there was no noise heard. All the materials for the building of the temple, all the stones and the wood, were measured and cut according to size in the mountains, before they were ever sent to Solomon. Every stone and piece of wood was properly coordinated together already. This was why at the time of the building of the temple, "there was neither hammer nor axe nor any tool of iron heard in the house" (1 Kings 6:7). God is doing the same work on earth today.

The book of Acts is an unfinished book. In the whole Bible, only this book does not have an ending; all the other books have an ending. The Pentateuch, the Gospel of Matthew, and the book of Revelation all have their endings. But the Acts of the Apostles is different. Many questions are left unanswered and unsolved. What happened to Paul later? How did his work end? These things are not recorded in Acts. The reason for their absence is that the Holy Spirit is still working today. In the church today, there is still the work of the Holy Spirit.

Submitting to Authority and Receiving the Riches of the Members

God's work today is the recovery of the testimony of the

Body. This Body testimony is not a doctrine, but a reality. In this Body, there is the perfecting ministry (Eph. 4:12), and there is spiritual authority. A close relationship exists between ministry and authority. Where there is ministry, there is authority. In fact, ministry is authority. In Ephesians 4, we see that the Body requires all kinds of gifts, the goal of which is the perfecting of all the saints. In order for the members to be perfected, there is the need to submit to authority. To submit to authority is to submit to the Head. Today, the sisters cover their heads with respect to the brothers. Actually, everyone should cover his head with respect to Christ. We do not have individual heads; only Christ is the Head. Those who want to retain their heads are trying to practice individualism. Those who promote individualism in the Body are trouble-makers. Only Christ is the Head; on the other hand, Christ covers His head before God. Although my hands and my feet are far away from my head, they are still under the direction of the head. Hence, for us to submit to the members is in reality for us to submit to the Head.

The mouth may be very important, but it still needs help from the other members. Without the eyes and the ears, the mouth alone will be useless. This is why I do not believe in the so-called personal revelation. In the Bible, there are such things as individuals receiving grace from the Lord, and there are such things as individuals being sanctified. Yet at the same time, there is the aspect of our relationship with the other members. What do we have today that is not received from others? The greatest heresies in the world came from those who received so-called direct revelations from the Lord. If an individual can receive revelation alone, then a person needs only to be a Christian individually; there is no need for us to come together to meet any longer, and all the "one another's," the "we's," and the "they's" in the Bible can be cut out. A man has to humble himself and has to receive what others have already received. When a person has received something, it is much easier for another to receive from this one. For example, twenty years ago, it was difficult to find a person who was clear about his salvation. But after we met one person like that, it became easier to meet more. This is true with the understanding of the truth of salvation. It is equally true with the understanding of all the other truths.

A STANDARD CHRISTIAN BEING ONE WHO BEARS THE BODY TESTIMONY

The Bible reveals one great truth: the kind of Christian God wants is one who is after a Body testimony. In other words, He wants Christians who will act as members of the one Body of Christ. What we need today are standard Christians. What does it mean to be a standard Christian? A standard Christian is one in whom others can detect certain characteristics. For example, when you sit down with a Presbyterian, he will tell you about God's predestination and will tell you that our salvation, regeneration, and justification are all based on God's predestination. However, if you sit down with a Methodist, he will tell you that everyone has to work out his own salvation, that repentance is an act of one's free will, that salvation is a result of one's willingness to be saved. Everything depends on ourselves; if we do not do anything, we cannot even be saved. Among certain kinds of Christians, you can find certain kinds of characteristics.

Christians today are not standard. They lack a few basic characteristics, such as selling their possessions, consecrating themselves, repentance and confession of sins, and experiences of deliverance from the power of sin. In addition, there is one characteristic that is lacking the most among them, which is the realization of the Body of Christ. We have to help the believers to experience these things as soon as we can. A newly saved person will do whatever you tell him to do at the initial stage of salvation. If he is allowed to go on for too long, he will become set, and it will become difficult to deal with him. Hence, we have to speak to the believers some of these truths as soon as possible. Everybody likes to be nice and to say nice words; everyone likes to be polite to one another. But a person cannot be an up-to-standard Christian this way. In the future we have to spend much time to study how to be a standard Christian, so that our next generation can become a brand-new breed of Christians.

Having the Reality of the Body of Christ and Experiencing It

The Body is not a doctrine, but a spiritual fact. If a spiritual matter is recovered, and it is real, it will surely be felt by others. This was the case with the release of the kingdom truth by Evan Roberts. He was sick for a long time. Later he began to realize the truth concerning the kingdom. When he stood up to speak, the message may have been only fifteen minutes long, but there was something real in what he said. Before him, there were people who had spoken about the truth of the kingdom, but the reality was not there. The same is true today with regard to the truth concerning the Body. Many people are able to speak about the Body, but they do not have the Body itself. Before Darby, many people preached this truth, but they did not have the thing itself. When Darby came, it was different; not only did he speak about the truth, but he presented before men the real thing itself that is conveyed by the truth.

A Believer Dropping What He Is Holding, and Experiencing What He Has Received Positionally

Does this mean that God is restricted by man? Of course not. If God wants to work, He will not be restricted. What a Christian receives on the day of salvation is the most that he will receive. What happens afterwards is that these riches are gradually lost. Why are they lost? It is because along the pathway of being a Christian, such a one picks up many other things. Both his hands are full, and he has no more capacity to receive anything more. This is the case with an individual, but the same is true with the church as a whole. The book of Ephesians describes the height of the attainment of the church. After that, things began to fall below that standard.

What a believer has received initially is something positional only. Afterwards, he begins to receive something experiential. However, in order for him to receive something experiential, he must first drop some other things. We must drop what we have in our hands before we can gain something more in our experience. When we leave this world one day, we will be able to say that all our losses are actually gains. Today, a believer must catch up with God's work and must go on with Him, and he should not be one who is falling back.

CHAPTER FORTY

THE RECOVERY OF THE BODY AND THE AUTHORITY OF THE MINISTRY

CO-WORKERS' MEETING (2)

Date: 9:00 a.m., April 10, 1948
Place: Hardoon Road, Shanghai
Speaker: Watchman Nee

Question One: Do we first know the individual life and then the Body life? Is the basis of the Body life the individual life?

Question Two: Is individualism a hindrance to the Body?

CONCERNING THE TRUTH

Not Arranging the Sequence of Truth according to One's Personal Experience

Brother Nee: At the time of the Reformation, Luther emphasized justification by faith. That was, of course, a recovery of the truth. However, at that time, men only saw that faith before God is needed, rather than work. Luther was supposed to have recovered the truth of justification by faith. Actually, he only emphasized faith; he did not fully realize what justification is. It was not until men like J. N. Darby were raised up in the last century that justification was covered. However, though the word "justification" was used, they had not touched the reality of justification. They did not know what in fact is justification. In spite of this, they spoke much on the truth of justification.

In the last century, some people began also to talk about the doctrine of regeneration. But what is the relationship between regeneration and justification? It is difficult to say which one comes first and which one comes later. There was a brother who once preached the doctrine of justification unceasingly; he had never heard of the doctrine of regeneration. After three years, he began to hear about the doctrine of regeneration, and he realized that he was regenerated. From that time on, whenever he preached the gospel, he would always tell others that a man is first justified and then regenerated. Not only was he preaching this, all the people around him began to preach the same thing. Actually, for a person to say that justification always comes first and regeneration afterwards is making too definite and too subjective a distinction.

A person who has no experience cannot preach God's word. But a person who trusts in his experience only cannot preach God's word either. A person who preaches God's word must be free from the limitation of his own experience. It is possible for a person to experience certain truths according to a certain sequence in time. But he must never think that the order of the truth is necessarily according to the way he experiences them.

The Two Sides of the Truth

There are two sides to the truth. Many times, some doctrines only cover one side of the truth. For example, we know that there are two aspects to the result of the cross. On the one hand, it removes our sins (Col. 2:14). On the other hand, it justifies us (Rom. 8:3-4). But you cannot say that the cross is clearly divided into these two things. They are actually two aspects of the one thing. We are actually justified from sin through the cross. We who are dead have been freed from sin and justified from sin. This does not mean that to be delivered from sin is one thing and to be free is another thing. Neither does it mean that to be delivered from sin is one thing and justification is another thing.

Not Sacrificing God's Word
on account of Our Own Experience

Many times, we sacrifice God's word on account of our personal experiences. Because our individual experiences are partial and fragmentary, we do not have a complete overall view of God's word. Men think that the sun comes out in the day and the moon comes out at night. They think that the moon only appears at night and disappears in the daytime. Actually, the moon is there both in the daytime and at night as well. When a person comes to God, he often makes judgments based on his own experiences. Most people like to arrange the truths in a sequence, such as putting justification first and sanctification afterwards. Yet the Bible puts sanctification before justification (1 Cor. 6:11). Actually, justification and sanctification are two sides of one truth.

Hence, we need to be delivered from human weaknesses. One cannot affect or sacrifice God's word on account of human weaknesses. Not only should we be delivered from doubting God's word; we must also be delivered from jeopardizing God's word. Under God's ordering, our knowledge of the individual life and our knowledge of the Body life should happen at the same time; we should not say which one comes first and which one comes later.

Not Taking What We See Today as the Whole Truth

We cannot judge God's word by what we see in this age. What we see today is still limited. Perhaps fifty years from now, other brothers will rise up to say that we are in darkness. We only wish we could climb higher than we are to see God's word. Just as we are not saved and then regenerated, in the same way we do not first receive an individual life and then come to realize the Body life. Just as salvation and regeneration happen at the same time, in the same way the realization of the individual life and that of the Body life happen at the same time (Acts 9:17-18). In every age, there are truths of that age. There are also errors of that age. We cannot make the truth of an age become an error just because we do not have enough knowledge about that truth. Take again the example of baptism and the laying on of hands. The two things should happen at the same time. After a person is baptized, immediately he should experience the laying on of hands, and immediately he should be brought to see the coordination, the Body, and to be joined to the brothers and sisters. Due to the fact that some truths were recovered first and some later, men set a sequence to the order of the truth. This is wrong. This is why we cannot consider what we have seen today as the whole truth, nor can we judge God's word by our own experience. Never forget that we are ministers of God's word.

The Need for a Clear Vision of the Body of Christ

The oneness of the Body is based on the knowledge of the life of the Body. First we have to see that we have received the same life. After this seeing, we become one in this life. Without this seeing, we have a big lack. A person who has not seen the Body will feel that he is not much different from a person who has seen the Body. But a person who has seen the Body will realize that with those who have not seen the Body, there is a big lack. This is like an unsaved person considering a saved person more or less the same as he is. Yet the saved person sees in the unsaved person a big lack.

CONCERNING THE PRACTICE

Finding the Ones to Submit To

After we have such a realization, we come to the second step. The first step has to do with God's word. The second step has to do with us. First we must have God's word. Then this word must be applied to us. In the Body, the first thing we have to learn is to find out who are those whom we have to submit ourselves to. We must know who are those who are ahead of us. All the authorities in the Bible are deputy authorities and not direct authorities. What we have to learn is not to have others submit to us, but to have ourselves submit to others. When I go to work, I do not first ask who my subordinates are. Rather, I must first ask who my superior is. If you go to another person's house to be the maid, you do not first ask who the children are, but who the lady of the house is. If we allow the inner life to operate freely, we will find out who are the ones we have to submit to. We may think that submission will make us unhappy. Actually, the opposite is true; submission makes a happy person, and insubordination makes an unhappy person. Only when we submit to one another will there be coordination one with another. This kind of coordination is most pleasant. The real submission is not one that is imposed from without, but one that comes as a result of the operation of the life within. It is wrong to submit to anyone because of his high position or material riches. To do so would make us no different from the political organizations of today. Our submission is not brought about by any outward factors, but by the demand of the life within.

This kind of submission may bring us tears. Yet, at the same time it brings us joy. We may feel that we are suffering, but we are at the same time rejoicing. Sometimes the ones whom you submit yourselves to may give you a hard time, but you can still say "amen." This is true submission. A true submission is one which neither makes a person suffer, nor causes him to feel happy. However, it draws an "amen" from his spirit and gives him peace in his spirit.

Fellowshipping and Coordinating Together

If you see the Body of Christ, you will see the matter of fellowship. The life that we received from the Lord makes us pliable and enables us to coordinate together. In this coordination, there is no friction, and there is no murmuring. To have such things in the Body would make us no different from the political organizations in the world.

In the Bible, many times the Lord did not speak to men directly. On the one hand, the New Testament does say that a man can know God from within. On the other hand, however, we have to see that after the Lord met Saul, He did not speak to him again directly. Instead, He asked Ananias to go to speak to Saul (Acts 9:6). On the one hand, the life that is seen in the New Testament is a very personal one. On the other hand, the Epistle of John also says that "you also may have fellowship with us" (1 John 1:3). This fellowship is mutual. On the one hand, we come to God individually by the blood and through the veil. On the other hand, we work together, walk together, coordinate together, and serve together. Here, there are those who serve and there are those who are served. From the records concerning Paul, Luke, Timothy, and others, we see that among them there was coordination. Whatever Paul suggested, the others would agree and would carry it out right away. Timothy was a good brother. He could have written a letter to Paul, saying, "Brother Paul, I have believed in the Lord for many years. I can pray, and I can seek after the Lord. Please give me some liberty!" But Timothy did not do this. On the one hand, every person comes to God independently and is individually responsible to God. On the other hand, no one can be independent, and no one can be free. If you are not coordinated with others, you do not have to tell others; within you, you know it yourself.

Being Delivered from the Self

A man's mouth may be very clever, but his mouth does not necessarily represent his person. Sometimes, a person may say yes with his mouth, yet disagree within. Some brothers and sisters only bring their mouths to the meetings; they themselves are not in the meetings. One sister once came to me to discuss the question of submission in the family. Her mouth was saying that she wanted me to handle the matter. But I knew clearly within me that her mouth and her ears had come, but her being had not come. Once a person has given up his personal opinions, though he may not readily consent with his mouth, within him he will acknowledge that this is the right thing to do.

We have to learn to be persons who are delivered from our selves. If fifty radios are receiving the same signal from a station, and my radio has a different signal from the same station, my radio is definitely not functioning properly. Although we live under the New Testament, and although we have the Lord within us, we are at the same time living in the Body. As such there is the need for us to be joined to the other members. In the coordination of the Body, we have to learn to care for the feeling of the other members of the Body. Only then can we have good coordination.

Not Being Individualistic

The body is the most beautiful thing there is on earth. Yet the body can also become the most ugly thing on earth.

A man looks very fine if he stands here with all his members attached. But if all I see is isolated members detached one from the other, this would be the most ugly sight. If I come into this house and I see two feet at the door, a pair of ears in the room, and a pair of arms at the stairs, how horrible a sight this would be. I will surely run away at once. In the same way, if a person acts independently and is not joined to the Body, he will become a most ugly member. It is one thing for a person to acknowledge that he is a member. It is another thing for this person to be coordinated as a member. Independent actions in the Body are the most ugly thing there is.

Submission to the Authority of the Ministry

1. Ministry Being the Authority

Authority is related to the Head. Authority is also related to ministry. Please remember that all the members have their special gifts. The ear, the eye, the mouth, the hands, and the feet all have their gifts. These gifts are the ministries. As long as there is the ministry, there is authority. Why does the ministry have the authority? It is because each one receives different ministries. The difference in ministries produces the authority. At the same time, with the authority in the ministry there are the limitations. God may grant grace to me to be an ear and to enable me to hear. On the one hand, He intends that I serve the Body with my hearing. On the other hand, He intends that I accept my own limitations. If I want to see, I have to ask the eyes to help me. The problem today is that those who cannot hear insist that they want to hear, those who cannot speak insist that they have to speak, and those who cannot run insist that they have to run. You have to realize that for others to do something is equal to your doing that same thing. Your gift is their gift. At the same time, you have to learn to be limited and to realize that the church is a Body.

2. The Need to See One's Limitations

Some people simply do not know how to study the Bible

or to teach the Bible. Yet they insist that they have to do it, and the result is many problems. If the Lord is gracious to you and He makes you a hand, you can raise up this hand as high as you want. But if you say that in addition to being a hand, you want to see also, you will not succeed even if you try it as long as you live. We should pray, "Lord, cause me to see my limitations." If you are all-inclusive, then you become the whole Body. The acceptance of our own limitations is a principle of coordination, and it is also the greatest test. Those who realize their own limitations will fellowship in everything and will seek help and counsel in everything.

We must realize that authority is in the ministry. The ear has a ministry of hearing. Hence, the ear has the authority of hearing. If you do not see your own limitations, you will not be able to submit to authority even if you want to. Only those who have seen their own limitations can coordinate with other members.

Some brothers think that they can expound the Bible. They think that they are Bible expositors. Actually, they do not know how to expound the Bible. Yet they insist that they have to do it. The result is many strange teachings. With a Christian, there is not much difference between the self and the individual life.

Some people never understand what Paul meant when he said that "all are yours" (1 Cor. 3:22). We have to realize that we are born into a rich family. You can rejoice because you are rich. Within you, there is always the feeling that you should accept authority. Your inner man always wants to submit and to accept the authority of the ministry. On the one hand, we have to see our limitations. On the other hand, we have to see that whatever the Lord has established is an authority. It is the Lord who gives some the ability to do something. That ability is that person's authority.

3. Submission to the Ministry Being Submission to God

While we are learning to submit to the ministry, we are submitting to God. A person cannot say that he will only submit to God directly. Of all the authorities that God has established on this earth, ninety-nine percent of them, that is, the overwhelming majority of them, are deputy authorities. The Bible says that we have to submit to our husband and our rulers, and the younger ones have to submit to the older ones. Other than one or two instances, all the cases of submission are submission to deputy authorities. Those who cannot submit to deputy authorities cannot submit to God. Although the eyes see, it is actually the head that is causing the eyes to see. If the eyes are separated from the head, they will be finished. What you touch may be the eyes, but behind the eyes is the head. If a person sees the Head behind the gifts, it will not be difficult for him to submit.

4. Submission Being a Joyful Matter

The teachings in the Sermon on the Mount in Matthew are not there to cause us to feel uncomfortable. Rather, they are there to make us happy. If you walk with others for a mile, it may make you feel uncomfortable. But if you walk with them the second mile, it will make you happy. The word "blessed" there can be translated as "joyous." Submission is a joyful matter. The life that the Lord gave us is a joyful life. The Head gives the ministry. Where there is the ministry, there is authority. When we submit to authority, we feel happy and joyful within.

5. Pursuing Submission

In the work of the Lord, we should find out who is ahead of us, and we have to seek for the opportunity to submit. I do not believe that there is any brother who is not under some other brothers. Something within you will demand that you find out who is the object of your submission. When the sisters cover their heads, they cannot do so with the hair that grows naturally from them; they have to find a handkerchief and cover their heads. The finding of the handkerchief means that a person has to pursue submission. Why should we not pursue submission in the same way that we pursue love or knowledge? Why would men not pay attention to submission in the same way that they pay attention to work? Why would we not love submission in the same way that we love the preaching of the gospel? A person has to learn to come under one or more authorities in the church. Let me repeat, where there is no ministry, there is no authority. Where ministry is, there is authority.

6. Honoring the Authority that God Has Established

In a local church, not only is there spiritual authority, but there is positional authority as well. Paul charged Titus and Timothy to appoint elders. These elders have positional authority. If you do not have the spiritual discernment and you appoint three elders, and after three years you find out that four other people are more advanced than these three, what should you do? Should you replace the old ones with the new ones? Should you ask the old ones to resign? We should honor all the authorities that God has established according to His will.

7. Submission Perfecting Ourselves and Others

I can testify that God has His arrangements in the church. If you go along with these arrangements, these arrangements will perfect you. Ministry is authority. When you submit to the authority of the ministry, you will be perfected. One sister was very capable of assuming headship. She came to see me because she wanted to submit to her husband. She told me that she could not submit to her husband, because her husband was too indecisive in everything. I answered, "Nevertheless, simply submit. Go and ask him everything. He cannot tell you every time that he does not know. By asking, you will force him to go to the Lord. You should learn to be godly and to fear God. When you submit, you are not debasing yourself. Rather, by so doing you are helping your husband. God has assigned you to be one who submits to others. If you would submit, you will help others." There is a reason for our being chosen: we are chosen to submit to others.

Paul could boldly say "my gospel" (Rom. 2:16; 16:25). He could also remind Timothy to know "from which ones you have learned" (2 Tim. 3:14). The reason he could say this is that he was a proper apostle, and he had the greatest ministry and the greatest gifts. Hence, he had the authority to remind others concerning his gospel, his ministry, and his teachings.

8. Submission Bringing In the Building of the Church

A person must put himself under a few persons and must submit to them. In this way, not only will he receive the benefit individually, but the church will also receive the benefit. A member in the Body is like a stone in the temple. The temple was built up because there were suitable stones that were coordinated and built up together. Building means that one stone is laid on top of another, and desolation means that no stone is laid on top of another.

THE WAY OF THE WORK TODAY

Going On with the Lord

The Lord is going on. What we considered as life yesterday may be death today. We must go on, and we must not stop at the past experiences. I believe that the Lord is doing a greater and richer work today than yesterday. All those who have their eyes opened will see that we are living in the richest age. Yet these riches are accumulated amidst desolation. On the one hand, the church is advancing and is progressing. On the other hand, the church is in an age of desolation. Some only see the desolation of the church and do not see the advance of the church. Others only see the advance of the church and do not see the desolation of the church. From the view of the Lord's work today, we can say that the Lord is advancing. But at the same time, when we consider everything around us, we can also say that the church is desolate.

The Testimony of the Local Church in an Age of Desolation

What God is doing today is to raise up the testimony of the local church in the midst of desolation, to answer God's call in an age of desolation with the local church, and to recover the church out of its desolation through the testimony of the local church. Christianity has been deformed and has fallen into desolation. For this reason, Christians today are not typical any longer. They have not come up to God's standard. A typical Christian is not only one who is a Christian individually, but one who is involved in the testimony of the church. Only the testimony of the church can bring the church back from desolation to abundance.

Maintaining the Lord's Testimony with the Ministry of the Church

The Lord says, "My Father is working until now, and I also am working" (John 5:17). The Father is always working; He never stops. For this reason we are also working today. Our work today is to secure for the Lord a testimony of the local church. Our ministry today is the ministry of the church, which is one that brings in a testimony of the church for the Lord.

Today the church is in a state of desolation. According to typology, the church has been captured to Babylon. The thriving condition of the church as seen by Paul in the first century was lost soon afterwards. From that time on, the church fell into a state of captivity, which continued until the time of Thyatira. After Thyatira, there was Sardis, where God began His work. Thyatira typifies Roman Catholicism, and Sardis typifies Protestantism. It was at the time of Sardis that God began His recovery work. Although the truths were buried for such a long time, when they were recovered, they immediately became actualities. When Paul spoke concerning the truth in the first century, those truths were spiritual realities, yet they were not actualities. For example, when he spoke about the church, it was a reality, but the actual church had not appeared yet. After the Reformation, not only were the truths recovered, but the actual things themselves were recovered. For example, justification by faith is no longer a truth only, but it has become an actual thing. If the Lord delays His coming, the church will never exhort men to be justified by works any longer. The actual matter of justification by faith has been recovered in the church.

What the church needs today is to raise up a ministry that will maintain the Lord's testimony. The problem with all the places today is that we only maintain a local church without maintaining a ministry that is for the Lord's testimony. Today's ministry must match God's work today. We cannot merely have a so-called ministry. We must have a ministry that is a proper testimony. Our ministry must be the ministry of the church, a ministry that is a testimony of the church.

God's ministry today is in the local church and is for the local church. The work of the ministry is to recover the proper testimony of the church. This is the real recovery. The unique ministry is for the unique testimony, and the content of the unique testimony is fulfilled in the local church.

Expressing the Reality of Christ's Body in the Local Church

These are not ordinary days. Our works today are not ordinary works. The way today is the way of the church. In this way, we must not act presumptuously or carelessly. Once we act carelessly, the Lord will have no way to go on. The Body described in 1 Corinthians 12 is a testimony that a local church should have; it is the testimony of the Body. In this Body, the eyes cannot say to the hands, "I have no need of you," nor can the head say to the feet, "I have no need of you" (1 Cor. 12:21). Every part must be in coordination. Ephesians 4 reveals to us the reality between the Head and the Body. The local church today must be a testimony that expresses the reality of this Body. It must be a practical and actual Body expressed in a locality.

CHAPTER FORTY-ONE

THE WAY OF THE CHURCH

CO-WORKERS' MEETING (3)

Date: The Lord's Day afternoon, April 11, 1948
Place: Hardoon Road, Shanghai
Speaker: Watchman Nee

THE TYPES IN THE OLD TESTAMENT

The Tabernacle and the Temple Typifying Two Aspects of the Church

Concerning the question of the desolation of the church, we must first consider the way of the church on earth. The way of the church on earth can be seen from the history of the tabernacle in the Old Testament. The tabernacle in the Old Testament was set up by God. The purpose of the tabernacle was for God to dwell with His people Israel (Exo. 25:8). There are many basic differences between the temple and the tabernacle. At the beginning, God dwelt in the tabernacle. After the temple was finished, God began to dwell in the temple (1 Kings 9:3). Both the tabernacle and the temple typify God's dwelling among men. The two appear to be a repetition in type. Actually, they are not repetitions. In the past, many people have written books concerning the tabernacle as a type. But few books have been written concerning the temple as a type. Actually, both things are types of the church. Yet there are some basic differences between the two things.

The Tabernacle Being in the Wilderness, Being Temporary and Movable, Whereas the Temple Being in the Holy Land, Being Eternal and Stable

The tabernacle was built in the wilderness under the

direction of Moses and Aaron. The temple was prepared by David and completed by Solomon in Jerusalem. The tabernacle does not have a floor. It has a cover and curtains. When a person enters the tabernacle, what his feet touch is the sand on the ground. This reminds him that the tabernacle is something transitory and movable. This is why it is called the tabernacle, or "the tent of meeting."

The temple has many similarities to the tabernacle. In the tabernacle, there are the gold, the silver, the brass, and the iron. In the temple, there are the wood and the stones. The stones are a crucial material. In the New Testament, the Lord called Peter, Cephas (John 1:42). The word Cephas means a stone. In the tabernacle there was no stone. Stones are immovable; they signify stability and solidarity. The tabernacle was designed for the wilderness; it was transitory in nature. The temple was designed for the kingdom; it was eternal in nature. David represents the Lord, and Solomon represents the Holy Spirit. The meaning of Solomon is the One who brings in peace. God sent the Holy Spirit of peace to build up the temple. David is a type of the incarnated Christ, and Solomon is a type of the Holy Spirit.

The Tabernacle Typifying God's Church on Earth, Whereas the Temple Typifying the Church as Christ's Unique Body

In the Bible, there are always two aspects to God's habitation. On the one hand, it is transitory and wandering, and it is typified by the tabernacle. The tabernacle moved as the people traveled along. Sometimes it was in Elim. At other times, it was in Kadesh-Barnea. Sometimes it was in the land of supply. At other times, it was in the land of the bitter water. However, the tabernacle itself did not change with the change of location. Wherever the Israelites pitched their tents, there was the tabernacle. Hence, the tabernacle typifies God's church on earth, or His church in the localities. In Shanghai there is the church, because in Shanghai there are God's people. Whenever God's people come together, there is the church. When they are separated, there is no church.

This is the aspect of the church as typified by the tabernacle. The temple is different from the tabernacle. The temple was established on the threshing floor of Ornan (2 Chron. 3:1) and was built with stones. It was built for the kingdom. It was the center of the life of the people of Israel. The temple is unique, eternal, and solid, and it cannot be divided. Even when the nation was divided politically, the temple could not be divided. There can be only one temple.

From this, we see that, on the one hand, the church appears in different localities. Yet the spiritual reality of the church is still one Body. It is unique and eternal. These are the two pictures of the church.

The Tabernacle Being in Ruins and the Ark Wandering, Typifying the Desolation of the Church

The visible church today is the tabernacle; it is already in ruins. At the same time, the temple is not yet manifest. In God's eyes, the church described in Ephesians 2 as God's habitation in the Holy Spirit is a fact. But in actuality, the church has not been fully manifested yet; it is still in its progressing stage. In 1924, we spoke of the history of the ark. The ark of the covenant was always advancing. First it passed through the river Jordan. Then it reached Shiloh (Josh. 18:1). At the time the Israelites went to war with the Philistines, the two sons of Eli had sinned, and Eli himself had become foolish and corrupt. He knew very well the reason the Israelites were defeated. Yet he still tried to use the ark to fight for them, with the hope that through the ark they would win the victory. But the Israelites failed. The ark was captured to the land of the Philistines, and it remained in the house of Dagon (1 Sam. 5:2). Later God brought in a curse, and the Philistines returned the ark on a cart drawn by cows (1 Sam. 4—6).

At that time, Samuel was raised up to fulfill his ministry. He was still a child and was girded with a small ephod (1 Sam. 2:18). Here was a minister who was set apart for the kingdom. The ark represents Christ. Wherever the ark was, there was the presence of Christ. The ark was known as the ark of the testimony. It was the center of God's testimony. Without the ark, the tabernacle was empty. The tabernacle was meaningful only when it had the ark inside it. After the ark was taken away from the tabernacle in Shiloh (1 Sam. 4:17), it never returned to the tabernacle. It continued to wander, until it was received into the temple when the temple was finished (1 Kings 8:1-11). Before David, there was Saul. At that time, Shiloh was already rejected. The ark did not return to the tabernacle, but remained rather in the house of Obed-edom (2 Sam 6:10) until the time of David, when David welcomed the ark into Jerusalem (2 Sam. 6:12-15). Jeremiah 7:12 and 14 speak of how God dealt with Shiloh, and Psalms 78:60 and 1 Samuel 4:3 speak of how the ark had left the tabernacle. Second Chronicles 5 speaks of how the ark was returned to the temple. God dealt with Shiloh not in the way of burning it down with fire, nor in the way of destroying the people there, but by removing the ark. To have a tabernacle without an ark—this is judgment, desolation, and punishment. Shiloh had the outward form of the tabernacle only; the ark was no longer there. It is like Christianity having only the name of the church, but the central testimony of the church is lost and God's testimony is removed.

When Solomon became king, he went to Gibeon to pray for wisdom in the tabernacle. Later, when he received the wisdom, he went to the ark (1 Kings 3:15). However, according to 1 Kings 3:4 and 2 Chronicles 1:3, the Gibeonites still made sacrifices and sought for God at the tabernacle. But from the day Solomon left the tabernacle, he never went back. Although in Gibeon there was still the outward human worship, all those who had received wisdom would never go back to the tabernacle. Those who had received wisdom went with the ark.

THE REALITY IN THE NEW TESTAMENT

The Normal Condition of the Church at the Beginning—Bearing a Testimony of Oneness in All the Places

The church on earth today is one. Those who are in the

church are men who are separated from the world. Under normal circumstances, every brother and sister should be serving God; this should be their proper occupation. Every one should be a consecrated one, and everyone should have everything in common. Under such a proper living, the gifted ministries such as the apostles, the prophets, the evangelists, the shepherds and teachers, as listed in Ephesians 4, are produced. Although these gifted ones are scattered in different places, they are still in the same church. This is like electric current being one, yet transmitted throughout many places. Although the intensity of light may be different from one house to the other, the electricity itself is one. The light expressed in different places is different, but the nature of the electricity is the same. This is the same with the church. Although the churches in the various localities are different as far as their localities are concerned, there is nevertheless only one church. The church exists for the testimony of oneness. When we say the "local church," our emphasis is the church and not the local-ness. The life that all the churches possess is a life of oneness. For this reason all the churches should be one among themselves. Although there were the manifested churches in Corinth, Ephesus, and other places, they were all one church. This is the normal situation.

The Desolation of the Church

However, when the church became desolate, conditions changed. At the time of Paul, the church was already falling into desolation. Paul said in the book of Philippians that "all seek their own things, not the things of Christ Jesus" (Phil. 2:21). In 2 Timothy he said that all who were in Asia had turned away from him and his ministry (1:15). The descriptions in Peter's epistles are no exception; they all mention the desolation of the church toward the end of the apostles' time. On the one hand, Peter speaks in his first epistle of the church as a spiritual house, or a spiritual temple (1 Pet. 2:5). On the other hand, Peter also spoke of the condition of degradation. John's epistles also speak of the coming of Antichrist and of apostasy in teachings (1 John 2:18; 4:3; 2 John 7). These are the conditions of the end times. In

Revelation 2 and 3, we see that the churches had become so desolate that the Lord could no longer write to the churches; He could only write to the messengers of the churches. The letter to Ephesus in Revelation 2 can be considered "The Second Epistle to the Ephesians." There the church had forsaken its original condition and had drifted farther and farther away.

God's Eyes upon the Spiritual Reality of the Church in the Age of Its Desolation

What we see today is merely a collection of human methods, doctrines, opinions, criticisms, and quibbles. Amidst the desolation of the church, we need to learn to exercise judgment. It is true that among all the denominations in Christianity, there are God's people who are still performing worship to God. You have to admit that there are still sacrifices. But the ark is not there any longer. There is no more testimony. The only thing that is left is an outward tabernacle. When God's tabernacle has become desolate, His eyes are turned to the temple. Today, we who are learning to follow the Lord have to make our choice between the tabernacle and the temple. Some like to follow what is on hand, what is visible, and what is available everywhere. Yet those who want to follow God have to choose the ark and to go on with it.

The position that we should take should be one of spiritual reality, that is, the position typified by the temple. Today the church is the habitation of the Holy Spirit. In this church, there is God's authority and the desire of God's heart. There is also the authority of the kingdom of the heavens. The Lord has given to the church the authority of the kingdom of the heavens. As such is the case, we can enjoy the power of the coming age in the church today. In the Old Testament, the temple and the kingdom are linked together; the temple is the most crucial element in the kingdom. In the same way, the church as the temple is linked to the power of the coming kingdom. This is where our way lies today. On the one hand, we have to leave the outward tabernacle. On the other hand, we have to seek after God's testimony. God has pronounced very clear judgment on the outward failures already. His judgment is His removal of the ark. Before God, to be without the ark is a shame. On the one hand, we have to leave the tabernacle. On the other hand, we have to seek after God's testimony.

What is God's testimony? In the Old Testament, God ordered Moses to make two tables of stones, which He called the tables of the law. On these stones were engraved the ten commandments. The tables of the law were also called the tables of testimony (Exo. 34:29). The ark that God commanded Moses to make was a type of Christ. Above the ark was the mercy seat. Within the ark was the law. However, God did not call the ark the ark of the law, but the ark of testimony (Exo. 25:22). Hence, the law is God's testimony.

The law is God's demand on man's conduct. How then can it be God's testimony? We have to realize that, on the one hand, God's testimony is the response of God's demand on man. On the other hand, God's demand is simply God's testimony. Where there are the divine demands, there is the divine testimony. Whatever demands God puts on man today, these demands are there to attest to God and to testify God. They testify God's glory, His holiness, and all that He is. The law declares God's demands, and the mercy seat bestows God's grace to man. The testimony is from man to God, and grace is from God to man. When God's glory is satisfied, there is the mercy seat. We have to know that the ten commandments do not refer to the dead laws, but to God's demand on man. This demand is itself a testimony, in which God testifies to Himself. The law maintains God's testimony, and it testifies for God. God has to explain to man His demands, and this explanation is God's testimony. Psalms 119 describes God's law as His testimony many times. When a man keeps God's law, he is keeping God's testimony. Every time the word *testimony* is mentioned in that psalm, it refers to the law.

Today the outward church has become weakened and has failed. It has lost the testimony of God and is not able to meet God's demand. For this reason, there are the disunity, divisions, denominations, and sects. God demands that man submit. But man cannot meet this demand. As a result, the testimony is lost, and division is produced. Although every revivalist comes along and builds a tabernacle, there is no ark of testimony in it. Even when there is a mercy seat, there is no ark. A man can go to different places to conduct conferences. What he is doing is merely moving the tabernacle from one place to another. What he is maintaining is merely a mercy seat without an ark. Although the ark is not there, the mercy seat is nevertheless put up. This is what men are doing today—replacing God's testimony with man's need. Whenever man's need replaces God's testimony, degradation begins, and problems arise. What then is the way for our work today?

THE WAY FOR OUR WORK TODAY

Realizing the Limitation of an Individual, and Being Delivered from Individualism

God has His specific demands; He wants man to learn coordination. God not only requires that man be delivered from sin, the world, and the flesh; He also asks that man be delivered from his individualism. With regard to the knowledge of the Body of Christ, man's problem lies in the fact that since the first day he has been taught the wrong things. Since the Reformation, man came to think that he can be a Christian individually, that he can be sanctified individually, justified individually, and work and serve God individually. Right from the very beginning, this realization has been wrong, and the way a person takes subsequent to this is also wrong. Man thinks that as soon as he believes in the Lord, all he has to do is to be zealous, to consecrate himself, and to give up everything. However, a man must realize that he is not only a man of unclean lips, but he also dwells in the midst of a people of unclean lips (Isa. 6:5). While it is wrong to have unclean lips individually, it is equally wrong to dwell in the midst of a people with unclean lips.

If we lay a good foundation today, within twenty or thirty years the situation will change drastically. We must see that a person cannot be a proper Christian individually; he must follow the footsteps of the flock, and he must never hold on to any form of individualism. After a person is saved, he must immediately be brought to see that he belongs to the Body. To be joined to the Body is the meaning of the laying on of hands. When a new believer is joined to the Body through the laying on of hands, he can no longer be an individual Christian.

We must be brought to a point where we acknowledge the limitation of the individual. This word is easy for the young ones, but it is difficult for the ones with considerable gifts. However, we must see that even members as great as the hands and the feet are but hands and feet only; they must accept the other members before they can become complete. We must recognize our own limitations. Problems arise in the church because some people think that they are all-inclusive; they want to do everything by themselves. However, the hand can only be the hand; it cannot see, and it cannot hear. It has to accept the seeing and the hearing of others before it can enjoy the riches. It does not matter how great a gift I am; in many areas I nevertheless have to accept others' supply. Some can only be the cells. Surely they need others. The question is whether or not they would ask others to help them. The basic need is that they have to acknowledge their own limitations. They have to acknowledge that they cannot see, speak, or hear.

We have to clearly identify our own limitations. We may not know something, but there are others in the church who will know. The fact that I do not know something does not mean that everyone else does not know about it. I have to live by others. I may not be able to walk, but others can walk. Never think that we can preach only the Head without preaching the Body. The more you depend on the Lord, the more you will realize that you have to depend on the members. If we do not accept our own limitations, we will never find the way that others have opened up already. As long as the question of limitation is not resolved, we can never advance. What we have individually is only very little. Do not think that you are so capable or clever, and do not think that you will never be wrong and that others are always wrong. We all have to humble ourselves and be delivered from our pride and our individualism to receive the supply from others. All those who are accustomed to their cleverness and who think highly of themselves should make a turn and have a change. This is the first point.

Submitting to the Authority of the Ministry

Second, not only do we have to acknowledge our own limitations; we have to know submission. In the Body of Christ, ministry means authority. Whoever can hear and speak is the authority. If a member can see, he is the authority. His being able to see is his authority. If a member can hear, his being able to hear is the authority. If you want to hear something, you have to submit to him. Either you walk blindly, or you have to submit to the eyes for your seeing. There is no one in the church who does not have to submit to anyone; everyone has to submit to those assigned by God. The problem today is that many brothers and sisters think that the supply others have received will not work in them. They think that they have to receive something directly from God. Man thinks that he can do without man's preaching, but God's commandments come through His ministers. For this reason, we must learn to submit.

Not Being Interested in Interfering with Others, but Always Seeking Help from Others

A minister cannot speak in a loose way, nor can he demand that others submit to him all the time without himself being first dealt with by the Lord. God will never entrust His authority to such kinds of people. If a man has a natural liking to put his hands on others' business, God will not be able to use such a person. Man has to be like God, who does not like to control anything. If God wanted to control anything, He could remove the tree of knowledge of good and evil, or He could put a fence around the tower of Babel. He could remove the fiery sword from the cherubim. But God would not do such kinds of things. He never likes to interfere with the liberty of others. Man has to make his own choices. Some brothers and sisters like to interfere with others' affairs. But God has no interest in such kinds of things. He never forces anyone to believe. He says, "Every one who believes ... would have eternal life" (John 3:16). Everyone who receives has eternal life. He does not force man to believe. If a man has been dealt with by God to such a degree that he no longer has a liking to interfere with others' business, God will entrust His authority to such a one.

A man should not have a desire to interfere with another member in the Body. If a man has been taught by God, he will firstly have no desire to interfere with others' affairs. Second, he will gladly seek advice from others concerning his own affairs. If we practice this, when thousands of members come together, with each one having no desire to interfere with others' business while gladly seeking advice from others, a beautiful Body life will be realized. If we do this, we will be balanced. God has no desire for us to be busybodies.

We have to be a person who has learned the lessons, and we have to reject and restrict all forms of individualism. On the one hand, we have to accept limitations. On the other hand, we have to learn submission. It is a joyful thing to pursue after submission. Today, in the whole world, in all the nations and among all the societies, there are all kinds of opinions, voices, expressions, and arguments. This is why all organizations have their rules, and when they conduct meetings, some are given permission to ask questions whereas others are given permission to answer. Those who speak cannot go on beyond a certain number of minutes. This proves that even in the world, an individual has to be limited by the group. Of course, this limitation is an artificial one, and not one that is done in submission.

Submitting to the Arrangement of the Head, and Receiving the Riches from the Members

The first sin of man was rebellion, lawlessness, and the overthrowing of authority. Satan's fall and rebellion were caused by his uplifting of himself to be above God. If we submit ourselves to God's authority today, we will have the proper testimony. We have to realize that not everyone has the authority, and not everyone has the word of God. The testimony of the Body today has nothing to do with numbers, but it is a matter of being in the Body. It is a matter of being willing to submit to the arrangement of the Head, as opposed to being free to make one's own choices and decisions. As a member of the Body, we cannot make any decision on our own. Christ has an immeasurably vast deposit in the church today. If we are in a receiving position, we will surely become very rich. If we insist on receiving only from God without receiving from the Body, we will become very poor. This is not a doctrine, but a fact. Not only is the thing I have my own, but what the brothers and sisters have is also my own. In many matters, other brothers and sisters have a clear discernment, but I do not have discernment. As such a one, I have to accept the discernment of the brothers and sisters. Some people know God's word. Some can discern the truth. I should gladly receive their discernment and judgment. What I do not know, someone else will know. If we will not receive from others, probably we will end up fifty years from now having the same as what we have now.

It is a strange thing that we have to exhort the brothers and sisters to receive from others. On the one hand, men say that they are poor and weak. On the other hand, they are not willing to receive riches from others. Is this not a strange thing? How rich are the ministries that God has raised up in the church today. Yet we are still in hunger. The reason for this is that we emphasize our own individualism too much. A man has to learn to bow down his head and to receive supply from others.

Accepting the Laying On of Hands—
Handing Over Oneself
to Accept God's Assigned Authority

Receiving the laying on of hands means accepting the judgment of the church. It means that one is willing to submit to the authority that God has put upon a person. We are ourselves responsible for handing ourselves over. In the Old Testament, when men laid their hands on the heads of the goats, it meant that they were willing to hand the goats over to the priests. If they wanted to keep the goats, they should not lay their hands on the goats, because they were not willing to hand the goats over. The Bible says that a man has to come to the altar willingly and offer his sacrifices willingly. God wants man to hand himself over in a voluntary way. The Acts of the Apostles records the matter of baptism; it also records the matter of the laying on of hands. The laying on of hands signifies the acceptance of the authority of the church. Today, man sees that baptism is a separation of the believers from the worldly system. But they do not see that the laying on of hands is an acceptance of God's authority that He establishes in the church. When a man refuses authority, confusion results. If a man is willing to hand himself over to the serving ones, it will become easy for the serving ones to do their job.

THE PRINCIPLE OF THE WORK—
THE CO-WORKERS HANDING OVER THEMSELVES

The principle in the work is the same. The co-workers in all the places should first hand themselves over and place themselves under the Head and be directed by the Head. Only then can the Lord do something, and only then will the work have a way to go on. We hope that in these days the Lord will at least give us a way to go on.

From now on, we have to accept the judgment of the Body. All major decisions and directions must be placed in the hands of the Body. If we do this, we will have life, power, and direction. Otherwise, there will be rebellion and insubordination. If we hand ourselves over, within us we will surely feel an "amen" and a sweet sense.

The situation in Foochow in the past has been one of confusion. The meetings there became a little kingdom by themselves. The saints were closed and would not fellowship with others. Their hearts were not broad enough and did not include all the believers; they did not see the unique Body of Christ. The way the Body will be manifested in the future is determined by the nature of the testimony of the local churches today. The local churches today are the models of the coming universal church. This is like an architect designing a house: first he builds a model. Although the model is not very big, what it represents is in nature the same as what will be built. First Corinthians 12 speaks of the universal Body, on the one hand, and on the other hand, the Body life in the local churches.

THE OUTLET OF THE WORK—
HANDING ONESELF OVER TO THE BODY
TO BE A THREE-DIMENSIONAL VESSEL

In our work we must find an outlet for the Lord. What we are lacking today is not power, but an outlet for the Lord. The problem among us is that the co-workers have not properly handed themselves over. Although there is a little power, this power is not great. A three-dimensional cup can hold a lot of water. But a flat piece of glass or a broken cup cannot hold any water. Because our work has been "flat," we have lost many blessings. The tabernacle and the temple in the Old Testament both typify the church, the Body of Christ, in the New Testament. Only when this Body becomes a three-dimensional Body can it be a vessel of God. Only then can it contain God's riches and be a strong and powerful testimony for the Lord.

Not only should the co-workers do this, the brothers and sisters should also consecrate themselves fully in this way. No matter where he or she is, every brother and sister should be a servant of God. Here all of us need a specific declaration, and should count the cost, and hand ourselves over.

THE DIRECTION OF THE WORK—
FROM THE CENTER TO THE CIRCUMFERENCE

The gospel spread from Jerusalem to Samaria, and then to the ends of the earth. This is God's way. If a man starts working from the ends of the earth, he is taking the wrong direction. We must work from the center to the circumference. At the same time, it would be equally wrong if all the believers were to remain in Jerusalem, for the intention of the Lord was that the gospel would be preached to the ends of the earth. For this reason, the Lord scattered the believers by raising up persecution in the environment. However, it was not wrong for the apostles to remain in Jerusalem. There should still be the apostles and the elders in Jerusalem, because Jerusalem was a center of testimony. In addition, Antioch was also a center of testimony. The problem today is that we do not have a Jerusalem, and we do not have an Antioch. All we have is simply local churches.

In the Bible, there was definitely a Jerusalem, and there was an Antioch. This is what needs to be recovered among us in these days. Our work today does not seem to have a Jerusalem. In 1937 we saw the ground of the church, but we did not see the light concerning Jerusalem. Nevertheless, we somehow felt then that the work should not belong to a locality. Thank God that He has led us on. What we have seen today is much more than what we saw then. We cannot change any part of God's Word, and we cannot skip any part of His Word. We should never forget that in the Bible there is still a church in Jerusalem.

Because our light was not adequate in the past, we suffered losses. From now on, we must have a fresh start. If we do not do this, the work will belong to the local church again, and the Lord will have no way to go on among us.

A TESTIMONY

Brother Witness Lee: Between 1940 and 1943, by the mercy of the Lord, we did quite a work there in Chefoo, Shantung. During those few years, many souls were saved, and many consecrated themselves. Of those brothers and sisters who were in Chefoo, ninety percent consecrated themselves. Later the migration started. Over one hundred people migrated to the northwest of China, and a few dozen migrated to Manchuria. With these migrating ones, their traveling expenses, ninety-five percent of them, were taken care of by the church. In the first three years after we began to have the testimony in Chefoo, about one hundred fifty brothers and sisters joined us in the breaking-of-bread meeting. This stirred up quite a lot of jealousy. Later the war started, and the Japanese began to persecute me. A dozen or more people in Christianity also began to join hands to attack me. The Japanese put me into prison for a month. After I was released from prison, I was not free from their hands. I was not the only one who was restricted; many other brothers and sisters also lost their freedom. At that time, the Lord prepared a way for me: I became ill and incurred tuberculosis of the lungs, and I had to rest for a year. During this period, I experienced many trials, and I was pressed on all sides. It was not until 1944 that I began to stand up to do a little speaking to the saints. I spent half of my life in Chefoo. In October of 1944, the Lord arranged for me to leave Chefoo to go to Tsingtao. At that time, I told the brothers and sisters that I had to go to take a rest. In this way, I left Chefoo, and I have never gone back.

CHAPTER FORTY-TWO

THE REQUIREMENTS OF THE KINGDOM

THE LORD'S DAY MORNING MESSAGE (1)

Date: Morning, The Lord's Day, April 11, 1948
Place: Hardoon Road, Shanghai
Speaker: Witness Lee

Scripture Reading: Matt. 3:1-2; 5:20; 7:21; 18:3; Luke 18:23-24; John 3:3

THE KINGDOM BEING THE CENTER OF THE NEW TESTAMENT

Today we want to consider the center of God's word in the New Testament. In the New Testament, the first thing that the Lord wants is the kingdom of God, or the kingdom of the heavens. As far as the subject itself is concerned, it is the kingdom. As far as its having to do with God is concerned, it is the kingdom of God, and as far as its having to do with the heavens is concerned, it is the kingdom of the heavens. Many people do not pay attention to this matter. They do not have the thought of the kingdom in their mind. When they study the Bible, they only find such things as love, patience, and humility. Others, when they read the four Gospels, find such things as the miracles, the healings, the casting out of the demons, or the virtues of Christ. Man is curious by nature, and he likes to study these things. But there is one great subject in the Bible, and that is the kingdom of God, or the kingdom of the heavens. This is the central thought of the four Gospels. After reading the four Gospels, if you are asked about their main subject, it would be natural for you to say that they contain records of miracles and works of wonder by the Lord. However, you have to realize that the main theme of the four Gospels, and especially that of the Gospel of Matthew, is the kingdom. The emphasis of the

Gospels is neither the miracles nor the works of wonder, but the kingdom of the heavens. The first message of John the Baptist was, "The kingdom of the heavens has drawn near" (Matt. 3:2). The first word that Christ uttered when He came out to preach was also, "The kingdom of the heavens has drawn near" (Matt. 4:17). Afterwards, when the disciples went out to preach, they preached first the gospel of God's kingdom (Acts 8:12). In order for a man to know the things of God, he must first enter God's kingdom. The story between God and man is a story about His kingdom. In the Gospel of John, we see the matter of the kingdom mentioned (John 3:3, 5). In the Gospel of Luke, what the rich man encountered was also the matter of the kingdom (Luke 18:24-25). Even the life mentioned in the Gospel of John is for the kingdom. I repeat the matter of the kingdom over and over again and come back always to the same subject because I want you to see that the main theme in the Bible is the kingdom.

THE KINGDOM BEING THE STARTING POINT AND THE MAIN POINT OF THE GOSPEL

What is the first thing that we present to others? In the New Testament, the first thing that the Gospels present is the kingdom. The principle of the New Testament is that whatever is mentioned first is the most important thing. The first mentioning of the gospel in the New Testament is the gospel of the kingdom. The first book in the New Testament, the book of Matthew, is a book that deals specifically with the kingdom. The first book of the New Testament is not the book of Romans. The New Testament does not deal firstly with sin or with the question of salvation. Nor is the first book the Gospel of John, which gives life. The first thing that God places before man is not salvation or baptism, but the kingdom. The first word that John the Baptist preached was not concerning sin, but concerning the kingdom. The first word that the Lord Jesus spoke to Nicodemus was also concerning the kingdom. To preach the gospel means to preach the kingdom. Regeneration is not for the purpose of dealing with the question of sin. It is to deal with the fact that the kingdom is ahead, and that we need to be regenerated to enter into this kingdom. A person repents, not because he is evil, nor because he has too many sins, but because there is a demand ahead of him that he has to enter into the kingdom. It is because there is a kingdom that a person needs life. Only when a person has life can he have the eyes to see the kingdom.

Today, when people preach the gospel, the first thing they present to others is heaven. Actually, in the New Testament where can you find heaven being presented first? Did the disciples or any other person present heaven? We are not saying that we do not need to mention sin or salvation when we preach the gospel. We are saying that the New Testament shows that the beginning of the gospel is the kingdom.

THE KINGDOM BEING
GOD'S REQUIREMENT TODAY

The kingdom is too great a subject. In the past, we thought that the kingdom is a matter of reward. It is true that the kingdom is a matter of reward. However, it is not simply a matter of future reward, but a matter of God's requirement today. The reason we need to repent and be regenerated is that we need to enter into the kingdom. The kingdom puts a requirement on man. It requires him to do this and that. The Lord said, "Unless your righteousness surpasses that of the scribes and Pharisees, you shall by no means enter into the kingdom of the heavens" (Matt. 5:20). This speaks not only of the condition for entering the kingdom, but the requirement of the kingdom itself. In the Bible, we see a rich young ruler who had a lot of money. When the kingdom put a demand on him, he was unable to meet the demand, and he left in sorrow (Matt. 19:16-22). The Lord also said that unless a man turns and becomes like a little child, he shall by no means enter into the kingdom of the heavens (Matt. 18:3). This is not only a condition, but a requirement.

GOD'S SALVATION MEETING
THE REQUIREMENT OF GOD'S KINGDOM

In preaching the gospel today, if we put heaven before

men as the first thing, our gospel is too low. If a man believes in Christ and is forgiven of his sins merely for the sake of going to heaven, such a standard is too low. The opposite of sin is the law. If salvation is merely for the forgiveness of sins, at the most it is to bring a person up to the standard of the law. The New Testament salvation is not merely for the satisfaction of the law, but to answer a higher demand. God's salvation is saving us to a point where we are higher than the law, the opposite of sin.

The Requirement of the Kingdom Being Higher Than That of the Law

Suppose two brothers are engaged in a business together, and suppose the first brother has taken advantage of the second brother. Others may say that the first brother is not right. This is the human way of speaking, but a Christian should have a higher standard than this. A Christian should say that if the first brother does not return what he has taken, he is not behaving like a brother. Suppose the first one took the second one's clothing. Humanly speaking, it would be right and just for the second brother to reason with the first. But a Christian should say that such behavior is not becoming to a brother or a Christian. However, even to do that does not meet the requirement of the kingdom. The kingdom requires that the second brother, in addition to giving up his reasoning, give another piece of clothing to the first one (Matt. 5:40). This is the requirement of the kingdom. What Christians have to come up to today is the standard of the kingdom. What they have to fulfill is the requirement of the kingdom. Most of the pulpits in Christianity today preach moral teachings. The purpose of such teachings is to turn lawless, evil, unjust people into good men. But the requirement of the kingdom is much higher than goodness and righteousness. The requirements of Matthew 5, 6, and 7 are much higher than the requirements of the law. According to the standard of the law, the goodness and righteousness of the young ruler were high enough. But as far as the requirement of the kingdom is concerned, they were still far too short.

The Requirement of the Kingdom Being the Ruling of the Heavens

As far as the law goes, it is right to demand payment of debts. Humanly speaking, it is right to be just, and wrong to be unjust. But as far as the kingdom goes, it is wrong to demand payment for debts. The requirement of the kingdom is not that a person cannot demand payment, but that he will not demand payment; and to go one step further, the requirement of the kingdom tells him to sell all he has and give it to others. Many people only know to teach others to be a gentleman, to teach an evil person to become a good person, and to teach an arguing couple to become a harmonious couple. This kind of sermon is welcomed by people. Yet, even if you are the best gentleman in Shanghai, you are still far off in the eyes of the Lord. Even if a man has not sinned, he still cannot enter the kingdom of the heavens. Those Christians who are living under the sense of heaven are those who are controlled by heaven. Man's view is to remove sin and to go to heaven, but the requirement of God's word in the New Testament is much stricter than this. God's requirement is not a question of morality, law, the conscience, or justice, but a question of the rule of the heavens. The kingdom is a matter of God's rule. Those who have a high moral standard may be justified before the law, but they come far short of the requirements of God. In order to satisfy God's requirement, a man cannot take the law as the standard, but he must take the kingdom as the standard.

If the standard of a Christian's living is his conscience, he will not be able to sell everything and give to the poor. At most, he will be able to be a moral person. He will never live out the life of Matthew 5 to 7. Today's civil law would never require a person to give his clothing to others. The requirement of the conscience at most asks that a man not argue with others, and that if one's clothing is taken away, he will let it go and will not pursue after it. This is the most that the conscience will do.

If an unreasonable husband argues with his wife, the wife can very well reason with him. If she asks any elderly pastor, she may be exhorted to be patient and may be told that unwavering patience is more precious than good treasure. However, such kinds of exhortation do not come up to the requirement of the kingdom. If the pastor is to present to her the requirement of the kingdom, he would ask the wife to love the husband all the more and to honor him all the more.

The Kingdom Being the Demand of Life, and Life Being the Supply for the Kingdom

If this is the case, who can enter the kingdom? Who can be saved? This question was raised two thousand years ago already. The Lord's disciples asked Him, "Who then can be saved?" The Lord answered, "With men this is impossible, but with God all things are possible" (Matt. 19:25, 26). Only God Himself can meet the requirement of the kingdom. The kingdom is intimately related to God's life. The kingdom is the demand of life, whereas life is the supply of the kingdom. On the one hand, the life we receive demands that we live out the kingdom. On the other hand, all the requirements of the kingdom are met by the supply of life. Regeneration is for a person to receive and to possess this life, and this life meets all the demands of the kingdom (John 3:3). Man thinks that a person climbs from a low point to a high point, and that improvement is gradual. But God gives to us a high life right from the beginning, so that we can live a high living of entering into the kingdom.

In the marriage life, you always encounter conflicts and tempers. Suppose a couple have believed in the Lord and are saved. At the beginning, they may still try to hold back their temper and to not give each other an unhappy look. But after a while, they will invariably come into conflicts. Our attitude at home toward our children and our servants often exposes where we are. If we cannot overcome in the small things, we will not be overcomers. In the New Testament, the Lord presented the kingdom right from the beginning. This kingdom requires that we take His life into us and live out a kingdom living. The kingdom life is able to take care of everything both great and small, and it is able to overcome everything.

Brothers who are engaged in business together may get along with each other well at the beginning. But after a while, they will start to argue with each other. They may argue so much that they have to bring the matter to some elderly brothers for arbitration. After the arbitration, they may be reconciled with each other for a while, and may agree with one another that they will henceforth not exercise their flesh, but will instead pray and confess their sins one to the other, and that by the grace of God they will no longer lose their temper. They may accept the word of exhortation of the elderly brothers. But after half an hour to an hour, while they are still talking, they may be provoked to argue with each other again. This is our real situation.

If one of these brothers would, on the contrary, answer the demand of the kingdom, not only would he stop arguing; he would even give what he has to the other. If we are only concerned about the conscience, the moral standards, and the public opinions, we are still not qualified to enter the kingdom. The life of Christ helps us not only to meet the standard of the conscience or of morality, but to meet the requirements of the kingdom.

If a husband loses his temper with his wife all the time, and a person comes along to exhort the wife to be patient and says that unwavering patience is more precious than good treasure, such an exhortation is like the barber's cutting of a person's hair; soon after he cuts the hair, the hair grows back again. If you can help the wife to see the requirement of the kingdom, everything will be fine. When the husband loses his temper, the wife can still smile at him. This shows that she is a person living in the kingdom, and that in everything she has overcome.

Answering the Demands of the Kingdom in a Desperate and Absolute Way

Today, God will not do anything to comply with our wish. All He wants is that we single-heartedly seek for the accomplishment of His will. If we seek for the accomplishment of God's will in this way, the kingdom will come. We must answer the demands of the kingdom in a desperate way. We must obey absolutely before we can meet the kingdom requirement. God's salvation does not bring us to the standard of the conscience, morality, or justice only. The requirement of God's kingdom is as "terrible" as an atomic bomb. We find many Christians who conduct themselves well in the first five or six years of their Christian life, but begin to fail by the seventh or eighth year. They begin to lose their patience and may even begin to lose their temper uncontrollably, or backslide or fall suddenly. Only those who answer the demand of the kingdom in an absolute way will overcome. The requirement of the kingdom is as high as heaven itself. The kingdom requires that we give all the reasons to others, and all the blame to ourselves. It requires that we give all the gains to others, and take all the losses to ourselves. If we do this, all the problems will be solved.

The same principle applies to our material offerings. Man considers it all right if he offers one-tenth of what he has. After he has tithed, he keeps the rest in his own pocket and considers it his. But the requirement of the kingdom is that you be separated from your money. It is not a question of giving up one-tenth, but a question of being delivered from the bondage of money. The way God wants us to take today is the way of answering the demand of the kingdom.

CHAPTER FORTY-THREE

GOD'S WORK OF RECOVERY

(1)

CO-WORKERS' MEETING (4)

Date: 6:30 a.m., April 12, 1948
Place: Hardoon Road, Shanghai
Speaker: Watchman Nee

THE BEGINNING OF THE RECOVERY—
MARTIN LUTHER

God's work of recovery began with Martin Luther. From that time on, God began to have distinct recoveries on the earth. This, of course, does not mean that the recovery began with Luther alone. At the same time that he was raised up, other people saw the same things that he did. He is merely taken as a representative of the recovery in that age. Before his time, the truth had become a kind of tradition, the apostolic ministry had become a system of popery, the oneness of the church had become an ecclesiastical ecumenism, and spiritual authority had become political authority. The church was taken captive to Babylon. The prevailing thought at that time was that the church ruled over the world; it declared that the whole world belonged to God. As a result, the Catholic church brought unconverted people into the church. As long as a person was a Roman citizen, he was automatically a member of the church. Spontaneously, infant baptism came in at that time. Originally, Christians were people who took the voluntary way of poverty. Christians and poor people are always linked together. But when the church opened its door to the world, voluntary poverty was lost, and the church became rich. Under normal circumstances, there should be two kinds of poor people in the church. One kind is the naturally poor ones, and the other kind is the voluntarily poor ones. Today in the church, we have the first kind of poor people. But there is no second kind of poor people. On the contrary, there are rich people in the church, and the church is filled with affluence. However, although many people are rich in material goods, they are poor in faith, and the inward spiritual content among them becomes more and more depleted.

THE RECOVERY OF VOLUNTARY POVERTY

Since the time of Clement, the truth became less and less clear. On the one hand, men became more and more capable of analysis and expositions, but at the same time they lacked life and did not have much grace or righteousness. Even at the time of Augustine, the truth was still unclear. Historically speaking, the church was always on the decline. Eventually it fell to such a low degree that reactions rose up within the Catholic church. One of these reacting ones was Francis of Assisi. He was dissatisfied with the outward riches of the church. He himself was originally a rich man, or at least the son of a rich man. Within a few days, he sold everything and gave to the poor. He himself began to practice a life of voluntary poverty. However, the things he wrote are unreadable. You may tolerate a line or two of his writings, but by the third line they become intolerable. Although we cannot tolerate his writings, the practice of voluntary poverty is nevertheless a right one.

In the church, those who receive little should not be in want, and those who receive much should not have an excess (2 Cor. 8:12). It is not a sin to receive much, but it is a sin to receive much and to have excess. If a man knows the Lord, he will invest everything in the Lord. If a man says that he loves the Lord, yet will not invest in the Lord, his love is false. The Lord says that the poor we always have with us (John 12:8). He did not say that we always have the poor brothers with us in the church. Rather, He says that the poor we always have with us. Among the brothers and sisters, it is not difficult to be without want. As long as those who have excess would give away, poor brothers will not appear among us. The Lord's principle is not to keep, but to give. If we all give, there will not be unnecessary riches in the church. It is abnormal that some people are too rich in the church. All excess riches have to be given away. In the world, people would throw away their lives in exchange for money. But in the Bible, God wants our lives instead of money. We cannot be a Christian in an uncertain way. Our God is not uncertain; He is very specific. He wants not only our money, but our lives also.

Later, in Moravia God raised up Count Zinzendorf of Saxony. He was originally an aristocrat and a man of learning. For the Lord's sake, he set aside his estate to receive all kinds of believers. Through his work, the Moravians were raised up. Out of this group, many people were sent to foreign lands. The number of those sent out from them exceeds that sent from any other group and ranks highest in terms of percentage. After this, there was Sister Eva, who was a German. She also took the way of voluntary poverty.

In the last century, the Brethren were raised up. They were very strong in the truth. Although they did not like to talk very much about themselves, a few dozen of their leaders also sold all their possessions at one time to follow the Lord. For a Christian, the question of money must be settled once for all. If it is not settled, the Lord cannot have a way to go on. What is the meaning of degradation in the church? It means that the principle of economy has come into the church. Once the principle of economy comes in, everything will be reckoned according to value, and the Lord will have no way to go on.

THE DEFICIENCY OF THE REFORMATION

A. The Recovery of Faith without a Clear Understanding of Justification

In Luther, we see the recovery of faith. However, Luther did not recover justification by faith. He only recovered faith, and he was not so clear concerning justification. History tells us that he once punished himself in order to be justified. In Rome, he once climbed up to a cathedral step by step in order to be justified. Later, he saw that a man is not justified by works, but by faith.

B. Bringing In National Churches

Luther came out of Babylon, but he did not return to Jerusalem yet. He brought politics into the church and thought that by so doing, it would help the church. Little did he realize that no political power can help the church. On the contrary, any political power will only damage the church. In the end, the national churches were formed. The national churches are partnerships between politicians and believers. The one contributed Germany whereas the other contributed the doctrines, and the result was the national churches. In Germany, the Lutheran church became the national church. The reason the Lutherans embraced the power of politics was that Roman Catholicism was too strong. But by so doing, what we see was a change of nationality instead of a change of the church. The church was changed from a Roman church to a German church. In England, it became the Anglican church. Every Englishman automatically became a member of the Anglican church. As soon as a person was born, he was baptized in the church. No question was asked as to whether or not such a person was regenerated. The only thing that mattered was whether or not such a person was an Englishman. As long as a person was an Englishman and was born in England, he was a member of the church. Consequently, the tradition of infant baptism by sprinkling became very prevailing.

THE RAISING UP OF INDEPENDENT CHURCHES

With the rising up of the national churches, many pure seekers and lovers of the Lord became dissatisfied. They did not want to remain in the national churches. As a result, some independent free churches were formed. Soon after the Reformation, there were over two thousand independent churches. In Switzerland alone, there were over two hundred such churches. During this period of time, the Roman Catholic church persecuted the Protestant churches, and the Protestant churches in turn persecuted the smaller independent churches. To stop these small churches from being established, the English Parliament even passed a law to unify all the churches in England. However, this produced the so-called Nonconformists. They were faithful lovers of the Lord raised up by Him, who would not cooperate with the national churches. The government persecuted them and ordered them to take jobs five miles away from their former places of occupation. They could not work for the government, and all of them who were government officers were removed from their posts. Those who opposed the law were condemned.

THE RECOVERY OF THE EQUALITY OF BELIEVERS AND THE TRUTH OF BAPTISM

After this, there were the Mennonites, who were the first group of believers to realize the error of a hierarchy. Among them, they recovered the title of "brothers," and they addressed each other as brothers. Some of them went to Russia to preach the gospel. In addition to them, the Baptists were also raised up. They saw the error of infant baptism, and they taught that a man must first be clear about the truth of baptism before he can be baptized. They were called the Anabaptists, and they were much persecuted at the beginning. These are recoveries of the outward things.

THE RECOVERY OF THE INNER LIFE

In addition, there was the recovery of the inner life. Madame Guyon, Father Fenelon, and others brought in a recovery of the spiritual condition. These ones are now generally called the mystics. They practiced denying their self, joining themselves with God to oppose their self, giving no excuse to the self, and not asking God to spare His hand on them. In every age, we can find followers of their practice. In addition to these, there were also the Pietists and the Quietists.

THE RAISING UP OF THE PURITANS

Later, the Puritans were raised up. Among them, some from Holland and England migrated separately to America. The ship *The Mayflower* was one of the vessels that carried these Puritan immigrants to the new land.

THE RECOVERY OF THE BRETHREN

A. The Heavenly Calling of the Church

In the last century, God began to have a special recovery. First, He recovered the heavenly calling of the church. The church is like the Israelites in the Old Testament. It should not at any time look to earthly blessings. The church is a group of people who have been called by heaven. It is not their aim to reform society. God's people are those who take the heavenly way on earth. They have given up all hope for the world and society. To them, the world is passing away, and everything therein will be judged. The church's view is different from that of the world. What the church expects is heaven, and not world reforms. These words are familiar to us today, and we may not feel the power behind these words. But at the beginning, this matter was a tremendous recovery.

B. The Oneness of the Church

The second thing the Brethren recovered was the oneness of the church. They saw the oneness of the Body of Christ and realized that the church today is in a state of ruin. Expositors such as J. N. Darby and F. W. Grant all agreed that the church today is in a state of ruin.

THE RAISING UP OF JOHN WESLEY— THE RECOVERY OF SANCTIFICATION BY FAITH

These recoveries occurred among the Brethren. In addition to them, John Wesley was raised up. He recovered the truth concerning sanctification. A man is not only justified by faith, but is also sanctified by faith. Wesley was indeed a servant of God, a dear brother, and a man greatly used by God. He bore the right testimony, but quoted the wrong Scriptures to prove his message. Although his quotations are wrong, the doctrine he preached was right. For example, he quoted 1 John 1:7 as a reference to sanctification. For this reason, some rejected his teachings altogether. This is to go too far. It is possible for a man to quote the wrong Scriptures. However, if he is the right person and he preaches the right doctrine, even if his quotations are wrong, the mistake is not fatal. On the other hand, if the quotations are correct, but the person is wrong, the problem is much more serious. We would rather see the person right and the quotations wrong, than to see the quotations right and the person wrong. Although he quoted the wrong Scriptures, God was still able to cause men to be sanctified.

THE RECOVERY OF SANCTIFICATION BY CONSECRATION

After this, there was Robert Pearsall Smith, a porcelain merchant. He was the husband of Mrs. Hannah Whitall Smith, the writer of the book *The Christian's Secret of a Happy Life*. At that time, men were not very clear concerning the doctrine of sanctification. He preached that man is not sanctified by faith only, but by consecration also. Sanctification does not come merely by faith, but by consecration as well.

THE KESWICK CONVENTION AND OTHERS

In addition to him, there were others like Evan Hopkins of England and Theodore Monod of France. These ones, together with Smith in America, formed the so-called Keswick movement. In addition, there was Andrew Murray, a Dutchman. The raising up of these brothers set the general scene for the recovery. However, their recoveries were not complete. There were still recoveries of other minor parts. For example, we have the recovery of the hymns by Frances Ridley Havergal, and some other contributions by other writers.

THE RECOVERY OF THE CRUCIFIXION OF THE OLD MAN

During the last century, God enlightened men concerning the matter of consecration and its importance through the brothers we have mentioned. However, their revelations were not deep enough. Consecration is not simply a kind of exchange, in which we offer to God all we have and all we are, and we take back from Him what He has and what He is. Darby told others that consecration is based on the casting off of the man of flesh and the removal of this man. The goal of the gospel is not only to forgive the sinner's sin, but to crucify the sinner. The gospel saves not merely by forgiving the sinner and delivering him from perdition, but by crucifying the sinner with the Lord. In preaching the gospel, we have to be careful. If we are not careful, we will easily preach the wrong thing. The gospel removes not only the sin in the flesh, but the person of the flesh. What goes to the heavens is the new man, and not the fleshly man. All spiritual lessons, including obedience and our service to the Lord, must be practiced in accordance with this principle. Even lessons as spiritual as those taught by Madame Guyon must be pursued according to the principle mentioned here by Darby.

Romans 7 says that we are dead to the law. This is why we can be married to Christ. Not only are our sins dead, but we ourselves are dead. If we were not dead, it would be unlawful and adulterous for us to be joined to Christ. If we are dead, we would not be our own person any longer, because the cross has removed our own person. Today there is no longer any need for this person to ask for forgiveness. Only a living person needs forgiveness; a dead person does not need forgiveness. The one who was dead in sin is the crucified old man, and the cross has removed this old man already. This was what Darby preached.

THE RECOVERY OF THE TRUTH OF THE CROSS

After this, we have Mrs. Penn-Lewis, who was raised up to preach the truth concerning the cross. She preached about the cross dealing with the old man. Her understanding was more advanced. Notwithstanding, today our understanding of the subject is more clear than that of Mrs. Penn-Lewis.

THE RECOVERY OF THE TRUTH OF RESURRECTION

After Mrs. Penn-Lewis, we have Mr. T. Austin-Sparks, who saw resurrection. We have been talking about resurrection for years, but we do not know what resurrection really is. Mrs. Penn-Lewis wrote two books about resurrection, but they are not very clear about the subject either. It was not until Brother T. Austin-Sparks wrote about resurrection in 1926 and published what he wrote in the *Overcomer* magazine that the world knew for the first time what resurrection is.

When Miss Barber and I read his writings, we began to pay attention to this matter. Many people talk about resurrection, but they have not presented to others resurrection—the real thing itself. When Brother Sparks talked about resurrection, light came. He presented to others the very resurrection itself. What is resurrection? It is life going into death and passing through death; in the process, what succumbs to death dies, and what cannot die comes out of death alive. This coming out of death is resurrection. Resurrection is anything that death cannot swallow up.

THE RECOVERY OF THE REALITY OF THE KINGDOM

The Welsh Revival

Let us go on to one more subject, the kingdom. The kingdom is a common subject, but to merely discuss the term "kingdom" is useless. The question is whether or not the kingdom as the very thing itself has been realized. When do men see the kingdom? I can say that it was during the Welsh revival that the kingdom as a real thing was recovered. Between 1901 and 1910, Evan Roberts brought in the Great Welsh Revival. This revival was unprecedented in church history. No other revival could match this one. Its effects cut far and deep. Roberts himself was a coal miner, and he did not receive much education. Yet God greatly used him. At that time he was only in his twenties, a very young man, and he was not eloquent at all in preaching. Yet his spirit was strong. His prayers were so powerful that it was said that even God had to answer these prayers. He learned from Mrs. Penn-Lewis and also from J. C. Williams. He did not have much schooling; yet when others touched him, they were saved and were brought to their knees. He was not eloquent; during the Welsh revival, he did not preach many messages. When he did stand up, his speaking lasted only fifteen minutes. Yet even those who dropped by to listen were known to be saved through his words.

Some have said that the Welsh revival was affected by China, because the revival broke out in 1901-1910, whereas in 1900 there was the Boxer Rebellion in China. During that rebellion, many Christians were martyred. After the rebellion, between 1901 and 1902, many Christians throughout the world began to pray for God's work. The answer to all those prayers was funnelled into one man. Roberts himself was confined to his bed because of illness between 1903 and 1904, and he was not released until 1909. When he finally got up, he began to speak to everyone he met concerning the things he saw. In the *Overcomer* magazine, it was mentioned that many times during the meetings others would ask what he was going to say, and he himself would also wonder at the same time what he was going to say. Yet once his mouth was opened, something came out, and men saw the light.

The Kingdom Being to Gain Ground for God

During the past few years, I have seen a little of what God's kingdom is. God's kingdom is a great matter. Now when I pray, I pray for God's kingdom. God desires that His kingdom come on earth. In order for God's kingdom to come on earth, there is the need for the church's prayer.

What is the kingdom? The kingdom is man gaining ground for God on earth. Where God's kingdom is, there God gains the ground. Today man thinks that the kingdom is a question of history. Actually, the kingdom is a question of geography.

The Kingdom Being a Matter of Spiritual Warfare

In order to have the kingdom and in order for God to gain the ground, there is the need for warfare. Hence, in order to recover the kingdom, we have to recover spiritual warfare. The messages on spiritual warfare were recovered by Mrs. Penn-Lewis. In her illness, she experienced spiritual warfare, and she saw that many people were deceived through their ignorance of spiritual warfare. Later, in collaboration with Evan Roberts, she wrote the book *War on the Saints* and released the truth concerning spiritual warfare. This light was hidden from man for two thousand years. Through Mrs. Penn-Lewis, it was recovered. Actually, this light was recorded in Ephesians 6 already, but no one before her had the experience of it.

THE RECOVERY OF THE REALITY OF THE BODY OF CHRIST

Messages concerning the Body of Christ

About 1930, Brother T. Austin-Sparks went on further to see the Body. From that time on, he continued to speak on the Body. He released over five or six hundred pages of messages on this subject. Yet what he released was but teachings only; the reality had not yet appeared.

The Body Life

The Lord's church is one Body because it has only one life. This Body comes out of one life. This life is the life of the Lord, which is the life of the Son of God. Since the Body comes out of one life, there is the need for coordination. We are not merely individuals, but we are parts of a whole. We are like the parts of a car; only when we come together can there be the whole car. We all come from one life. We need to realize today that the life we received is a Body life. What we have received individually is a "partial" life. Hence, we do not receive personal edification first and then become coordinated afterwards. Rather, in and by coordination we grow up to receive everything. If we see this fact, all those who will be saved after us will immediately see the reality of this fact and enter into it. As soon as they are saved, they will become persons who voluntarily hand themselves over to the Body.

The Proper Body Life Not Yet Realized

The gospel is not prevailing today because the proper church is not yet manifested. In a proper church, as soon as a person is saved, he hands himself over to the church and sees the Body. Today, men do not have a proper consecration after they are saved. As a result, we have to go back and help them to make up their consecration. There is no proper church today. Hence, there is no place where you can show a saved person the normal condition of the church. The hindrance today is with us; we have not provided others with the necessary make-up lessons. If enough brothers and sisters would take the ground of God's absolute salvation and consecrate themselves fully to the Lord right after they are saved, and they would hand themselves over fully, the church will find the power and the authority to testify for the Lord and will bring others to the proper stand from the first day on.

THE RESPONSIBILITY OF THE RECOVERY TODAY BEING ON OUR SHOULDERS

Today, the responsibility of the recovery is on our shoulders. All the questions related to the recovery have to do with us. God's work in the world, and in China in particular, depends entirely on us. The responsibility has fallen on us. We have to see that in the Body there is only one life. If we see this, we will see the need for coordination. The problem that exists among the brothers and sisters reflects the problem that exists with us. If we are not the right kind of persons, we will not be able to preach the right kind of gospel. The gospel not only delivers men from sin, the world, and the self; it also delivers men from individualism, from money, and from everything else, into the Body.

The Last Recovery— the Coordination in the Body and the Manifestation of Authority

With each step that the Lord has taken in His recovery, the content of His recovery has become richer and richer. Today, it seems as if there is nothing more to be recovered. The recovery today has reached the stage of the Body. Perhaps this will be the last recovery. There may be other items of recovery, but as far as we know, when we reach the recovery of the coordination of the Body and the manifestation of authority, we have reached the final recovery.

Taking the Way of Submission

In order to arrive at this recovery, God requires that there be the manifestation of authority among us. We have to take the way of submission. If we submit, God will take the way of increase among us. The need today is that such a recovery be realized in us individually first. We have to be an all-inclusive person, and we should have all-inclusive experiences. The gospel we preach should be an all-inclusive gospel. When a man receives this gospel, not only are his sins forgiven, but he is brought into the Body. If we do this, in a few years' time the condition of the church will be entirely different. Today, the responsibility rests entirely on us.

Having the Body Consciousness

What we need today is a Body consciousness. The reality of the Body life lies in the Body consciousness. This is something that cannot be copied or imitated. In Kuling, one brother asked what his future holds. Once this brother asked this question, his future was finished already. In the Body we do not have an individual future; we only have the future of the Body. We would rather be wrong in the Body than be wrong in ourselves. I would rather submit to the Body than to seek for my personal future and offend the Body.

LEADING IN THE BODY

Brother David Hsu asked: How do I know that I will not lead others into mistakes?

The Judgment of the Body Being More Reliable

Brother Nee: Actually, we are not aware of all the mistakes we make in our own lives. Who is responsible for these mistakes? Of course, we are responsible for them ourselves. Since we make mistakes in any case, I would rather make them in the Body. It is better to make mistakes in the Body than to make them in ourselves. If in the church today three or five people, or thirty or fifty people, know the will of God, and I do not have the right judgment concerning certain matters or persons, is it not better that I take their judgment than to make a judgment myself? In the Body, sometimes we become more clear when we do not know something, and we become unclear when we know too much. When a judgment is made by the Body, the responsibility rests on the Body. Sometimes when things happen to us and we are directly involved with them, we become affected by the factors involved and fail to have a clear discernment concerning the matters. But the Body is not affected by personal factors. It is not as easily influenced, and as such, its judgment is more reliable. If we do not have any spiritual reality with us, these words may sound like the Catholic teachings. If we do not have any spiritual reality, Catholicism will indeed come in. But if spiritual reality is with us, we will realize that no matter how good our personal judgments may be, they can never be compared to the judgments of those with spiritual discernment in the Body. You cannot fight against the Body consciousness. Whenever you feel uncomfortable or uneasy, you have to give up and submit yourself to the Body.

Learning to Submit to Authority

Today we have to learn to submit to God's authority. Everywhere we see man's rebellion. In any kind of human institution, we see rebellion and insubordination. Man wants to be free and to be independent. He has his own proposals, views, and judgments. But there are no such things in the kingdom of God. In God's kingdom there is only order and submission. There is nothing better in the whole world than submission, and there is nothing more beautiful in the whole world than order. Here we have submission, and we submit one to another. Here we have no arguments, and no one strives to be the greatest. There is only divine order. What a beautiful thing it is when everyone is pursuing after submission!

Allow me to give a little testimony of my own. I began to learn this lesson in 1922. At that time, I was learning it in tears. Although the person to whom I had to submit might not necessarily be right, and although I might be right instead, if I refused to submit, I would not receive the discipline of the Body. Perhaps at that time, there was not the discipline of the Body yet. But at least, there was the discipline of the Holy Spirit. When I first began to work for the Lord, I was quite young. Another co-worker was five years older than I was. At the beginning he was quite zealous, but he did not have much light. However, God gave me quite a lot of light. At that time, many people exhorted men to believe in Jesus without being able to explain what they said. But I saw more light than others did with regard to the truth of the gospel. At one point, over sixty people wanted to be baptized, of whom ninety percent were saved through me. Since I had brought them to salvation, naturally I should have been the one to baptize them. But that other brother insisted that he would baptize them, for the reason that he was the older of us two. The Bible clearly indicates that whoever preaches the gospel also baptizes the ones he preaches to (Acts 8:35-38). I thought it was quite reasonable that I should baptize them. Later I went to Miss Barber, and she said that I should let the other brother baptize these ones. I asked her why, and she told me that the other brother was older than I was. Later I found another brother who was older than this one, and suggested that this second brother should carry out the baptizing. But Miss Barber insisted that the first one should carry out the baptizing. I was quite bothered. She told me that I should not reason, and she said, "Listen! From today on, you have to learn to listen to your brother." I thought that this brother was not clear about the truth or the way of God. Why then should I listen to him? This went on for three years. Every Sunday I fasted. God was teaching me the lesson of submission. Today I can work together with others because I have learned this lesson.

The Bible mentioned the centurion's word, "For I also am a man under authority, having soldiers under me" (Matt. 8:9). This is submission. Brother Witness Lee once said to me, "You are very severe when you speak on the platform, but you are not so severe when you step off the platform." Whether I am severe or not, I do feel that a person who will not submit to authority is a wild and disorderly person. Those who live in the church should submit to authority. A person who does not submit to authority may be saved, but he does not act like a regenerated person. Any time a person is free from any authority, he has no way to go on, and he does not have the reality of the church with him.

With God there is the anointing, and this anointing is poured upon the church. On the one hand, we have to submit to the anointing within us. On the other hand, we have to submit to the anointing in the church.

Protection and Blessings in the Body

A Christian is most safe today, because for him, there is the protection of the Body. A man can be miles off the target if a boundary is not defined for him. Today, many truths have been established already, and there is no reason for us to stray off any longer. As long as we remain in the Body, the blessings and the anointing are here.

BEING AN ABSOLUTE PERSON

We have to see that the whole problem rests with us today. We have to realize how great our responsibility is. Because of our unfaithfulness, we dare not preach the complete gospel to the sinners. You must be a transformed person before you can preach a transforming gospel. You must be a different person before you can preach a different gospel. There must be a recovered person before there can be a recovered gospel. There must be men who are coordinated before there can be the gospel that brings in coordination. If we are not a certain type of person, we can never preach that certain type of gospel. We must be men of Acts 2 before we can preach the gospel of Acts 2. Only then will we produce more men of Acts 2. If your family, career, money, or position is your center, I have nothing to say. But I can tell you that you cannot be a co-worker. Unless we ourselves are the right kind of person, we can never expect others to be the right kind of persons. If we are not absolute, in twenty or thirty years God will raise up men who will be absolute. Whether or not God will find a way in this generation depends on whether or not there are absolute people in this generation.

THE IMPACT OF THE GOSPEL

In the early churches, although the number of saved ones was not too great, they were all men who were on fire. Although many of them did not preach much, what they did say at the time of their martyrdom spoke louder than what we preach for a whole lifetime. What is needed today is nothing less than absolute obedience and absolute consecration. These are the things that will bring in the power. In his book *The Decline and Fall of the Roman Empire,* Edward Gibbons described the sufferings of the martyrs. They were persecuted, exiled, and many times abused by the Roman soldiers. Yet the more the persecution came, the more people were saved. The question today is how much has the gospel laid hold of us. The more the gospel lays hold of us, the greater the impact of the gospel will be.

Whether or not we can cause the next generation to be a people of Acts 2 depends on how well we perform today. The question is whether or not we are willing to be torn down. The recovery may come to a halt when it comes to us, or it may have a new breakthrough from us. If God gains His way through us, those who are saved after us will not be like the saved ones we see today; a better breed will emerge. What others say and criticize is not important to us. The important thing is the kind of persons we are before God.

Our God is a God who is always going on. The Father works until now, and the Son also works (John 5:17). If we offer up all our time, money, and everything, power will come. At the beginning, the Lord demanded that the believers sacrifice their lives for following Him. The calling today is more serious than it was then. Formerly, we may have exhorted others to believe in the Lord by giving them a pat on the back and saying nice words to them. But today, to ask others to believe in the Lord is to ask of them their lives. Formerly, we were begging others to believe; it was as if they were granting us a favor to believe in the Lord. Today, the situation is turned; a man has to realize that to believe in the Lord will cost his very life. I am afraid that there are not many places on earth where the kind of message we have today would be preached.

THE WAY TO GO ON

In order to match God's work, the way before us needs some adjustments. I can mention a few of these. First, there is the need to train people. In training people, we need to pay attention to the vessels themselves. The vessels must be right before the work can be right. Second, we have to strengthen our existing works. Third, we have to learn to judge others and to deal with others. We have to stop those who are too much and strengthen those who are not enough. In the future, we will judge the world and the angels (1 Cor. 6:2-3). For this reason, we have to learn to judge today. The first one we have to learn to judge is ourselves. If we do not judge ourselves, our judgment will not be clear. If we ourselves have been dealt with, our judgments will be accurate. Those who are the ministers of the word should especially learn the proper lessons. At the same time, all the brothers and sisters should learn to receive the portion of the ministers of the word.

Fourth, money must have no place in the heart of the co-workers. The co-workers must be delivered from the bondage of money. Any feeling for money in the co-workers must be completely taken away. We hope that the Lord will work to such an extent that we can have all things in common in the church.

Fifth, the local churches should pay much attention to the newly saved ones, to properly equip them and to render them the clear teachings. Two kinds of perfectings are necessary. One is the preaching of the gospel. This must be done year round in all the places. The other is the edification of the new believers. This needs a few dozen topics with which we educate the new believers week after week. These topics are fixed topics; there is no need to devise more advanced topics. The same topics can be used year round. Those who will serve as the speaking vessels need to learn the topics first. They should also know how to use the adequate materials.

Some brothers should remain in a place to wait on the Lord. Some should spend more time traveling to other places, while the rest stay in one place. Everyone should learn to work together as a Body. There should not be a church that is only tied to its own "turf," one that is closed to outsiders.

AS CONSECRATED ONES, LIVING FULLY FOR GOD

There are certain things concerning consecration that are difficult to speak about. According to the Bible, there is no such thing as an unconsecrated saved one. Everyone who is saved is consecrated to the Lord. All the brothers and sisters who have consecrated themselves should move and act together with the co-workers.

The Bible says that the poor we have always with us. It is wrong for us to pile up goods in our houses. The basic principle and requirement of the Scriptures is that we should help the poor. Whether or not a poor person is one among us, the Bible requires that we give to him. If you have never remembered the poor, your heart will not be enlarged. When you give things away, you will learn to have an enlarged heart, and you will develop an enlarged view. Today it is difficult to find people with large hearts and broad views. The Bible teaches us not to be bound by material riches. Every commandment in the Bible is there for us to keep. If we fail to keep any one of them, we will suffer loss. It is easy to give to our own brothers, but it is not easy to give to outsiders. Nevertheless, the requirement of the Scriptures is that we remember the poor.

Many brothers and sisters do not realize how the co-workers live. Some co-workers have no fire on their stove five days in a row. Others do not have money to provide education for their children or adequate support for their family's livelihood.

We should help the brothers and sisters to choose their jobs in a proper way. In this kind of coordination, it is right for some to devote themselves to making money. But who should be the ones to make money? Only those who are fully consecrated are qualified to make money. Only this kind of money-making will be of any use. When the Israelites left Egypt, they took all the money with them (Exo. 12:36). When they crossed the Red Sea, the money crossed over with them. Any money that was left in Egypt, regardless of how much it was, was useless. Only those who have passed the Red Sea can employ their money to the proper use for the building up of the tabernacle. What is needed first is for the person himself to be delivered. Second, the money has to follow. Then third, there is the building up of the tabernacle. Formerly, we did not have the boldness to say this. But now we do. A person must first consecrate himself. If he does not do this,

God will not want his money. The sin of the golden calf must first be exposed, and a person must first be delivered from such sin, before the question of the gold can be settled. It was because man had first worshipped idols that the gold went to the calf. The gold should have been given to the tabernacle. But because of idolatry, the gold went to the calf. Hence, the worship of the golden calf was not only a matter of sin, but a loss for the tabernacle. It was the same gold. But when it was placed on the golden calf, it was wrong, and it had to be ground into powder. On the contrary, when it was placed in the tabernacle, it was right. The same material could be directed toward different objects. One object was the idol. The other object was the tabernacle. In the New Testament, covetousness is placed side by side with idolatry. Idolatry is linked to covetousness (Col. 3:5). Where there is deliverance from idolatry, there is deliverance from money.

Today, all the co-workers should go on despite all kinds of sufferings. However, the rest of the brothers and sisters should also learn to be consecrated ones. This does not mean that everyone has to be a preacher. However, it means that everyone has to be a consecrated person. What is needed today are fully consecrated people. Not everyone is a preacher, but everyone should be for God full-time.

As long as there is a group of people who will go on in this way, wherever they may be, we will see the emergence of Acts 2 Christians. If we are consecrated, God will have a way to go on. If we do not consecrate ourselves, God's word will be jeopardized and will be depreciated. Acts 2 Christians are those who are at a crossroad; they see exactly the way ahead, and they have the boldness to tell others the right way to go. The more we fear that others will not believe, the more we will beg others to believe. But if we have enough deposit within us and we are clear about the way ahead of us, we will have the assurance to speak, and others will have the confidence to believe us. The reason others cannot have faith in us is that we do not have faith in the first place. However, if we are clear, others will follow us. If we ourselves are not clear, we will surely depreciate and discredit God's word. The issue today is fully with us.

CHAPTER FORTY-FOUR

GOD'S WORK OF RECOVERY

(2)

CO-WORKERS' MEETING (5)

Date: Monday, 6:30 p.m., April 12, 1948
Place: Hardoon Road, Shanghai
Speaker: Watchman Nee

Brother Chu-en asked: Will the church in Jerusalem and the church in Antioch become another form of a "central" church or "head" church?

SEEING THE BODY LIFE

The Holy Spirit Being the Starting Point of the Work

Brother Nee answered: Our work today does not begin from Antioch. Nor does it begin from Jerusalem. Our work today begins from the Holy Spirit. The basic question is the starting point of our work.

The Work Being Carried Out in the Body

We have to realize that the church is a Body. As such is the case, our work cannot be carried out individually, but it must be carried out in a corporate way. Neither can we be a Christian individually. Perhaps a person is a well-behaved Christian. However, he must be put together with others before his real condition is made manifest. Only those who know the Body will deal with themselves and coordinate with others. A man may have the greatest achievements and may appear to be very spiritual. But this should not be mistaken as true progress and true spirituality. Only by working with others will we realize whether there is true progress and whether the self is truly dealt with. When the self assumes the throne, it sees no one but itself. But if the self is dealt with, we will see others and will not see ourselves.

The Body Being the Test of Spirituality

We must always bear in mind that our life is but a part of the whole. We must live together with the whole. There are severe disciplines in the Body. The way of the Body is the cross. Those who have not seen the cross do not see the Body. When relatives live far away from one another, they maintain good harmony. But when they move close together, they become enemies. When a person lives in a house by himself, there is comfort and bliss. But when two brothers live together, they have to learn to take the cross. The more people live together and the closer they are to one another, the more crosses there are. Sometimes a person is put in a situation where he has crosses all over him. What man considers as spiritual progress does not count unless it can pass the test of the Body. The only thing that will count is that which can pass the test of the Body. No matter how great a person's works are, how many gifts he has, and how much life he possesses, if he is not in the Body, none of these matters count. Only when a person puts himself among the co-workers and the brothers and sisters will he know how much he has been delivered from the self and how much he knows about the cross.

Accepting the Limitations and the Coordination in the Body

The first thing we have to know is the Body of Christ. Once a person sees the Body of Christ, spontaneously he will see coordination. In the Body, the Lord has His assigned authorities. Who is an authority? Whoever has the ministry has the authority. Ministry is authority. We have to accept our own limitations. We must realize that we are only one minister before the Lord and that we have to work together with other ministers before we can meet the need. We should seek for coordination. When one member cannot meet the need, he needs the coordination of the other members. Only by coordination can we receive the supply from the Body everywhere we go. A man needs the coordination of the other members. At the same time, he needs to accept the limitations of the Body.

Submission to Authority
Being Submission to the Head

Authority is the deputy of the Head. When the eyes see, it is actually not the eyes that are seeing, but the head that sees. When the limbs move, they are not the ones that are moving, but it is the head that is moving. All the movements of the body are headed up by the head. What is ministry? Ministry is the movement of the Head. Whenever we are at odds with the ministry, we are at odds with the Head. In the Bible, the overwhelming majority of authorities are deputy authorities. When we speak about submission to authority, we mean submission to deputy authorities. The real manifestation of authority is the expression of the Head. To submit to authority is to submit to the Head. For this reason, God's children ought to learn submission.

Accepting the Ministry
Rather Than Repeating the Ministry

Ministry is expressed in two things: gift and authority. The gift is the power of the ministry. It is also the expression of authority. A man cannot accept the gift while rejecting the authority. For example, on the one hand, the eyes have the gift of seeing. On the other hand, they have the authority, and other members have to accept them. If other members do not accept the eyes, they will not receive the supply of their gift. As long as you are a member of the Body, you have to accept the gifts of the other members. There is no need for you to repeat their gifts. Concerning the ministry, there is only the question of accepting; there is no need of repeating. What we have to do today is not a matter of repeating others' ministries, like copying writing with carbon paper. All we have to do is to accept.

Always remember that you are only a member; you are not the whole Body. No one is all-inclusive. If a person is all-inclusive, he is no longer a member. The parts of a car are only the parts; they are not the whole. The parts cannot equal the whole car.

Every Member Enjoying the Riches of the Body

Although I am only a member, I can share the riches of the Body. Every member in the Body shares the riches of the Body. My fingers never complain that they cannot see. My ears never complain that they cannot walk. They never say, "How come I cannot walk as the feet do?" The many gifts in the Body are there to perfect the saints. This is why there is no division in the Body, and there are no conflicting ideologies. Although the position of the hand dictates that it cannot be the speaking member, as long as the mouth can speak, the hand is satisfied. For the mouth to speak is the same as for the hand to speak. The life that we received is a partial life; it is not the whole life. When we experience the riches of the other members in this way, the Body is perfected. Under such circumstances, how can the individual members be poor, and how can they be useless?

Coordination Dealing with the Self

Many people think that what they have is their own, and that what others have is not theirs. However, we have to realize that individualism is the worst thing there is in the Body. In the Body of Christ, individualism must be removed. The greatest test to the self is in the meetings, in the church, and among the brothers and sisters. On the one hand, we have to see that we are members individually. On the other hand, we have to see that we are a Body together with many other members. It is easy to deal with unbelievers; the minute they walk through the door, they will realize that they have the wrong address and have stumbled into the wrong place. But it is not so easy to deal with individualism. Many times, individualism creeps into the church without one realizing it. It is when a person is being coordinated together that his self life is most severely dealt with. The minute a man lives in coordination, his self is dealt with.

LIVING IN THE REALITY OF THE BODY LIFE

We must see the Body life before we can consider the question of the church in Antioch. First, there is the Body life; then we have the church in Antioch. For this reason, before we discuss the question of Antioch, we must first have some make-up lessons. If the reality of the Holy Spirit is present in the church, the question of central control no longer exists. However, if there is not the reality of the Holy Spirit, instead only approval by vote, planning, and resolutions in our work, what we have will be more than central organizations; it will be Roman Catholicism.

The Catholics say that there is only one church, that their priests are the only kind of people who can understand the Bible, and that their church is the only true church. It is true that there is only one church. But the way the Roman Catholics interpret this oneness is not the right one. How can something right become not right in the hands of the Catholics? We have to realize that it is right for the church to be one. But in the Catholic church, there are the human ideas, methods, and organizations. As a result, that which is right becomes wrong. Luther gave us two things: justification by faith and an open Bible. It is true that the Lord's recovery has made it possible for everyone to read the Bible, but this does not mean that everyone is able to interpret the Bible. Some do not have the gift of interpretation, yet they insist on interpreting the Bible. The result is errors. Some think that by putting together a few verses they can come up with a new doctrine. To do so not only produces wrong teachings, but it takes men out of the sphere of God's grace. Some would not be subdued even when others have pointed out the error in their teachings; they would still insist on speaking. These people can never be taught.

God has set up teachers in the church (1 Cor. 12:28). The teachers are those who interpret the Bible. In the church, some have been set up to interpret the Bible. The meeting spoken of in 1 Corinthians 14 has the prophets as its center. Not everyone can interpret the Scriptures. In the meeting, when those who can interpret the Scriptures stand up to speak, the others should discern. However, this does not mean that the interpretation of one or two, or of a few, will ascertain a truth. The speaking is done by one or two, but the others have to discern. Even when the congregation is not able to discern, the words of the prophets must still be judged by the Spirit of the Lord.

Antioch was not a center, because it was not the product of an organization, but the product of the Holy Spirit. Once the church is separate from the Holy Spirit and once it has lost its spiritual reality, it becomes the Roman Catholic Church. It is possible for Catholicism to be found among us. The basic question today is not the method of Antioch, but the kind of person we are. Are we a person living in the spiritual reality? This is the basic issue. Whether or not a local church can become a central church depends basically on whether or not that church is spiritual. This is the foremost issue.

NO LOCAL CHURCH BECOMING A HEAD CHURCH

Factually speaking, the church in Antioch could not have become a head church either. Antioch in fact had never exercised supervision over other churches. One local church cannot exercise supervision over another church. However, the work has the right to exercise supervision over a local church. The church in Antioch never exercised supervision over another church, but the apostles who went out from Antioch did exercise supervision over other churches. When a problem arises in a local church, the matter has to be brought to the attention of the workers. First Timothy says that an accusation against an elder must be accompanied by the word of two or three witnesses (5:19). An accusation cannot be based on rumors or hearsay; there must be witnesses, and the accusations must be presented to Timothy. Timothy was a worker. This is why he could deal with the problem of the elders in a locality. Antioch was only one local church. Jerusalem was also another local church. As far as their being a church is concerned, the question of a head church never existed. But as far as the work is concerned, it is something different.

THE STARTING POINT OF THE WORK BEING THE ONENESS OF THE BODY

The starting point of the work in Antioch was the sending forth of two or three men. However, if workers are sent out by the work, the question of organization may come in. When we are having our gathering this time, brothers from different localities have come on their own accord. Such a kind of gathering is not a product of organizations, teachings, or doctrines. It is a product of the Body's need. There is only one Body. What is manifested in all the places is the same life. This life is the reality of this Body. The work is produced out of this reality. This is the Lord's standard. If we compare our work with the Lord's standard, we will see that we have surely come short. The Lord has shown us today that individual works can never come up to the standard of the Body. If we do not see this, but insist instead on our individual works, we will face a stone wall. All works that are not the issue of the Body life will sooner or later hit a stone wall. The Lord will lead us to the point where we have to take the way of the Body. He will lead us to the point where we will not be able to go on or even to live if we do not take the way of the Body. If a man falls into the river, surely he will cry out for help. In the same way, the Lord will force us to cry out for help and for rescue out of our individual works. This is the starting point of the work. The starting point of the work is the oneness of the Body.

The electricity that comes from the power plant is one, yet the places where it shines are many. Although it shines in many places, the electricity in these many places is under the control of the same power plant. Today, the works in all the localities should be under the fellowship of the one Body. No place should set up its own bunker or defense line. Today, we should express the life of the Body in the different localities. If we make the churches in our localities little kingdoms and territories bounded by their own "turfs," we are wrong.

THE TWO LINES OF THE WORK

In the Bible, there are only two groups of workers. Other than these two groups, God did not have His eyes on any other institution of Christian work. These two groups of workers are the group from Jerusalem and the group from Antioch. In addition to these two groups, there were other workers. For example, the book of Philippians mentions some others who preached Christ (Phil 1:15-17). Yet the Lord did not pay much attention to these ones; He only paid attention to the workers from Jerusalem and those from Antioch. Since the Bible pays little attention to these other ones, we pay little attention to them also. The Lord emphatically placed in the Bible two lines composed of two groups of workers, the line of Paul and the line of Peter. For this reason, we have to be clear about these two lines.

ORGANIZATION BEING THE RESULT OF THE LACK OF LIFE

The reason there are headquarters is that there is the lack of life. Once life is lacking, organization comes in. In the Body of Christ, organization is the heaviest burden. When a person is healthy, he does not feel the weight of his body. Once a person is ill, he feels the weight of his body. The more a person is ill, the heavier his body is to him. When a person dies, his body becomes the heaviest. It becomes so heavy that he has to be lifted up by others. When there is life, the body is a body. When life is gone, the body becomes a corpse. In the same principle, without life, headquarters appear. Once life is gone, there is the need for an organization to come in to arrange everything. As long as there is life in the Body of Christ, it will not be a problem even if this Body becomes very large. This is like saying that as long as there is life in the human body, a person does not feel the weight of this body no matter how heavy and big this body becomes. But as soon as this body becomes a corpse, it will become very difficult to lift it.

THE LOCAL CHURCHES NOT BECOMING A METHOD

Today we cannot make the truth concerning the local churches a method. If we make it a method, it will become very dead indeed. The question is not Catholicism or local churches. The question is the church being in doctrine or in life. I fear method as much as I fear Catholicism. The local church cannot become a method. Once it becomes a method, it will become very, very heavy. This is our basic problem today.

We cannot say that the Catholic church is all wrong. If the Catholic church would remove her idols, the oneness that she talks about is right.

CONCERNING "HANDING OVER"

I still need to say something concerning the question of "handing over."

Handing Over Being a Make-up Lesson and Not a Teaching

The matter of "handing over" must never become our teaching. It is not a teaching, but a "make-up" lesson. The reason there is the need for such a make-up lesson is that the matter was not taken care of properly at the beginning. It is like a man riding on a train; he should first buy the ticket and then board the train. However, some people have boarded the train without paying for the ticket. As a result, there is the need for some kind of make-up measure. Originally, tickets should be bought at the train station. After a man is saved, he should immediately consecrate himself (Rom. 6:6, 12-13), and he should not have to wait until a later date to make it up. But many Christians have not done this properly, and the church has not presented this need to them properly right from the beginning. We can say that today the church has given the believers a "bonus ride"; they board the train without paying for the ticket. But sooner or later, they still must pay for the ticket.

For the new ones who have just come in, we do not need to ask them to hand themselves over. What they need is to consecrate themselves. The reason there is a "handing over" is that the consecration was not done properly at the beginning. As a result, there is the need for such a make-up lesson. The standard of salvation is not high enough today, and many of the items a person should have acquired at the time of salvation are lost. Strictly speaking, when a man is saved, he should be fully consecrated and should be a person who lives fully for the spread of the gospel. As soon as a person comes in, we should lay the full demand on his shoulder. If we can do this, none among us will still be holding hands with the world after we are saved, or will have to come back at a later date to consecrate ourselves.

In the Gospels, when men thronged to follow the Lord, He presented His requirements to them. He explained that a man must take up his own cross before he can follow Him (Matt. 10:38; 16:24). The Lord never lowers His standard. On the contrary, He lifts the standard high. He says that man should follow Him, and that if a man is to follow Him, he has to do this and do that. Let me emphasize that after a man is saved, unless he consecrates himself, he cannot go on. Unless he takes up his cross, he cannot go on. If you want to come to the Lord, you have to consecrate yourself, and you have to take up your cross and give up the world and your individualism. All these things must be clearly dealt with at the time a person is saved.

The matter of "handing oneself over" is a measure taken because nothing else could be done. It is like a man boarding a train without a ticket. Since he cannot get off the train again, the only way is for him to buy a ticket then. For now, we try to settle for the term "handing over." One day, when everyone is consecrated as soon as he is saved, there will be no need for anyone to "hand themselves over" any longer. It is because the things that should be there on the first day are lost, and everyone has boarded the train without a ticket; some have climbed into the carriages through the windows, while others have walked in without any ticket. Although these have boarded the train without any ticket, they cannot go on with their free ride the rest of the time. Sooner or later, they nevertheless have to pay for their tickets. There is a difference between buying a ticket on the train and buying it at the station. To buy it on the train is abnormal, whereas to buy it at the station is normal. If everyone buys his ticket on the train, there will be no need for a ticket booth at the station any longer. If everyone buys his ticket on the train, you might just as well move the ticket booth into the train.

I am afraid that after some time the matter of "handing over" will become a new terminology among us. It is possible that in the future the matter of "handing over" will become a peculiar thing among us. If this happens, those teachers who come after us will write and ask us about the scriptural foundation for the practice of "handing oneself over." There is no such doctrinal term as "handing over." We borrow this term today because men do not have a proper and good beginning. If everyone begins in a proper way, there is no need to bring up this question any longer.

A Proper Start for the New Believers

There is a big difference between a proper salvation and an improper salvation. One woman can give birth to a twelve-ounce baby, whereas another can give birth to a twelve-pound baby. The church should bear the responsibility in its ministry to help the new ones to have a good beginning. There is a great difference between the way taken by those who have a proper beginning and those who do not. Among the ones raised up by the Lord throughout the ages, many did have a good beginning. Once a person has a good beginning, he can go on in a proper way. As long as the beginning is clean-cut, that one can go on properly no matter how little he understands and sees at the beginning. There are others who dragged their feet along when they first came in. With such, their way cannot be straight. Once a person is saved, he should have a clear-cut separation from sin and the world. The question of money has to be settled. The question of consecration has to be settled, and the question of individualism also has to be settled. What the future holds for a person depends on God. After Paul brought others to salvation, he committed those saved to the grace of God (Acts 12:43; 20:32). No doubt in the way ahead a person needs God's grace. But in the initial stage, there must be a clear-cut salvation. If the beginning is not good, the make-up lesson later will not be easy.

Brother Tang asked: Is it one thing to go to God and another thing to go before man?

THE MINISTERS OF THE GOSPEL

The Need for the Work of the Holy Spirit in the Gospel

Brother Nee answered: There are six lines to take in preaching the gospel. One can start from love, righteousness, judgment, sin, the world, or vanity. However, no matter which line you take, there is the need of the work of the Holy Spirit. The result of the work of the Holy Spirit is just one thing: to subdue a person. The real gospel is one that subdues and softens a person. All those who think that they are doing God a favor by believing in Him are unqualified ones. Once a person sees the gospel, whether it is through the preaching of love, righteousness, or judgment, he will surely be softened and subdued.

The Center of the Gospel Being God

When we preach the gospel, we have to present the proper way to others. The question of the world and of our service to the Lord must be dealt with together. We have to see that the center of the gospel is God and not ourselves. It is not that we gain something for ourselves, but that God gains something for Himself. As soon as a person is saved, he has to realize that everything belongs to God. Our occupations are not ours; they are God's. The doctors have to see that their occupation is not to be a doctor, but to serve God. They are only working as a doctor on the side. If a man is not willing to take this way or to accept the Lord and be baptized, we will not force him to do so. But we cannot lower the standard. As soon as a person is saved, we have to tell him that from now on he is no longer an individual person, but a member in the Body. As such, he needs to learn to listen to others and to submit to others.

If the church will not take this way, it will always remain sub-standard. If Brother Tang drinks cow's milk today, no one would laugh at him. But if he still takes his mother's milk, it would be a big joke. Strictly speaking, the church should have learned obedience already. But now it is going back to re-learn this lesson. This is why, in order to take the straight way today, we have to put everything upon a person the day that he is saved. Those who are saved must begin in a proper way.

A Minister of the Gospel Being One Who Lives the Gospel

We must be a certain kind of person before we can produce that kind of person. The gospel demands not only that we preach it, but that we live it. The gospel must not only be heard, but must also be seen. No preaching can match the act of a martyr. More people are gained through an act of martyrdom than through the work of preaching.

There was a sister who was nineteen or twenty years old. For the Lord's sake, she was banished to Siberia. On her way in the train, she comforted her family and said to them, "Do not cry for me. Cry instead for those who do not have God. What I have far exceeds what they have. I am happy to suffer for the sake of my beloved Lord. The suffering that I endure can never match that of my Lord." A young thirteen-year-old boy sitting close by heard this word, and he was greatly moved to believe in the Lord. Later, he became one of the great workers used by the Lord in southern Czarist Russia.

The Need for Impact in the Gospel

Strictly speaking, we need men of Acts 2 before we can have messages of Acts 2. What we have to do today is not simply to preach, but to have an impact on others. If we preach the gospel in this way, a fleshly man will not even be able to come into the church, let alone to go on afterwards. If there are such men and there are those who live this kind of life, corporately there will be the impact and the influence, and others will catch on to the warmth and the joy. Life is a matter of consciousness and feeling. With some people, you can only shake their hands; you cannot touch their spirit or their real person. If what a person has are the things of God, what others will sense in him will only be the things of God. If what a person has is the life of God, what others will sense in him will be life.

THE MINISTRY BEING A MATTER OF THE INWARD BURDEN

All proper ministers are burdened with a message. If a man has a ministry, he will always be burdened with a few strong words that always remain with him. These few words become his burden. Sometimes the burden may appear very small, but the more the person explains it, the more words there will be. It is like a woolen yarn; the more you pull it, the more yarn you see. Any ministry that is of any worth is a ministry with a burden. Within that ministry, there is a specific burden.

With some people, all the time they are preaching on the podium, their minds are spinning. With some others, all that comes out of them is empty words. When others listen to the words, they do not receive any Spirit; all that they receive is the sounds. All real ministries have a burden within their words. The ones speaking may come feeling heavy, but they should leave feeling light. When they speak, they speak with a burden from within. If a man does not have a burden, any preaching he conducts with his mind and thoughts will be useless. A ministry must have a ministry's burden. The greatest suffering is for a person to come with something but to find no one to pick up his words. In the end, he carries back the same burden that he brings with him.

CONCERNING THE MOVE OF THE LOCAL CHURCHES

The problem of the move of the local churches must be solved in the Body. It is useless to try to solve it separately. The Lord must first have a way among us. Only when He has a way among us will He have a way among the churches. If He does not get through with us, He will not be able to solve the problems separately in the different localities.

THE NEED TODAY

A. Committing Oneself to the Body

I see clearly that with our present condition, we need a second salvation. This is a great matter. The term "handing over" is only our borrowed term. I do not wish that it be taken by others and used as a standard terminology. Originally, man was rebellious, individual, and unwilling to hand himself over. Now through the work of the Lord, he is willing to drop everything and to hand himself over voluntarily. Today, if a man wants to hand himself over willingly, he has to do it; and if he does not want to hand himself over, he nevertheless has to do it. Some may think that they cannot hand themselves over, but they should go ahead and try it. Once a sacrifice is on the altar, the altar will sanctify the sacrifice. This is like some people saying that they cannot believe and that they have too many questions. But once they decide to believe, all their questions are solved. A person can believe even though he has many doubts and questions. As long as a person is willing, God can work on him. If a man thinks that he cannot hand himself over, all he has to do is to place himself in the church. The church will help him to become able. If one individual has some problem, he can ask for help from the church; a few others can come along to help him to hand himself over. Today, as long as man makes a little move, God will move along with him. The handing over that we speak of today is not an individual handing over, but a handing over that is done in fellowship. Such handing over is a kind of committing of ourselves. It may seem that a person is only putting himself on the altar on a trial basis, and it may seem that God is only accepting such a one on a trial basis. Actually, whether or not a man considers his move a trial effort, God takes it up seriously. He takes up those who do it whole-heartedly, and He also takes up those who do it half-heartedly. Today, when we hand ourselves over, we are committing ourselves to the Body. The Body is our greatest protection. In the coming days, we shall see that those who do not live in the Body will suffer great loss. The supply of the ministry is in the Body. Once we are separated from the Body, we are cut off from the supply of the ministry.

B. Realizing the Supply of the Body

The book of Acts indicates that when Paul was in Athens, he was provoked in his spirit and was ill at ease (Acts 17:16). Yet when Timothy joined him in Corinth, he immediately received the supply (Acts 18:5). This is like a certain brother passing by your locality, or a new one joining your meeting. Immediately, you can feel the supply. Sometimes, when a few brothers visit a locality, supply follows them wherever they go. The brothers may not even need to say anything. All they have to do is to sit there, and the supply is there. Many times, as long as there is the proper audience, a speaker will be able to release his burden. The thing that causes the most suffering is for a person to come with a burden and to go home with the same burden on him.

Since we are a Body, we affect one another. However, we are not very clear how we affect one another. Sometimes we feel that our fellowship with the Lord is particularly intimate. At other times, we have some inexplicable feelings. The reason for these phenomena is that there exists a supply in the Body. With the Body life there is a supply. This supply is a reality. However, we do not know how this supply affects the members. In the Body, we should not be a brother or sister who consumes others' supply; we should have a clear realization of the Body. All our failures and weakenings today are due to the fact that we behave as individual Christians. There are some things that we cannot explain very clearly today. In the days ahead, perhaps there will be the opportunity for us to speak about them in a clearer and more precise way.

During the Boxer Rebellion in 1900, many Christians were martyred. At the same time that this was going on, many churches around the world had the feeling that something was happening. Many people were depressed in their spirit for many days, and they felt the need for prayer. This feeling was not something that came from the physical eyes or the ears. It was a feeling of the Body. Who can say that the faithful martyrs were not supplied during those hours by the effect of these prayers? Miss Barber was in England at that time, and she was oppressed in her spirit. She felt the need to pray. Soon after that, she found out what had happened.

Whenever one part of our body becomes sick, the other parts of the body will come to the sick member's aid and will try to deal with the sickness. In the same way, there is a supply in the Body of Christ. The Body life is not a term, but a reality. Many people think that the church is only a mysterious and abstract Body. They do not realize that this Body is a reality.

First Corinthians 11:29 mentions the discerning of "the body." The Body denotes two things: the Lord's Body, and the Body of Christ. Here it only mentions the body, without making reference to either the Lord's Body or the Body of Christ. Therefore, on the one hand, it refers to the Lord's Body, whereas, on the other hand, to the Body of Christ. Within this Body, there are the riches of the Lord, and there are the riches of Christ. Every Christian can receive the benefits of the Holy Spirit and of the Lord's grace in this Body. The greatest lack among Christians today is the supply of the Body. May the Lord open our eyes to see this Body and to realize the supply in this Body.

PRINCIPLES OF OFFERING

Let us also consider a little the principles of offering.

Material Offerings—
Not a Matter of Amount,
but a Question of Where the Heart Lies

The Bible speaks about offerings with respect to a few things. The first is material offerings. There is no set principle as to the amount one should offer. Some offer more, others offer less. Some time ago, a few brothers in Ku-tien sold all their possessions. At that time, I stopped them temporarily from doing this. There is no set principle to offering. Some offer everything they have. Christ says that a man must sell everything to follow Him. John the Baptist said that those who have two garments should give one away (Luke 3:11).

The Gospels tell us to care for the poor. In the Epistles, we see that the church should care for the widows among us. However, a person must first care for his own household (1 Tim. 5:16, 8). Second Corinthians 8:15 says that "he who gathered much had no excess, and he who gathered little had no lack."

The problem today is not how much a person should offer, but the fact that money has laid hold of man's heart. In God's work, no one can keep his money, on the one hand, and say that his heart loves the Lord, on the other hand. The Bible says that where our money is, there is the heart also (Matt. 6:21). In order for our hearts not to be ensnared by money, we have to let the money go. If the money goes out of our pocket, the heart goes out with it. If a man loves the Lord, he will be able to choose voluntary poverty. Voluntary poverty is the way for the heart to be released. Sometimes God will ask a person to sell all he has. Sometimes He will only ask a person to give what he has in excess. Whatever it may be, the heart has to be released. In Acts, the apostle rebuked Ananias for keeping back what he had in excess (Acts 5:4-5). Today we should not have anything in excess. To have anything in excess is a shame in the church. The church should not see any excess. If there is any excess, it should be given away.

Sister Eva said that every time she went to bed, she would always consider how she could save something more from her spending in order that others may receive more. We need to take care of our livelihood, and we need to take care of our family. But that is not this issue today. As long as we would set aside a portion from our income and would lower our standard of living a little, we will be able to give away all our excess.

Today, when we speak of handing ourselves over, we are not talking about what we have to do to take care of our money. Rather, we are saying that a person has to offer himself up for the Lord and for the gospel. Brothers and sisters who are engaged in an occupation, the Lord needs your ministry in your job! These few years we are short of new co-workers. Formerly, at its peak we had about four hundred co-workers. Today we only have about two hundred, with two hundred short. In order to fill up the gap of these two hundred workers, there must be a group of people who would go to make money. Formerly, I dared not say such a word. But today I dare to say such a word. Some should go to make money and offer their money to the Lord's service. They should consecrate themselves to make money for the Lord's service. Perhaps such a one can make a million dollars. He will only take what he needs to sustain his livelihood. The rest he will give to the church. If you are only a spectator here, nothing will happen to you. But if you want to give yourselves for the co-workers' need, it demands your life.

Of course, God does not want us to go to the extremes. He wants us to be in moderation. First He wants us; then He wants what is ours. We ourselves have to come to Him first before we can bring what we have to Him. If we do not come, God will not accept what we have. All the brothers and sisters have to see that everything is for the Lord and that everything has to center around the Lord. We must have the same center. Although some function in their money-making ministry while others function in their ministry of the word, the center for both must be the same.

Offering Up Our Occupation—
Taking Up Occupations Approved by God

Other than material offerings, the Bible also mentions the offering up of our occupations. The Bible shows us that many occupations are not suitable for a Christian to engage in. It is true that we have to make money, but we have to consider how our money is made. Some means of making money are not approved by the Lord. We can only keep the occupations that God approves, and we can never engage in works that God does not approve. Today, some leading ones in some localities have wrong concepts about occupations. They bring these wrong concepts to the church. As a result, the church is ill-affected. May the Lord be merciful to us.

A PRAYER

Concluding prayer: The Lord of all our works, we beseech

for men on behalf of the church. Today the church is in a state of desolation. There is a lack of men in the church. May the Lord grant us men, and may the church be filled with men. Give many gifts to the church. Be merciful to us, so that there will be consecrated ones who will hand themselves over. May we find men who would submit under Your mighty hand, so that we can serve You together with all the saints. In this age of desolation, we ask especially that You raise up not just the young ones or the co-workers, but a church that would uphold Your testimony. May more people put themselves into Your hands, so that their jobs, positions, and living can become worthy of the gospel. May there be young ones raised up to work for You, and may all the brothers and sisters rise up to match the move of the gospel. We believe that You can fulfill the work of Your recovery. May You do a greater work, and may You raise up more men to give all their time to serve You and to go out with the gospel. We ask that You raise up a great multitude of men. We are not asking first for their money or their time. We are asking for their whole person. May there be some who would offer themselves to You in a thorough way, and may they do it right now. We pray that You would remove from us the desolation and would give us men. Lord, be gracious to us; we are inquiring of You men. Only You are worthy to gain us. Only You can cause us to serve You unreservedly and single-heartedly. We would pour out the water of the well of Bethlehem here on the ground. May none among us be a withdrawing one, a hiding one, or a spectator. May the Lord be merciful to us. In the name of the Lord Jesus Christ we pray, amen.

CHAPTER FORTY-FIVE

TESTIMONIES OF CO-WORKERS AND COMMENTS

CO-WORKERS' MEETING (6)

Date: Evening, April 13, 1948
Place: Hardoon Road, Shanghai
Speaker: Watchman Nee

Brother Watchman Nee: In tonight's meeting, we would like the co-workers to give their own testimonies. Those brothers and sisters who are joining us as guests should only come with their ears. They should not be the mouths, nor should they take what they hear and use it as subjects for gossip. Tonight we want to speak honest words before the Lord and to speak the truth in love.

NOT BEING CONTROLLED BY EMOTIONS

Brother Chang Yu-chi testified: (1) I find it easy for me to lose my temper and to criticize; (2) I always have strong feelings for injustice in others.

Brother Nee: Brother Chang is easily swayed by his emotions. He does not have much problem with his will. We cannot be influenced by our emotions. What we learn in sickness is a discipline from God through our environment.

BEING DIRECT AND SIMPLE IN ONE'S MIND

Brother David Hsu testified: (1) I always experience conflicts of various kinds; (2) whenever something happens, I would fall into much consideration and find my thoughts very complicated; (3) I also experience conflict between my heart and my head.

Brother Nee: We should have thoughts that are like straight lines. A straight line is the shortest distance between two points. We should not have circumventing thoughts. Once light comes in and we see ourselves, we should apply the dealing right away. If we do this, our mind will become simple.

HAVING A DEFINITE BURDEN IN OUR SPIRIT AND SPEAKING INTO OTHERS' SPIRIT

In serving the Lord, we have to seek for definite burdens in our spirit. We must have the Lord's words within before we can speak His word without. Our words are not just spoken for the ears of others. The real speaking is one in which the deep calls unto the deep. On the one hand, we should have the spiritual burden within us. On the other hand, our words should be conveyed to the depths of others.

THE NEED FOR OUR SPEAKING TO BE SHORT AND DIRECT

The problem with Brother Hsu is the conveying. I have no way of knowing how much burden there is within him. However, he has used so many words and so much time, and yet that which is in his spirit is not yet conveyed to others. The reason for this is that there is not enough practice. As a result, his mind is poor. When we speak, our words have to be short and simple. Brother Hsu's problem is not a problem in the basic matter; it is a problem with his speaking. If he practices more, he will avoid the complications and the hesitations. Brother Witness Lee's prayers are "light" in time and "heavy" in content. If a man needs a glass of water, simply give him a glass. There is no need to lay a fifty yard pipeline first and then put the glass to it.

It is not easy for you to take such words. It is not easy for me to speak such words either.

THE NEED FOR A STRONG SPIRIT TO RENDER OTHERS THE PRACTICAL HELP

Brother Jih Yung-tung testified: I am learning to mingle myself with the other co-workers. But sometimes I become withdrawn because of others.

Brother Nee: Brother Jih needs to be strengthened in his spirit. The real love for the brothers has to do with our being absolute toward the Lord. This requires that our spirit be strong. Those who do not have a strong spirit cannot render others much help in the church. They cannot build others up, and they cannot cause others to waste themselves on the Lord. Only those who have a strong spirit can render others the greatest amount of help. We should not give others fragmentary and defective help. Rather, we should render them practical and definite help. This requires a strong spirit on our part.